Angela Valentine

The Dark Edge of the Rainbow

novum pro

© 2016 novum publishing

ISBN 978-3-99048-586-6
Editing: Nicola Ratcliff, BA
Cover photo: Angela Valentine
Cover design, layout & typesetting: novum publishing
Internal illustrations:
Angela Valentine (19)

The images provided by the author have been printed in the highest possible quality.

www.novum-publishing.co.uk

All rights of distribution, including via film, radio, and television, photomechanical reproduction, audio storage media, electronic data storage media, and the reprinting of portions of text, are reserved

Printed in the European Union on environmentally friendly, chlorine- and acid-free paper.

Newton Abbot
2015
To Sabine and Christiane
My sisters

✸✸✸

This book is dedicated to my mother.
She helped me greatly with the events I was too young to remember.
My clear memory starts with my father and
myself at the Brandenburg gate
In 1939

✸✸✸

The strong character and determination of my mother was
Instrumental in all of us coming through these difficult
Times. My mother died in 1994.

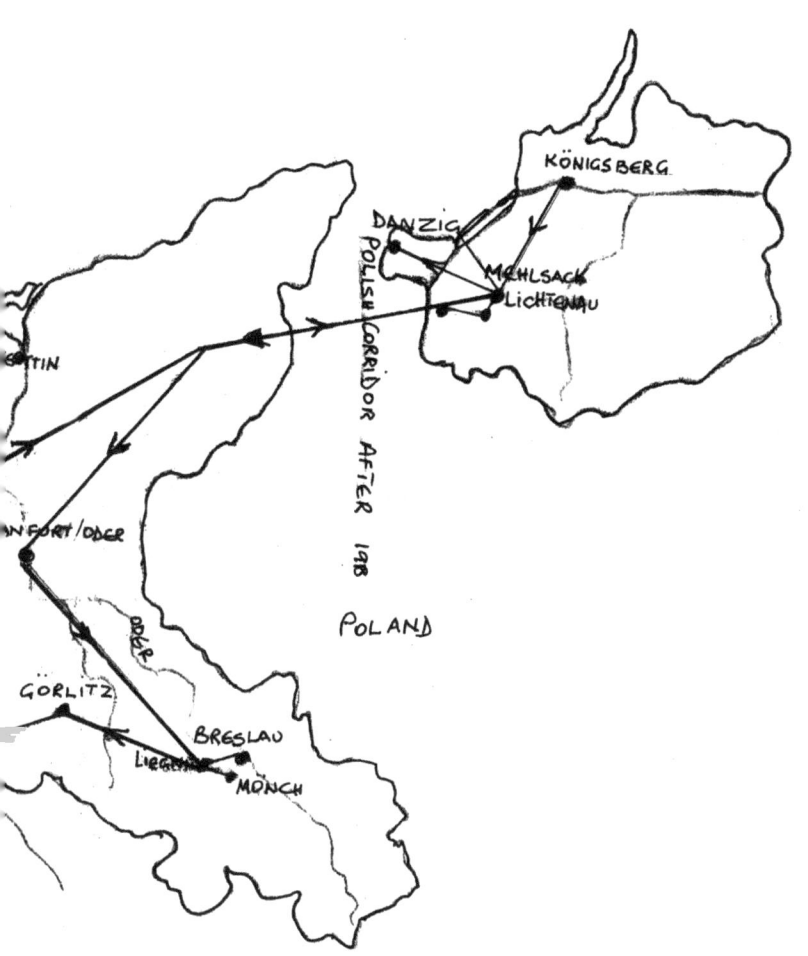

The Dark Edge of the Rainbow
Angela Valentine

Du hast sie zerstört
Die schöne Welt,
Mit mächtiger Faust,
Sie stürzt, sie zerfällt!
Ein Halbgott hat sie zerschlagen!
Wir tragen
Die Trümmern in Nichts hinüber
Und klagen
Über die verlorne Schöne.
Mächtiger
Der Erdensöhne
Prächtiger
Baue sie wieder
In deinem Busen baue sie auf!
Neuen Lebenslauf
Beginne,
Mit hellem Sinne,
Und neue Lieder
Tönen darauf.

Goethe, Faust, I
You have destroyed her
This beautiful world
With a mighty fist
She crashes, she crumbles!
A demigod has shattered all.
We carry
The fragments across to the void
And lament
The lost beauty
Oh mightiest
Son of the earth
Magnificent
Create her again
In your heart create her anew!
A new course of life
Begin,
With a shining new spirit
And new songs
Shall sound thereafter.

(*My own translation*)

Foreword

When I asked my ten year old son to tidy his room and then do his homework, he clicked his heals and lifted his arm and shouted: "Heil Hitler!"

I looked at him, pulled him close and asked "What's all this about?" It turned out that one of his friends had asked what it was like to have a Nazi as a mother.

I explained that neither his granny nor I, were ever Nazis and that I was only as old as he was, when the war came to an end. I also explained that my father belonged to the Nazi party, because if he hadn't, he would have been out of work and so he had to go to fight in the war in 1942. I explained I never saw him again after that.

My daughter had also had to put up with listening to silly questions at school. But being older, she'd been able to put it aside. She knew and loved her relatives in Germany. I answered their questions and we had a long talk.

Not knowing what war is like, how could they understand what I was talking about? What their mother, their aunts and their granny went through, was so unbelievable, that it did not make sense. They were too small and too protected.

After the war and the years that followed the monetary reform on the 20th June 1948, we did not talk about the bombing and the loss of our relatives and possessions, anymore. We talked instead, about the loss of our homeland and whether we could ever return to the land that was our home for so many generations. We carried the trauma of what happened inside us, buried, as if it never happened. The trauma of what happened to the Jews in Germany, was so unbelievable that many of us were unable to come to terms with it.

We were truly hoping, that as soon as things were sorted, we could return home. But home did not exist anymore, it was given to foreigners and the rest was rubble and ash.

Most dispossessed Germans felt the same.

What so many of us thought and hoped for, was that if we suppressed it, it would go away. Not surprisingly, this didn't happen. The years went by and we kept ourselves occupied by helping rebuild houses. We scraped the bricks of the rubble heaps clean, and replanted forests and picked Colorado beetle off the potato plants, which had been sprayed by enemy planes, just before the end of the war.

We went out into the world, got married and had children. But deep inside us, was a wound that would not heal. Noises and certain smells brought events back so clearly, as if they were happening at that moment.

I had come to Britain to work and then got married here and my children were born here. I would never have believed this would happen at the time, when the events described in this book took place.

I soon found out that people here, who were not involved in politics, had no idea of what really happened to ordinary German people. I learned quickly, not to answer questions about what happened to us. I really didn't know where to start and when I was told that I must have been too young to remember the war, I left it at that.

My New Zealand father-in-law only ever referred to my countrymen as the "Bloody Hun", but then turned round and said that his best friend in New Zealand was a German.

When asked whether I came from East or West Germany and then trying to explain, when the next question came about the wall, I found that people didn't know or care about east or west. They weren't interested in the iron curtain or the Island of West Berlin, isolated in the middle of the cold war, Communist East Germany.

In June of 1989 I finished my Access Course at Dartington/Totnes with an installation. I built a large replica of part of the Berlin Wall, in front of the Brandenburg Gate and broke it down. At the time, I, or anyone else for that matter, had no idea it would fall six months later, so dramatically and completely. My fellow students were intrigued and I explained, but they had no idea where it was.

So for my children and my fellow students and anybody else who would be interested, I wrote the story of an ordinary family from Berlin, having been bombed and evacuated to East Prussia in 1943 which is now Russia. Then in 1944, to Silesia, which is now Poland and finally in 1944/45, to Bavaria, where we waited for the Americans to finish that terrible war. The bombing, the shooting, the killing and the dead, three children under ten and one brave mother and other happy and sad events are described in this book.

I also illustrated it with pencil drawings, some from photographs and some from memory.

My heart was a lot lighter when I finished the book.

✱✱✱

1

The rain had stopped and grey clouds were racing across a blue sky, chased by brilliant sunshine, sleet and snow. It was cold outside, Mother had put on her warm coat and boots. She had to go to feed the rabbits in our garden, and left me in charge of my two little sisters.

I was standing by the window, resting my chin on the windowsill looking out, feeling very bored. The weather wasn't nice enough to be outside. I had lifted the lace curtain over my head to get a better view of the clouds as they hurried across the sky. The strong wind changed their shape constantly. I turned round and through the patterns of the curtains I watched Bine and Tissi.

Before Mother left, she had put Tissi on the pot. She was a nervous baby and soiled her nappies as soon as she heard the siren or the doorbell. A constant string of nappies hung to dry in the bathroom, and to save even more nappies, Tissi spent a lot of time on the pot, surrounded by her toys with Bine or myself playing with her. She was wrapped in a lovely pink blanket, which used to be my favourite, then Bine's and now Tissi's. It had fairy tale characters woven into it, like Snow White and the Seven Dwarfs, *Dornröschen* and the *Froschkönig*.

A strange noise made me look out of the window again.

Suddenly, small and very dark grey clouds appeared. They just popped out of nowhere and there they were. Lots of them. I called Bine over and we watched together, fascinated. Each little cloud was accompanied with an ak sound. Ak-ak-ak. We tried to count them, but as soon as they appeared, the wind blew them away again. The sound was muffled through the double windows.

Another strange noise took our attention. Over the roofs of the apartment houses opposite, planes appeared, row upon row. A droning sound filled the air. Slowly, the sky darkened with these menacing planes, and just as we were trying to work out what they were, I heard the siren. A prickling went down my back. Tissi started crying, I looked at her. Mother hadn't gone all that long ago. She would turn back and come home, surely.

How many raids had we survived? I looked back through the window. The first planes had disappeared over our roof and they were still advancing over the roofs opposite. How many were there? A hundred? At least a hundred. There were no gaps in the sky. Suddenly, one changed into a fiery ball and crashed into many pieces, behind the blocks opposite. Laboriously, the others continued to cross the sky over our street.

The Doorbell rang. Bine rushed to the door, yelling: "Mutti, Mutti", but it was Frau Meier, Roland's mother.

"Why aren't you downstairs? Where is your mother?" Not waiting for an answer, she picked up Tissi, potty and all. Bine picked up some toys. I picked up the first aid case, which was always ready by the door and we went down into the cellar. As I came out of the back door, before turning into the basement shelter, I could see, that the blanket of planes, had disappeared over the horizon of the bombed and burnt out apartment blocks at the back and were still coming on, overhead. The air was filled with snarling engine noises. Hypnotised, I watched.

Frau Meier shouted: "Come quickly, don't stand there. You'll get killed." I turned and ran down the stairs into the basement shelter. Where were so many planes headed? What was the target? Where was Mother? I listened to every little noise. Frau Meier asked again where Mother was, and I said: "She has gone to feed the Angora's. Will she be alright?"

Frau Meier nodded her head.

"She has gone into somebody else's shelter. Anywhere between here and the Colony." (We called all the gardens the Colony).

Frau Pfeiffer, from the second floor, put new nappies on Tissi. She was still fretting, I went over and put my arm around her. Bine's eyes were dark and huge. She was watching everybody and although she said nothing I could read her question. Where was Mother? I took Bine's hand, there was safety and reassurance in just sticking together. The din outside had become deafening. There was the smell of cement and dust trickling from the ceiling. We had all landed on the floor involuntarily. The three of us huddled together, Frau Meier close with Roland. The other members of the apartments above, also huddled on benches along the wall, barely visible in the dingy light.

Suddenly, it was very still outside. Nothing could be heard and no one uttered a word. Then the door was flung open and Mother rushed in. She was out of breath, bleeding slightly on her forehead, her clothes were torn, and she was very dirty.

She put out her arms and Bine and I flew into them: "Where were you?"

She put her hand up to the mass of plaited hair, which was hanging down her back, pins sticking out here and there. She tried hard to pin it up again.

"I ducked from doorway to doorway, but I got hit by small pieces of shrapnel. It looks as though they are attacking Tempelhof again. But where they are going with all those planes, goodness knows." The neighbours asked a lot more questions. Frau Meier was cross with Mother, because she came back in that hellish inferno.

"You know we will always look after the children, we would have been quicker had we known you were not here."

"I didn't think there would be a raid so soon again and I simply had to come back for the children. The rabbits have to go. I cannot leave the children again."

We loved the rabbits, their soft, warm fur and strawberry red eyes. Their twitching pink noses when they ate. Bine's eyes filled with silent tears, and my heart sank.

"It is much better they go, *Kinderchen*, they are not safe in the garden here in the city. We take them to Silesia."

Mother went over to the bunkbeds and fetched the Grimms Fairy Tales book. Roland came too, and we all settled down to listen, including the adults.

Mother read the story of someone who went forth to learn how it feels to make his flesh creep.

The chap in the story was fearless. His bravery knew no bounds, and his adventures were horrific, and still he had not learned what fear was. Nothing made his flesh creep. Eventually, he met a miller who hired him as an apprentice. While they were all sitting down for the evening meal, he told the family of his quest, and how he had wandered through the world and still had not yet learned what fear was.

That night, the miller's daughter went out and filled a bucket from the cold stream with water. She had also inadvertently caught some tiny fishes in her bucket. She poured the bucket over the sleeping lad, who woke up shuddering and said: "Why, now I know what it feels like."

We thought this story was a little strange, but also funny, and asked for it often.

The book of 'Grimms Fairy Tales' was part of the first aid kit and always came with us into the cellar and made the time we spent there more cosy. It made us forget what was going on outside.

Half way through the next story, the siren announced the end of the raid.

We went straight upstairs and Mother started to cook lunch. We were so hungry. We all sat in the kitchen quietly, watching her.

"Minka, go and lay the table, Bine can help." she said, but Bine had a very special knack of suddenly and quietly disappearing.

This meal was only potato soup with lots of parsley in it. We added a lot of Maggi, which was always on the table. We added it to everything. Normally, lunch would have been a vegetable stew with any amount of vegetable from the garden plus potatoes, and for the evening meal, two slices of bread with either cheese, or jam, or *Kunsthonig* which was the best thing we could buy. It was artificial honey and came in blocks and was simply delicious.

In the mornings, we were bribed with *Kunsthonig* to have one spoon of cod liver oil. I retched every time I swallowed that.

We had just settled down to our meal when the bell rang. Mother opened the door and we could hear voices. After what seemed, to us children, a long time, Mother came back, very upset.

The colony had been hit by several bombs. Frau Sauer had been buried under her garden house, Emil was dead too. He had been on his way to Frau Sauer, when he was killed. They were our next door neighbours in the colony. Omi Pless, an old lady whom we had befriended and called Granny Pless, had been hit and wounded. She couldn't get to the shelter in time.

I could not imagine Emil and Frau Sauer dead. They had been there on the day when Mother first wheeled me into our garden in the ancient pram.

❋❋❋

2

I possess a beautifully leather-bound diary, which was started by my grandmother, Margarete von Stückerodt, for my mother, who was born in 1907. She had kept it up for a while, and then she had become ill with Tuberculosis and had to spend two years in a Sanatorium. When she was cured, my grandfather took her to the Baltic Sea for a holiday, but sadly she was swept away by a freak wave, which almost took my grandfather too, in his attempt to save her.

This diary was only used up by a third, and my mother carried on after my birth to record little things when my life started.

Times were confused and unsettled, when I was born. People were confused about what was happening in Germany at the time, and slow to realise the size of the monster that was awakening.

There were also preparations in full swing for the Berlin Olympics. The great excitement was visible on everybody's face, and troubles were momentarily forgotten.

Mother also told me in the diary, that the 1st of July was the birthday of my great grandmother and my great great grandmother, Mother's side. I was always very impressed by this.

I was born on a Wednesday afternoon at five, in my *Onkel Kurt von Stückerodt's* clinic in Wilmersdorf. He was a gynaecologist and my grandfather's nephew. A terrible 'tropical' thunderstorm raged outside, it was 'greenhouse-weather" and flooding followed. Berlin is built on ancient swampland with rivers, lakes and canals in abundance. Some people called it little Venice. My father always said there were more trees and gardens in Berlin than in Venice and just as many bridges.

The French windows in Mother's room, in the clinic, were open all night and the wonderful fragrant smell of strawberries and warm, damp earth filled her room. She got up early with the rising sun, looked into my little cot, saw that I was happily asleep, and walked out a little into the garden, letting the soft warm earth caress her bare feet. She pulled a few weeds and admired the many raindrops, as they sparkled and glittered in all the rainbow colours in the first rays of the sun.

Onkel Kurt, watching her from his apartment upstairs, pulled up the venetian blind furiously and told her to get back into bed immediately. A nurse appeared with a bowl, to wash her muddy feet, grumbling something in Silesian dialect. Mother felt totally at home. *Onkel Kurt* had to have his good natured grumble.

I had spent my first night on earth.

On the third of August, the day the Olympiad opened, I was christened in the *Passionskirche am Marheinike Platz*. I was given many godparents, because Mother didn't want to hurt any of her cousins, and, as she put it, one can never have enough. There was Onkel *Max von Stückerodt, Tante Ria's son, Tante Ria von Stückerodt, Tante Elisabeth von Heigedorn, Onkel Max Ludwig von Gerebrecht, who was Mother's cousin from Mönchgut, and my father's brother, Onkel Holder*. I was wearing the traditional *von Tilemann* christening dress, in which my grandmother and my mother were christened, and my *Onkel Max Ludwig* drove us to the church in his car. It was a beautiful, carefree day and my family looked with some sense of hope into the future. Our roots went back a long way, our family had been closely knit over many generations.

On 20 October 1936, I took my first flight on Heinkel HE III Lufthansa to Breslau in Silesia to visit my father's parents and other relatives. Mother got terribly ill on the plane; flying in those days was quite an adventure.

Silesia was my second home. Mother's relatives lived there. Mother's father was born there too. Mother grew up in a beautiful *Schloss, Mönchgut*, which was owned by her mother's sister.

After my grandmother's death, my mother went to live there, until Grandfather married again. Mother didn't get on at all with her stepmother, so she went back to Mönchgut and a string of cousins and her own grandmother. It became her home. Often, in later years, we would sit together and she would tell of all the things that had happened in that rambling, friendly and happy place. When I was a little older, Mother's cousin's children were there, all about my age, and the same customs and habits continued. Nothing ever changed there from generation to generation. There was always room for everybody.

It used to be an old monastery, renovated and rebuilt in the baroque style, but was abandoned by the monks and bought by a younger son of a Silesian landowner. He married, but only had one daughter, who married an ancestor of the present owner, the husband of my great-aunt. The estate had been in that family for one hundred and seven years. It was wonderful to have a home that was forever.

The house was a long, two storey building with two rows of fifteen windows either side; and two graceful little towers on each end of the roof. One was a little clock tower, the other carried a bell.

There was a large park with a lake on one side of the house. The front of the house, with the open stairs leading to the entrance door, faced a large court area, surrounded by farm buildings. Standing on the open staircase, looking into the court, immediately in front was the drive. On the other side of the road was a giant trough, with clear well water, running constantly for longer than history was recorded at Mönchgut. The work horses, returning in the evening, would drink there before going into their stables, which were in a large building, dominating the entire opposite side of the court. It housed the field and carriage horses. It also housed the cows and oxen. It was designed and built by my great grandfather, Tante Mieze's father, who was an architect-builder, and many famous buildings in Berlin and other cities were built by him. These stables had wonderful, vaulted ceilings and roped pillars and intricately tiled floors. The stables and the cow house always reminded me of a palace.

Four very tall chestnut trees, two on either side of the trough, divided the courtyard. To the right, making it an enclosed yard, the entire side was taken up by what looked like a big wall with windows and two large carriage entrances with domestics-and servants' quarters either side and above. It also housed the riding horses. At the very end, was a water mill and the mill pond, with the leat running past the entire length of the back of the manor house. A little bridge, from where we used to drop leaves and sticks, led from the French windows into the park, past the orchard with apple and pear trees. One could lose oneself entirely for days in that area, and always find something to do.

Adjoining, was the cherry orchard from which a gate opened into the fields. A path carried on past greenhouses and the birch wood to the fishpond and the play lawn and into the park property, eventually leading to the pastures where there were horses grazing, often with foals. Closing the half circle here, one would arrive at the back of the huge barns, which also housed the woodwork shop.

A little further on, was the large sheep house, the foreman's house, the farmworker's cottages, the village street, leading to the little village where some of the farmworkers lived, the bake house and brewery, and the many village children, with whom we often played. The village street entered this enclosed yard from the rear and finished the square. This place was my entire world, as it had been to my mother, who still called this place home. I too would regard visiting Mönchgut the same as going home.

❋❋❋

Not far from our apartment block in Berlin, there was 'a garden colony'. Many Berliners had their own garden where they grew most things for their own use, and with the arrival of the first swallows, the apartments emptied, and the Berliners would move into their summer-houses for the summer. They were small, very cosy and comforts were basic. But the Berliner likes his own bit of earth. Berlin is the Garden City, the Green City.

We too had such a garden. Ours was surrounded by other gardens and so gave the illusion of being in the middle of a wonderful jungle. Every garden had lots of fruit trees and berry bushes. Our little summerhouse consisted of a lounge, a bedroom and a kitchen, and outside, adjoining the entrance into the lounge, we had a grape-arbour from which we harvested the most succulent grapes just before we returned back to our apartment in the autumn. We lived in that arbour and only went indoors when it rained too much and the drops found their way through the thick leaves, and at night. I loved to hear the raindrops tapping gently onto the roof, with the doors wide open into the arbour and the air filled with the aromatic scent of the wet fresh earth.

Since the kitchen was the first room when entering, it was almost, as if the cooking took place outdoors.

A trap door in the kitchen led down into a little cellar, containing some wine, bottled fruit and jam, potatoes and bottles of juice.

Father had built a sandpit filled with the shining golden and silver grey sand, native to some parts of Berlin. He also built a swimming pool for my second birthday. It wasn't very big, but it had a shallow end, into which led some steps from the sandpit, and a deep end for the parents.

I celebrated all my birthdays in this paradise garden and we had noisy parties with lanterns and many of the children from neighbouring gardens. Emil, one of the neighbours, always brought a Punch and Judy show. Mother traditionally made a birthday crown from all the different flowers growing in our garden in July. A birthday without the crown was not a birthday.

I was given my first doll, which had a porcelain head and jointed arms and legs and real hair. I had her for many years. My mother's half-sister visited us on these occasions; she was ten years younger than my mother and much shorter and very round. She had beautiful small but very hard hands, which she used frequently to slap me with when I did something she thought

I shouldn't. She was employed as a governess to the children of a count, which would explain her strict behaviour with me. She was the daughter of my grandfather's second wife, who was born *Gräfin von Helmstatt* (Countess of Helmstatt).

There were plenty of strawberries from the garden, with real whipped cream, two very wobbly mysteriously shaped pink *Götterspeisen, Streuselkuchen and Sahnetorten* (ambrosia pudding, crumble cake and gateaux). For the children, there was barley coffee, and real coffee for the adults. And lemonade!

Six weeks after my second birthday party, my sister, Sabine arrived. She had black hair and huge dark brown eyes. With those eyes she followed me around. For days I would just lie on my tummy and look at her in her cot. I thought she was a little miracle. I had been given a baby doll at the same time. I named her Sabine, and copied everything my mother did. Sabine was also delivered by *Onkel Kurt*, and I stayed in the apartment above with *Tante Guste*, short for Auguste. *Tante Guste* had two teenage daughters and two sons. One son, Hermann, was only two years older than I, a latecomer; there was a nine year gap between him and his brother.

Over time, Hermann and I, played together in the large private and clinic garden, when we visited. There was a little wooden gate which separated the two gardens. We often hid among the bushes and watched the patients, against *Onkel Kurt's* orders.

He was strict, where his patients were concerned, but I wanted to know where he stored the new babies. I was convinced that we were all from Onkel Kurt, and I wanted to know where he got the babies from. My father thought it was sweet and nobody would explain to me what really happened. Onkel Kurt would laugh good naturedly, pick me up and hug me. I loved that big and cuddly man. What interested me was, why my parents chose Bine and me!

✸✸✸

3

On a clear, hot summer's day in 1939, I was sitting astride my father's shoulders. We were standing very close to the Brandenburg Gate. Huge crowds lined the street. All the buildings behind us and the Brandenburg Gate were completely covered with giant swastika flags. Everything was draped in red. All along from *Unter Den Linden* up to the Brandenburg Gate and down to the *Siegessäule,* the red flags on the flagpoles were gently waving in the breeze. The golden Angel of Peace on top of the *Siegessäule* caught the light and glistened like a sunbeam. It was almost too bright for my eyes, but I kept blinking towards the angel, because he looked so beautiful. The people around us were laughing and joking. Everybody was in a festive mood.

I was wearing my 'princess dress', so called because in one of my fairy-tale books, Snow White was wearing a similar dress. In my hand, I clutched a little round handbag with a big tassel on the bottom. Best of all, I had three bananas in that bag and I was eating one, very slowly, scraping the banana little by little, with my teeth, savouring every bit of it, holding the banana carefully with the peel, neatly hanging over my fist. My father was holding me firmly by my feet to stop me from over balancing.

From my lofty height, I could see column after column of soldiers in their gala-uniform marching past. A few men were assembled on the balcony of a large building opposite, and, as the columns came abreast, they all looked right, and as if by some secret signal, lifted their arms. All the men on the balcony lifted their arms too, except one, who only held his arm up a little.

I wondered why. The soldiers looked proud, some carried huge banners of various colours. There were musicians and the men were singing. Soldiers on horses. It went on and on, I was on my last banana. Father was happy and excited.

"These are *unsere Jungs*" (our boys) my father said proudly. Standing next to my father was a friend of his, Onkel Rolf. He had a very deep dimple in his chin, through which he said he could whistle. I didn't really believe it, but he was very convincing.

When the parade was over, we went into an open cafe in the *Tiergarten*, where we sat on white wooden chairs and tables with white cloths under chestnut trees. Little bits of the trees drifted down and landed on my ice cream. Father and Onkel Rolf drank a *Berliner Weisse* which was served in a wide glass goblet. It was an exciting day and I wished for it never to end. So many people in beautiful clothes and summer shoes were happily and slowly walking past. There was a fountain not very far from where we were sitting and the sun was playing in the water as it gracefully fell back into the big basin from which it had sprouted up. We sauntered slowly through the Tiergarten to the underground and there Onkel Rolf left us.

By the time we came out of the underground, I was almost asleep and Father carried me home.

❋❋❋

My hair was light blonde and thick and growing fast. Mother used to weave huge blue ribbons into my plaits to match my eyes. Bine's hair turned out to be very dark brown, almost black to match her dark eyes. She had a tiny curl at the top of her head, and Mother tied it up with a small red bow. I did the same to my doll.

As the summer of thirty nine came to an end, Mother had a letter from her father, who lived at this time, at the Chiemsee, just south of Munich.

After Grandfather lost his third wife, he employed a housekeeper, who consequently had fallen in love with him and he didn't know how to get out of this embarrassing situation.

Father took leave from work and stayed with us while Mother took a coach to Munich where my grandfather collected her in his Nimrod, which was a very racy sports car.

Ten days later, Father took us on a whim, which he could not explain later, to join Mother in Prien.

Grandfather and Father were happy to see each other and 'behaved like schoolboys', Mother said. They went out together, slapping each other's shoulders and came back late, laughing even more loudly. Everybody was happy, and Father spoiled us, which didn't happen very often.

Grandfather rented the rear of his house to some strange people. The woman was friendly in a quiet way. Her husband was a wrestler from Italy. There also lived a black man, Ali ben Abdul, who wore long white robes, like sheets, draped around him. He washed these large pieces of material with his feet in a big bowl in the garden. On his head, he wore a colourful skullcap, beautifully embroidered.

He was a gentle giant and spoke German with a very guttural accent. People often asked me what he had said, because I could understand him better than others. We went on long walks together. My hand disappeared almost to the elbow, in his hand. I had a little brown birthmark on my left hand, and people teased me, that his colour was rubbing off, onto me. I believed it, and watched myself very carefully after that, but the mark never grew any bigger.

I was very fond of Ali. When he stood up with his arms stretched out, my father fitted underneath. He was fond of Bine too, because, as he put it: "she black like me." She wasn't really, only her eyes and hair.

In early autumn, the family was sitting round the table, finishing lunch, with the *Volksempfänger,* the people's radio, which stood in the other room, making little nondescript noises, when suddenly, there was a loud fanfare which made us all sit up and listen.

Grandfather left the table and turned up the radio. A male voice prepared us for a *Sondermeldung*, a special announcement.

The German *Wehrmacht* was advancing into Poland. England had declared WAR!

Everybody was listening to this, but Grandfather turned the radio off. His dear, friendly face had changed. His eyes were like black coals. He said nothing, just looked at each one of us around the table. Father said:

"It had to come. We can't sit back and let the Poles murder the German people. The Poles should not be so ungrateful. Over the centuries we have brought them culture and wealth, stability and government. Without us, what has Poland got? They would soon go to the dogs."

Grandfather stopped in front of my father and said:

"Those are rumours, put about by warmongers and propagandists. There is no proof about the horror stories. I have heard them too. I have worked and lived in Poland, I know these people. Polish blood runs in our veins also." He had difficulty controlling his anger, turned his back on my father, and left the room. Grandfather and Father were no longer friends, it seemed.

I went out and found my friend, Helga, from next door, and we shared a caramel which she had been chewing, and bit it in half. I picked my half from her lips. It was wet, but delicious.

Father went back to Berlin that same day, but we stayed on in Prien.

Two days later Father rang and said we should stay, it would be safer, and he would keep us informed.

Nobody knew what was going to happen. The adults talked a lot in whispers, we were sent out of the room, and of course we were curious and also worried. What was a war? I thought to myself. What happened in a war? Nobody seemed able to tell me.

I asked Helga what she had heard, but she didn't know anything. Her Bavarian dialect was fascinating. She thought I sounded ridiculous, with the way I spoke. She said her mother told her off for asking so many questions.

We sat, looking at the Alps, which completely blocked out the world like a wall, the Kampen Wand, which rose high into the sky. Often, they seemed very close and at other times, they were much further away. I had never seen anything like these jagged big mountains before, strange and mysterious. I often looked at them and wanted to go into them.

One day, Ali took me in Herr Salvatore's car. I asked him what he was doing here and where his home was. He said he was a wrestling partner of Herr Salvatore, the man he shared the flat with. Herr Salvatore and Ali trained together.

Herr Salvatore was a hot-tempered and unpredictable man, and his wife had a very difficult time. She called her husband Stinky. Ali intervened many times, and stopped Herr Salvatore from beating up his wife. There was a lot of shouting in the Salvatore household, and Ali would often be found walking in the garden, or by the lake.

Ali was the one who explained to me what war was. He said that in the hot and dry desert, where he lived, there could be a war just because somebody used their well without permission from the chief. If somebody comes and takes something which is not his, the owners fight for it, and kill for it, and the stronger wins, whether he was right or not. Because the winner is right. He said those were the rules, no matter how big the war, or how many tribes or countries got involved. I sat on his knee, pondering over what he'd said. It seemed unfair.

Sitting on Ali's lap, I temporarily forgot the war that seemed to threaten our lives. He told me a lot about his people and the desert. He said they lived together in tribes, and travelled across the desert on camels. The sun would burn the sand, the heat from the ground would meet the heat from above and the air would be too hot to breathe in. That is why the desert people would wrap themselves in so many sheets of cloth, showing only their eyes. Ali said it was to keep the heat out. I explained to him, that we take our clothes off because of the heat, and he laughed. It was fascinating to listen to him. I would like to see the desert. At times, he took me through the garden to the lake, boating and fishing.

***

Winter came with so much snow! This soft and fluffy whiteness muffled all sound.

I was given brightly coloured mittens, a matching hat and scarf, warm socks and boots, and Grandfather produced a wonderful sledge, with colourful webbing to sit on. The sledge runners came round in a big arch, to make it easier to hold on to. A curved back rest stopped us from falling off. Bine and I were put into Grandfather's furry foot bag, which he had, from the times when he drove in open, horse drawn carriages, in the winter. We spent endless hours out in the snow.

When mother pulled us up the long hill, for our run down on the sled, huge amounts of snow fell down on us from the overhanging fir tree branches. It was a magical Christmas and fairy land, all rolled into one. We took mouthfuls of fluffy, virgin snow and it tasted special. The first signs of war to reach us, in this remote wonderland, was rationing. Suddenly, Grandfather and Mother could not buy what we wanted in the shops, only what the authorities permitted us to have.

But with Grandfather around, things were not so harsh. He would take his rucksack off the hook, put on his green hunting hat with the bushy Gamsbart, (goats beard), and his mountain boots, and go into the mountains to visit the Alm farms. On his return, there would be smoked ham, cheese, butter, a six pounder, charcoal baked rye bread and with any luck, a chicken. I always loved the crafty smile on his face when he returned, and we all surrounded him, full of expectation.

Close to where Grandfather's house stood, passed the newly built Autobahn, there was also an ancient Inn, and this Inn became the first Autobahn *Raststätte* (Motorway service station). It kept the adjoining farm, which produced most of the meat and vegetables, consumed by the Autobahn users.

Very soon, we saw column after column of military vehicles going south. Finished with the Polish invasion, they were now headed for Italy. Mother said the soldiers were so very young, with boy's faces.

Grandfather, feeling restless, decided to go to Monte Carlo for the rest of the winter, which left us free to return to Berlin.

Ali was very sad to see us go, but he said he would not stay for very much longer himself. "When there is a war, one has to be in one's own country." he told me. He said he would write. Mother sent a telegram to Father, announcing our arrival time in Berlin. We took the train via Munich. There was utter chaos at the Munich railway station, and there were soldiers everywhere.

✳ ✳ ✳

4

We soon realised that our scheduled connection from Munich to Berlin, as such, did not exist and that we had to line up with many other stranded passengers, and see which train to the Capital had space for us.

After a lot of running back and forth, with the suitcases and Bine in a Rucksack on her back, myself trying to keep up, Mother headed for the *Bahnhofsmission,* where we were given some space to sit and a bowl of soup, with a slice of bread.

A sawdust stove radiated cosy warmth. A nurse with a red cross on her nurse's cap, came over and told us there would be a train in the morning. She pointed to a corner with a mattress and two children already asleep on it and said to my mother:

"You can put your two alongside those two. I am afraid I haven't anything for you to sleep on." Grateful, Mother put us on the mattress and settled us down. It was a very noisy night, but we slept, even in the bright light of the mission's shade-less bulbs.

In the very early morning, Mother was there, with a bowl of porridge and even a little lump of margarine floating on top, with some milk and a slice of bread. It tasted very good. She hurried us, because the train was already on the platform, and she said:

"We will have to share a compartment with some soldiers. I asked them to keep seats for us and they are looking after our luggage too." I got all exited and couldn't wait to get on the train. I said I couldn't eat anymore, but Mother insisted I finish the porridge and milk. The bread she wrapped up and put into her pocket. Then, she picked up Bine and we all went to the mission's loo, before boarding the train. Mother washed our faces and hands. We were black from the soot of the trains.

When we entered the station again, there was steam hissing everywhere. We ran along the train and in the distance, I saw a soldier leaning out of the window waving. Mother smiled and waved back. She lifted us up and handed us in through the window. The train was already so packed, that we could not get in through the doors. The Soldiers had made beds for us in the luggage nets, above the seats with their overcoats, and lifted us straight into our nests, since there was little room below. From there, I watched how they heaved Mother in through the window too. Everybody laughed, and a man with a red cap helped push her up from outside. Finally, we were all in, the window closed and the door to the corridor was closed too. A miracle, everybody had a seat. Two soldiers sat astride our suitcases, in the middle of the compartment, leaving very little room for the feet of the other passengers, on the wooden benches. They were all soldiers returning from one front, to go straight to another one.

Slowly, the train started to roll out of the station, gathering speed. We were on our way home.

Excitement and laughter filled the compartment. One of the soldiers had some chocolate, which he shared between my sister and myself. It tasted delicious. There were bits of nuts in it too. I let the chocolate melt slowly in my mouth, until only the nuts remained, which I took out and looked at, very carefully, before I ate them, one by one. Bine had long finished hers and had ended up with a chocolate beard.

Another of the soldiers made hats, boats and aeroplanes, out of newspaper. The planes were best because I could fly them from my lofty position and the soldiers would catch them and hand them back. It was great fun in the luggage nets and so cosy.

When it was lunchtime, one by one, the soldiers came up with bits of their rationing. Everybody opened up what they had. Mother had two loaves of bread, big six pounders, which she had hoped to bring back to Berlin. One of the soldiers produced a knife and started to slice up one loaf, holding it against his chest and turning the loaf as he drove the knife through it. Another opened some tins, someone sliced some Salami, and somewhere, some *Speck* appeared, got sliced and shared. Another had a tin of *Saure Gurken* (gherkins).

It turned into a lengthy feast. The food was plentiful. There were even desserts and a bottle of wine, but no glasses, so everybody had to drink from the bottle. There was lemonade for us, some more chocolate and some tinned peaches. Someone suggested to leave some for later.

After that, everybody went to sleep. Legs came up and crisscrossed over to the other seats, past the soldiers in the middle, who rested their bottoms on our suitcases, but leaned over onto the other soldiers laps, with their feet on the laps of their comrades opposite. It looked just like the tin of worms, which Ali had, when we went fishing on the Chiemsee. Mother had a seat in the corner, into which she could lean, and one soldier leaned against her shoulder. Everybody, except Mother, snored. I lay on my tummy and looked down on this human salad. But soon, I too fell asleep.

When I woke up, I could hear muffled laughter and whispering down below. Everybody was sorting out their limbs and fishing for more food. One by one, they woke up, yawned and stretched, as best they could. There was a lot of pushing and shoving amongst the soldiers and Mother climbed over some people and finally disappeared down the corridor. When she came back, Bine needed to go to the loo. One soldier stood up, lifted her from the net and handed her out of the door to another soldier:

"Hand her down the line. One package for drainage." Bine's large eyes looked at Mother who nodded at her and laughed. Before I knew what was happening, the same soldiers had picked me up and handed me over and said:

"And another one." I went from hand to hand, following Bine who still looked worried. When we arrived at the loo, one soldier was told he had to put us on the loo. I turned round and told him we didn't need his help for this. I laboured with Bine. She was wearing nappies, but they were still dry. I lifted her onto the seat and held onto her until she had finished. It was difficult putting the nappies back on, and the soldier by the door, laughed, lifted her up, loose nappy and all, and handed her back. I closed the door for myself. When I came out again, I was handed back as well, surrounded by a lot of good natured, laughing soldiers.

Soon we settled down to another meal. It was quite dark outside now. While we slept, we had passed Regensburg, Nürnberg and Hof, and were now heading for Leipzig. The soldiers were telling jokes and stories, we weren't allowed to hear. I listened intently, but when everybody laughed, I wondered why.

Many hours went by. Some of our companions got ready to leave, as Leipzig was the point where they gathered, as one of the soldiers explained to me, to go back to protect the East of Germany, against the Russians. I was sad to see them leave, they exchanged addresses with my mother and everybody promised to write. Mother often wondered later, if any of them had survived.

I slept again until we reached Berlin.

Father was not at the station, and we took a taxi home, which wasn't very far. When she opened the door, she found utter chaos. Nothing had been tidied. In the kitchen, the dirty dishes were piled high. She started in the bathroom to make room to give us a bath. While we were in the warm water, she went to the kitchen and busied herself there. Her head came round the corner every now and then, to see if we were still all right. Soon she came to dry us and put us to bed with a pile of books. I never tired of books, and I was glad to see all my old favourites again.

Cooking smells came through from the kitchen. I could hear the vacuum cleaner in between times.

When Father came home, the place looked spick and span, as if we had never been away. Mother didn't say a word, and neither did Father. He took it for granted, that the place would look like a battle ground, when Mother was not around, and that she would quietly tidy it up when she got back. I expected Mother to be really cross, as she was when we didn't tidy our room. I was disappointed when she said nothing to Father.

✱✱✱

With the first swallows, we returned to live in our garden, in the spring of 1940. There were reunion celebrations, and visiting neighbours. The neighbour at the back of our garden was a large and very fat lady. Frau Sauer lived in her garden all the time, summer and winter. It fascinated me to see her sitting down, because one couldn't see the chair. She had difficulty walking. She was friendly and jolly, perhaps a little loud and had a strong Berlin accent, into which she weaved a constant string of little jokes. Listening to her, one had to laugh all the time. Even when she said serious things, she was funny. People said she had *Galgen Humor*, (gallows humour).

I used to ask her what she was doing when she was just sitting there, and the answer was usually the same: "I am ironing, see?" And when she got up, there would be a neatly folded pile of laundry, perfectly flat on her seat, which she picked up and put away in her chest.

She always used to say: "*Kauft Kämme, es kommen lausige Zeiten,*" 'Buy combs, there are lousy times ahead.' It was a saying which we all soon adopted.

Most times when I visited, Emil, our other neighbour, was there.

"*Na Kleene*, little one, come here," and with a sweep of his big hand, I would land on his lap. There wasn't much room there, because he had a big belly on his lap already. He was always around, and helping if there was the need. He had time for everybody.

We spent a perfectly relaxed summer in our garden. Relatives came to visit us all summer, glad to escape their city apartments for the day. Their visits were always a cause to celebrate, and we celebrated, a lot.

Playing in the large sandpit, we could watch the planes as they lined up for landing at Tempelhof. Often there would be an airship slowly purring across the sky. The adults called those a 'Churchill Zigarre'.

We grew strawberries, cherries, yellow and blue plums, apples and pears, red and black currents, gooseberries and peaches and even apricots. Mother allowed us to go to the bushes and help ourselves, to anything which grew there and still, there would be plenty to bottle for the winter, or eat raw as a dessert with sour milk or *Quark* (cream cottage cheese).

The idyllic summer of 1940 came to an abrupt end however, when a week after Bine's second birthday, something happened, none of us at first expected or understood, except Father.

There was a strange and frightening noise in the air. Father was the first to realise what was happening and made us all go down into the little cellar in our garden house. There, we sat worried and confused and waited, and Father said:

"I expect, there will be a lot of this now. I didn't expect it so soon. We have to move back to the apartment, it is too dangerous to stay here." Mother looked at Father but said nothing.

"What is happening?" I asked.

"The Tommies are dropping bombs on Berlin." Father said. "They took us by surprise, it won't happen again." Father sounded cross. His finger came up and he wagged it, as he said "Just wait."

"Come, come, calm down," said my mother, "I wonder who dropped the first bombs."

Father replied to Mother, "That is not the point anymore. Since we lost the First World War, and that war was not of our making, but they would have us believe that it was, they have exploited us financially, crippled us, milked us dry, and they do not understand, or don't want to understand, the serious threat we are facing in the east. They should be helping us. It is time they looked to Europe. All they can see is their precious empire. What they don't realise is, that they are threatened the same as we are. Communism is marching, it won't stop until it has conquered the world. They had better watch out. They will wake up with a thump."

Seldom had I seen my father so worked up. He was short sighted and that made his eyes look small behind the lenses, which always looked strange in any case, and now they were two dark glittering dots. He was impatient with Mother. She didn't seem to agree with him.

"What is that noise?" I asked and Father, calming down a little, explained that it was a siren, announcing the end of the raid. We climbed out of the little cellar through the trapdoor; nothing outside had changed! So what was it all about?

From then on, the raids continued irregularly and we had to leave our garden early that year, but still spent most of the daytime out there, only at night we had to be back in the apartment block for better shelter. There, we had proper bunk beds and the noise outside was muffled. The walls in the cellar were thick concrete and there were iron doors and air filters. We all had coal central heating in our apartments and the big boiler was in the basement. Hence the iron doors for fire safety.

On a visit to Onkel Kurt, shortly after that, I saw what the bombs had already done. I couldn't believe that something falling from a plane could break a house so completely. Houses that had looked so safe and strong! If such a thing fell on our house, would it break like that too? Mother said "yes it would." I was very worried. There were many nights though, when there was no raid, and I thought the war was over.

❋❋❋

5

Father took us all on a holiday to the Wannsee, where we kept a large paddling boat. Since the raids were few and mostly at night, we had relatively peaceful and wonderful days. Days I would never forget.

Out on the quiet lake, the water surface was so still, it looked like mirrored glass. When my parents stopped paddling, with the paddles just resting across the boat, the drops made a chain of ever increasing perfect circles. It was fascinating and putting one finger into this smoothness, I watched as the v my finger created, grew and grew. Leaning over the edge, I could see the endless sunlit greenness of the water, some fish darting out of sight and the boat making a shadow. I loved these moments, and when my father ordered: "Come on, one – two, one – two, pull hard!" the paddles would slice into the water, in unison, leaving big swirls and the boat would rush forward. I could feel the wind on my forehead, imagining myself as a viking on the high seas or Siegfried, going to Iceland to find Brünhild. Our trips were highlighted when we 'dropped anchor' at the *Pfaueninsel*, Peacock Island, which was also a truly magical place. The peacocks there seemed unreal, they were so beautiful. I liked to imagine, that they were enchanted princes and princesses, and the white *Schloss* on the island was also enchanted, and one day, the magic would break and the palace and the peacocks would return to their original forms and live happily ever after.

There was a big aqua slide in beautifully carved, smooth wood, towering, soaring and long. You reached the top platform via a ladder. Before splashing into the lake, you had to negotiate a bump in the middle of the slide. My woollen bathing suit wore out completely, several times, and Mother had to knit new bottoms. Every Berliner seemed to come here and be happy.

Potsdam was near the Wannsee, and we often went there too. It was where Frederik the Great's Residence stood, surrounded by many palaces and stately buildings, dotted with clean and shining simple homes, for the ordinary citizens of Potsdam.

The summer palace of König Friedrich II, known as the *Alte Fritz*, was there too. It was called Sanscouci, and built like a miniature Versailles, set in a dense parklike forest which suddenly opened up, and amidst beautiful gardens with the scent of many flower beds filling the hot air, stood the little palace, with fountains, where one could cool off, dotted here and there.

We entered into a graceful, colonnaded semicircle and approached the front entrance. I was always in awe of the grace and beauty of the place. *Onkel Max* told me that the columns were Korinthian, which was a place in Greece, and that we had adopted their way of building things, because no one found a better way of producing beautiful monumental buildings, since ancient Grecian times.

It was usually a little gloomy, after the bright sunlight, and on the marble floor, immediately in front of us, we found a mountain of huge felt slippers, big enough for me to sit in and go paddling. The floors in Sanscouci were highly polished parquet or marble flooring, intricately inlaid with different varieties of wood or marble. One room was magically decorated with mirrors and crystal chandeliers. It was the so called *Spiegelsaal*. I imagined it to be like the Ice Palace in the fairy tale of Anderson's 'Snow Queen'.

The garden side of the palace led onto a terrace, which ended in a wide staircase sweeping downhill, on which, used to grow grapes. Either side of the staircase were greenhouses, which hugged the hillside like giant glass steps. The hot air which emanated from the glasshouses, was filled with the scent of thyme and lavender. In the Orangery, real oranges grew. Marble kings and princes on horseback, further documented Germany's history in the garden. At the foot of the sweeping staircase of green houses, was an enormous artificial, perfectly round lake with rounded marble benches and statues in between. Here, Mother used to sit down and unpack our sandwiches and bring out the lemonade. Bine and I ran around the lake and glanced up at the glittering glass houses. The light would catch the glass and a million suns shone down on us. This palace was a magic jewel and favourite place of excursion for us.

Not far from Tempelhof and easily reached by the *U-Bahn*, was the Lustgarten with the Royal Museum and its many columns, flanked by two enormous bowls of water with fountains in the middle. Fountains fascinated me. I loved water, and often tried to create the fountain effect with our garden hose to make a rainbow. I always circled round a fountain to find the rainbow.

The Dom to the right of the Lustgarten, dwarfed everything within its sight. The Royal Palace next and opposite the Kaiser Wilhelm I National Memorial, jutted out into the River Spree. A bridge, adorned with many snow white marble statues, on tall square pillars, spread like an extension of the square, across the river. There were statues everywhere, a lot of the heroes, kings and queens that ever ruled over Germany, were there to be remembered and admired.

An enormous park in the centre of Berlin, leading away from the Brandenburg Gate down to the Siegessäule was called the *Tiergarten* (Animal Garden). Formerly, this was the hunting forest for the kings and princes. The main entrance, with gigantic marble elephants on both sides, and a Chinese pagoda-like gate, faced the platform, where you left the train. Great excitement came over me, every time we entered through the gate. What sort of adventure would I have today?

One way to reach the zoo, was to walk through the *Tiergarten*. There were strange and exotic animals and smells and sounds. Different species of trees grew around a lake and along intricate waterways, where one could hire boats.

The ultimate delight was a camel or elephant ride, and the Reptile House, with snakes so enormous, they could have eaten me, sent shivers down my spine. Huge butterflies and birds, no bigger than bees were found in a gigantic glass house. More white marble statues of the famous, Richard Wagner, Queen Luise, Kurprinz Friedrich Wilhelm, the young Wilhelm and Goethe, Schiller, and so many more adorned the *Tiergarten*. There were fountains and one was called the Roland Brunnen and Roland looked such a proud knight in armour.

There was never a dull building, a dull moment or a dull day.

Berlin, the Garden City, the Beautiful! There was no place more exciting or beloved.

We used the underground to travel to most places in Berlin, and often visited Onkel Kurt. He was a gentle man, wise and loving and made time for all the family, even though he was a busy doctor. He could be so funny, there was much laughter in his house, and Tante Guste, his wife, moved quietly among the family with a mysterious, happy smile.

Her two daughters, in their late teens, were serene and beautiful. Kurt, their teenage brother was in the *Hitler Jugend* and proudly displayed a swastika armband. There was a certain authority about him.

Hermann, the youngest, and I were good friends and teamed up together as a rule. He was going to be a gynaecologist, like his father. They had two large German Bulldogs, which were very beautiful to look at, except for their mouths. They seemed too big for their faces and often a tooth would stick out. It reminded me of an aunt we had, who also had a tooth which didn't go behind her lips, but always sat on the bottom lip. Mother called it the 'cake tooth'.

***

There was a marked change in the autumn of 1941. The adults huddled worriedly, discussing events, making sure we weren't listening. When they saw us, they sent us away to play. Hermann had overheard some things and took me to his room.

His mother had started to collect warm clothing, because, as Hermann explained to me, 'our boys' were going to Moscow. Winter was near and they had no winter clothes. He told me a lot about strategy, which I did not understand. He knew so much more, having grown-up sisters and an older brother, they included him in their conversations. Once he said:

"Oh you wouldn't understand anyway, you are a girl," and I said crossly "No, I am not." I hated to be put down as 'a girl'.

We went down again and tried to listen to the adults, discussing the situation. Tante Guste had organised collections in her area for scarves, mittens, socks and long johns, sweaters and pullovers, in fact, anything warm.

"It won't be enough" I heard her say.

"They'll never survive the Russian winter."

Hermann told me that his uncle, his mother's brother and two of her cousins were heading to Russia and Tante Guste was afraid for them.

"Stups is going to Moscow (he was one of my godfathers), did you know Gittel?" Onkel Kurt asked my mother. She nodded.

"Max Ludwig is going too," Mother said, "he wrote to ask us to come to Silesia before he leaves."

"I hope Hitler remembers what happened to Napoleon's Army, and doesn't make the same mistake." Onkel Kurt said.

(Many years later I remembered that remark, when I learned about my great-great-great grandfather, a tactician in the Prussian Army. He took his leave to join the Russian Army, after the Prussian treaty with Napoleon. His King thought him a traitor, and only many years later, was he hailed as a hero. It was he and Clausewitz who advised the Tsar to let Napoleon advance as far as Moscow and let the Russian winter do the rest).

Mother was very quiet on the way home. I heard her later discuss the situation with my father. He was optimistic and full of enthusiasm. He only talked of winning the war. He said he wished he could be there. Mother was sad and I saw tears in her eyes, which she wiped away very quickly, when she saw me in the darkness of the corridor.

"Shouldn't you be in bed," Father said, as he led me back to my bed and tucked me in. Things were not the same anymore. Father too, wasn't the same. I even heard my parents quarrel, on some occasions. One day, when I entered the drawing room, I actually saw them with raised hands, and eyes flashing. But as soon as they saw me, they were soft and cosy again. I wondered what was going on. Mother explained later, as we were going to the garden, what was happening:

"Your father and I don't agree over some things concerning this war. Your father thinks we have to fight this war, but I think there is another way to solve the differences we have with our enemies."

Our enemy! I saw posters everywhere on the sides of houses and the many advertisement pillars, where a German soldier was stabbed in the back by a monster, which was the enemy. One had to fight that enemy. I was inclined to be on my father's side.

❋❋❋

In the late summer of 1941, Mother went back to Onkel Kurt and returned with a baby. Bine and I had a sister, Christiane.

As winter set in, we heard the situation reports daily, the tactical withdrawls by the Russians, the dreadful cold and the suffering of the German Army, their weakened combat ability. Everybody in the neighbourhood spoke about the blinding snow-storms, unstopped, across the Russian plains and how the ground was too frozen to dig in for shelter. Temperatures were so cold, the guns froze and their vehicles would not move. Some of those poor soldiers came back with their legs frozen so badly, they had to be amputated. They would tell of such cold, where their breath would make icicles on their eyelashes. So cold, that their lungs would freeze and their noses fell off, if they didn't warn each other, to keep rubbing them, when they became white. I couldn't imagine it. It was sickening.

I collected all my warm things and gave them to my mother for her to pass them on to the people who collected for the soldiers.

"They won't fit, my little heart, but maybe one can unravel the wool and knit something else." My warm things disappeared, leaving me with only one of each. The Berlin winters were also very cold, the canals and rivers froze over, and there was lots of snow. As I built a large snowman outside our front entrance, I had to think of the men on the Eastern front. Would my uncles be safe?

✱✱✱

6

Easter 1942 came and I couldn't wait for my first school day. It wasn't school so much, as what came with it. Most of all, the wonders of the *Schultüte*, which was a large paper cone, almost as tall as I was, and filled to the brim with chocolates, sweets, all sorts of biscuits, little toys and things for school. Apart from that, a brand new shiny leather satchel with a slate, slate pencils in a carved wooden pencil box, and dangling from the slate on a piece of string, a large yellow sponge and cloth. With envy, I had watched other children walk to school, past our apartment, carrying their satchels on their back with their sponge and cloth dangling in the wind. Now it was my turn. My *Schultüte* was as big as everyone else's. My friendship with Reni started here as we compared what we had in our cone on that first day.

The school was not very far, only down two blocks, crossing a wide semi-circle street, called *Damm*, through a little park, over the *Tempelhofer Damm* to the Schwiebusser and Jüteboger Strasse where the school was.

Reni and I became best friends. Her full name was Reni Peresselenkow, her dark hair was cut into a neat bob. I begged my mother to allow my hair to be cut too, but she wouldn't hear of it. Reni and I played after school until the raids became too frequent. She lived halfway between my house and the school, but I needed to be with my family when there was a raid, and Mother soon insisted that I come straight home from school. Reni and I were both sad, that we couldn't play together more.

Then came the letter, which called Father to war. It had never occurred to me that he might have to leave us. He was always at home in the evenings, and at weekends, we often met him in town and spent an hour with him in the park, eating sandwiches. But he was being called away, and he couldn't tell us where he was going or for how long. It was a secret. All I knew, was he was with the Air Force Ministry.

"Must you go?" I asked him, sitting on his knee, with my arm around his neck, cuddling up to him. His face came close to mine and he rocked me a little back and forth.

"Well, my little Minka," as he used to call me, "when my Führer calls me, I have to go. I have no choice. Everybody has to do his duty. Your mother will have a difficult time now, and you as the oldest, must help her. She will be relying on you, and so will I."

Those were his last words to me.

And so Father went to war. I missed him very much and looked more and more for Emil in his garden, but mostly, I found him with Frau Sauer, or *die Sauern*, as most people around used to call her.

I asked Emil, why he didn't have to go to war and he lifted up one trouser leg and knocked on a wooden leg, which ended in a leather bucket where his real leg rested, just below the knee.

"That's why. *Weltkrieg*."

"What is *Weltkrieg*?" I had heard that before I thought to myself.

"That is the war your grandfather fought in, when your mother was little. It was a bad, unjust, unfair, terrible war. Too many people got hurt and died and now our 'glorious Führer' is trying to put things right for the German people, but he is doing it all wrong."

The way Emil said 'glorious Führer' I could tell he didn't like him. But Father does. I didn't understand.

"Why don't you like the Führer?" I asked. I could see Frau Sauer looking at Emil and shaking her head a little. Emil gave me a hug, dug into his large pockets and found some fruit drops.

"Here, have these and now be off with you and play. I will tell you one day." Puzzled, I left. There were always things we children were not allowed to know. There were many times adult conversation stopped, when we came into the room. It was puzzling and worrying.

I was slowly walking down the path to the garden gate, when Emil, limping hard, caught up with me. He hardly limped at all, when he walked properly, only when he ran.

"Don't be sad *Kleene* (little one), I will be here, even if your father isn't, and you can come to me any time. If your mother needs any help in the garden, just come round, I have nothing much to do nowadays."

"Did it hurt when you lost your leg?" I asked him, taking his hand and remembering how my knee hurt, when I fell and took off all my skin.

"Well," he laughed "first it was very painful, and my leg hurt, even though it wasn't there anymore. I could see it wasn't there, but it still hurt. Now," he laughed and squeezed my hand "it only hurts when the weather changes."

"Why when the weather changes?" It didn't make sense. But Emil laughed and said: "That's when the wood expands." I would never be an adult, I thought to myself, there was too much to learn.

❋❋❋

A large, formal envelope, containing an invitation, arrived by post one day. It was really a summons, and we dressed as if we were going visiting on Sundays. Christiane in the pram, Bine sitting on a seat across the pram between the handlebars, and myself walking beside the pram holding on, we took the underground from Papestrasse, our local stop.

Emerging from the underground at our destination, we saw a big building, resembling a palace, which we entered. I felt excited. Mother left Tissi's pram in the lobby, with the other prams, and we went inside. It was a large theatre which we entered at the top, and way down the sloping floor was the stage. There were many red flags with the black Swastika on white ground, men in mustard coloured uniforms with a Swastika armband, women and children. We sat down, and I wondered what was going to happen. Would there be a show? I slid around, excitedly on my seat, looking around at so many children. They too were all excited and there was a din like in the big wave pool in the swimming baths.

A man walked onto the stage and climbed onto a little tower with only his head and chest showing. Everybody became quiet and he began a long and boring speech. When he had finally finished, a military band played and played, followed by the "Horst Wessel Lied", which everybody sang and Deutschland Deutschland über allies.

Eventually the man came back on stage and read out a name and one by one, mothers and children went down to the stage, received something and came back to their seats. It went on for ages. Finally, our turn came. Mother took Christiane in her arm, Bine's hand in her free hand and I trotted on my own after them. I always walked on my own, after Tissi's arrival.

'I only have two hands' was Mother's new phrase.

Mother let go of Bine's hand, and a mustard coloured man shook her free hand, smiled at all of us and proceeded to put a blue and white cross with the same coloured ribbon around Mother's neck and then handed her a piece of paper with a signature of Hitler on it and congratulated her on the four children, born for Hitler and the Reich.

Four children! For the first time I became truly conscious, that I have a brother, older than I, and never at home. It made Mother sad to talk about it. He visited us quite regularly, but it was just a visit. It never felt as if he was a brother. He lived with my father's mother in Silesia, but we didn't visit them often. I didn't like my grandmother at all, and I am sure it was because she didn't like me. She didn't like Bine either. Suddenly, I felt very sorry for my brother, who had to live there all the time.

Much later, I found out why there was such a lot of quarrelling between my parents. Father's mother was convinced, that because my brother was the first born and a male child, he had to be brought up properly. Mother was judged by her mother in law, not to be a fit person to do so, because she grew up as, in her words, "a spoilt baroness, brought up by governesses and servants."

※※※

Mother packed a lot into the year of 1942. Father wasn't at home anymore, though there were lots of letters. Presents arrived from Paris and Rome, a shining silver blue bicycle for Bine, but she was still too little to ride it, so I was allowed to use it. There were roller skates running on ball bearings; extreme luxury, and mine too!

The wide, smooth road outside our apartment was my skating rink and I raced around the entire block. There were hardly any cars on the road, except the greengrocer's three wheeler or the whining post van, which had an electric engine. The bicycle took me to school and to the garden, on many errands and joyrides. Reni had a bike too, and together we explored Tempelhof. We found Hasenheide Park and the Rixdorfer height, the Landwehr Canal and on the other side of the airport the Teltow Canal. Once, we nearly got lost, and Reni was afraid there might be a raid and we wouldn't make it back home. But then I recognised the back end of our colony and found the way home very quickly.

It was a special treat to visit Tante Ria von Stückerodt. She lived in the middle of the city. Her apartment was in a large building that always reminded me of a grand palace. The double entrance door opened mysteriously, after a little buzz and led into a marbled lobby. About six steps up, were two enormous mirrors on the wall opposite each other and standing on tiptoe, I could see my head disappearing into the distance forever.

Four more marble steps up, was a glass lift, inside a beautifully wrought iron cage. At the push of a button, the door opened and we stepped in. The stairwell was open and one could see the staircase winding itself all the way up around the lift. We had to glide up 4 floors and I wished it went on forever.

Tante Ria was always waiting with outstretched arms at her door when we arrived in the lift. She had snow white shining wavy hair, tied up high in a big knot. Her dress was black with white trimmings, usually high at the neck with white lace ruffles, pinned into place with a cameo brooch at her throat. She was quite tall and wore pearls hanging down over her well-shaped bosom to her belt. She was warm and kind, and I never misbehaved in her home. There was something about her which made us respect and love her.

We entered a long, highly polished corridor on which we slid along at high speed. She always rolled up the runner to expose the parquet floor, and produced some rags which she tied around our feet.

Tante Ria's table, laid for the afternoon *Kaffee und Kuchen*, glistened. Everything on the table, except the cups we drank from, was of silver. The cups were all different, and of the thinnest china. I liked the smooth porcelain against my lips, when I sipped the chocolate, which was prepared for the children and tasted like heaven. Cream foam floated on the top, with minute particles of brown chocolate in white foam. There was nothing I could compare it with, and no chocolate in later years tasted the same. There were usually three cakes to choose from; fresh cream cake, *Gugelhupf* and a fresh fruit cake. There was whipped cream to go on the cake and into the coffee and chocolate. There was plenty to go round, even if there was a string of cousins, visiting at the same time.

In a glass cabinet, was an ostrich egg, on silver legs, with beautiful carvings on the eggshell. There were other exotic things to look at. One of her ancestors had fought at Ladysmith in South Africa, and there were African carvings and weapons hanging on the wall.

Now one of her sons was in Stalingrad. A shadow had come over our happy gatherings, and the conversation invariably turned to her sons and my uncles, Mother's cousins and my father. Tante Ria was as sweet as ever, but she did not smile as often and we had to ask for the rags to go sliding. She forgot things like that now.

War turned out to be sad and horrible, making people unhappy. The smiling soldiers were in great danger. Did the adults not know that beforehand? Was there no way to talk to the enemy and work things out? Did one have to kill? I asked myself. I was leaning against Tante Ria's knee, and she had her hand on my head, stroking it gently.

"You are far too small to understand it all. Don't worry your little heart over it. All will be well, you will see." she said.

But it wasn't. As the weeks went on, the bombing got worse and worse. Regularly, every night, near to eight o' clock, we would end up in the cellar.

✹✹✹

7

The screaming siren, announcing the air raids, always caused a sinking sensation in my tummy. Mother decided, after a while, that it would be better to put us to bed in the cellar, rather than having to wake us up, take us down and put us back to sleep. I hated having to sleep down there. There was a musty smell, which irritated my nose and the bunk beds were not very cosy. But Mother insisted. There were children from the other apartments too. Roland was a friend of mine, who lived above us. He was younger and frightened. I always felt I had to protect him.

The adults huddled on benches and deckchairs and the odd cast off armchair, but there was not enough room to have beds for the adults too. We had only two men among them, and one of those was the shelter warden. He had to see that everybody in the block was in the air raid shelter, with the doors closed and air vents shut, should there be a gas bomb. He had a device which warned him of such a bomb. He also had to check that everybody carried their gasmasks. People looked like monster elephants with those masks on their faces.

One morning, on waking up, I found the cellar empty, except for the children in their beds. I was alarmed and climbed out of bed. Bine's big black eyes were watching me, as I reached down with my foot, from the upper bed.

"I am just checking to see what is happening. Stay here." I whispered to her, trying not to wake Tissi, who shared Bine's bed.

I went along the dark and musty passage, to the double iron door which I found slightly ajar. As I climbed the stairs, into the open court, it was still night, except for a red glow above the rooftops. It reminded me of the brilliant sunsets I had watched at the Wannsee. But this was not a sunset. I could hear a frightening roar and crackling, and then I discovered that this red glow came from behind windows at the apartments, adjoining ours and that flames were shooting and bellowing from the roof and windows. In fact two thirds of the square was on fire. I was very frightened.

I ran in at the back door, through the entrance hall, onto the street and there, I saw a long double chain of people. Everybody from our block, in fact, all the women from the neighbourhood, were passing buckets, and anything that would hold water, up one side and empty down the other to a gushing hydrant. Everybody worked with a frantic speed. I walked along the chain and looked at all the women. They were so busy passing buckets, they didn't seem to see me. I saw Mother through the staircase window on the second floor of a building, just as the fire engines came racing round the corner. Everything shone in the crimson glow. The firemen had been so busy all night and only just managed to come to us. Mother waved to me and yelled something. It looked like: "Go back", but I couldn't hear it. The roaring and cracking of the fire was fascinating. I stood and watched, feeling the immense heat. I noticed more burning houses down the other street, and more people passing buckets. I saw the little bit of water that each bucket held, and it didn't make any difference at all as the person at the top chucked it into the inferno. A few sparks, a little bit of black smoke, but the fire roared on just as before.

My whole world was on fire!

Mother had left the chain and came down to me. She was black and had lots of patches on her face, arms and hands. Those were bits of burning wood, which had dropped onto her and charred her skin. She was excited and out of breath and yelled over the din:

"Go back and look after the children. We have to stop the fire before it catches our house. You can help by keeping the children in the cellar, we need all the adults here." You are now *die*

Grosse." She gave me a big hug and looked at me. "I am counting on you, Minka."

Slowly, I went back. I had lost my sense of safety. I hoped that our house would not catch fire. I could see what it had done to the other houses. Where Reni lived, there was only a black stalky emptiness, where we used to stand on the balcony, there was nothing and the windows were just gaping holes. What happened to Reni's toys? Had she saved her dolls and her beautiful dollhouse? As soon as I got back to our apartment, I would pack all my precious things and take them to the basement. Would they be safe there? Was anything safe now, with all this destruction? But first, I had to go down and see to the children. As I came out of the back door, I saw Bine clutching Tissi, barely being able to hold her up. Both were crying bitterly, and the other children huddled at the top of the stairs. Bine was trying to cope with the snot that was running down her nose, not having a hand free to wipe it. I took Tissi and we all went back to the basement, and Bine wiped her nose on her sleeve. I found some sandwiches and some milk, and all the children settled down on one bed in a tight circle with a blanket over our heads covering everybody. In this safe darkness we ate the bread and in a whispering voice I told them what I had seen. I reassured them, that all the mothers were safe, and that they would soon be back. The smoke started to seep into the basement, but we felt safe under the blanket tent. We didn't move until the adults came back. Smiling, they pulled the blanket away and took us back to our apartments.

We had barely got in when the alarm went again. Tissi smelled and needed new nappies. Bine and I had a race to the loo, Mother grabbed some bread and some nappies and soon we were all back in the basement. Nobody spoke. The children were sitting on adult's laps and Tissi cried and hiccupped. Mother rocked her gently. There were some dreadful blasts. My ears hurt. I felt sick in my stomach, and soon I had such a headache that I vomited and couldn't open my eyes. The air raid warden put me to bed with a wet, cool cloth on my face, which was very soothing, and I fell asleep.

When I woke up, there was no electric light, but a candle was burning on the table. There was hardly any air, it was so hot, the warden was pumping filtered air into our cellar, but it stank. The adults looked very white with dark hollow eyes. I heard an eerie whistling and then a bang which gave me such a pain in my head, that tears streamed down my face. I closed my eyes and thought that maybe, we were now going to die.

When the raid had finished and we finally came up, we had been down there for fourteen hours except for the short interval.

Our side of the street lost all its windows, some tiles on the roof, but all the apartments were intact except for the doors. They were all torn off the hinges. Left and right and the back of our square was in ruins. People simply stayed in the shelter and continued to live there and called themselves voles. Others who had no room found some with us and our neighbours until they were rehoused.

There were big craters and mountains of brick and rubble in our road, and I could not roller-skate or cycle, the beautiful bicycle was crushed when the front door fell on it.

School went on as usual. After school, the children would go and search in the ruins for belongings. We would find the owner and offer it back and often we would earn some bread and butter or an apple, a carrot on a saucer with a little sugar from the delighted owners. But that soon came to a stop, when someone found an unexploded bomb, and we were not allowed into the ruins anymore.

Because of the regular, intensive night bombing, we children were ordered to sleep in the Bunker of Tempelhof Airport. There were large underground shelters with cells of 4 bunkbeds in each, and hundreds of children came to sleep there every night. Bine and I came too, Tissi stayed with Mother because she was still an infant.

We were given thick slimy porridge for breakfast, and I went to school from there, which was just across the square, seeing Mother briefly when she fetched Bine. I only spent my afternoons and early evening at home now. I hated it.

At the Tempelhof bunker a female warden would close the iron window shutter from the inside when there was a raid and there was no noise after that. I felt secure, except that it worried me that our mother and Tissi could not join us, and every night when there was a raid and the iron shutter was closed, I prayed that Mother and Tissi would be safe.

✳✳✳

The first Christmas without Father, we had an invitation to come to Mönchgut and took an overcrowded train to Wohlau in Silesia. Somebody in the compartment wondered whether Hitler was aware of the condition of the German trains. Everybody laughed. I could see signs saying: *"Räder müssen rollen für den Sieg"*, wheels must roll for victory.

We also visited my brother who lived very nearby in Obernigk. He came back with us to Mönchgut for a few days, and we had a carefree, happy time.

Having learned to ice skate on the many canals in Berlin, I found it easy to skate on the millpond. We also took the sledges into the deep snow. There was laughter and shouting, red cheeks and frozen mittens, cold feet and happy hearts. Not a minute was wasted.

Going into the forest with Härtel Kolle on the horse drawn sledge, with hay and nuts, to feed the wild deer and the birds who found nothing in the deep snow, was greeted with delight. We would be as quiet as possible so as not to frighten the animals, and found that they were quite tame and unafraid, knowing that we would not harm them.

We looked forward to Christmas Eve with trepidation. None of the men had been able to come home on leave, for the celebration. We spent a lot of time remembering everybody, and trying to work out what they would be doing, and if they would have a fair Christmas. Would they have a tree? Had they received their parcels with the *Stollen*, Wurst (smoked sausage) and cookies? Everybody had someone in the war.

We remembered my godfather, Onkel Max Ludwig, Tante Mieze's son who had died on the 4th December the year before, in 1941. Mother, Onkel Max and Onkel Martin were more like brothers and sister than cousins. We all hoped that nobody else would die and that the rest would soon be safely home again. We sang a Christmas Carol for everybody who was not there, remembering which song was their favourite.

Tante Mieze managed to have a goose stuffed with prunes, apples and onions for Christmas Day with red cabbage and potato dumplings, pink angels delight and homemade ice cream, which I helped make with Tante Mieze's ice cream maker. There was plenty of *Stollen* and cookies.

On the second Christmas day, a man came to the door, wearing a uniform, carrying an envelope. He stood in the great entrance hall, smartly getting his heels together and lifting up his right arm and saying "Heil Hitler."

Everybody knew that the envelope meant terrible news. Tante Mieze sat down, holding the envelope. Haertel Kolle, the foreman came over and gently took the envelope from her shaking hand, opened it and read aloud:

"We regret to inform you that Lieutenant Martin von Gerebrecht has been killed in action, exact date unknown."

Christmas was suddenly over. Tante Fee and Tante Gretel had lost a brother, Tante Mieze another son, Mother a cousin, I a godfather. The man in uniform was still standing there. What was he waiting for? Did he enjoy all this grief? No, it didn't mean a thing to him. He produced another piece of paper.

"Herr Karl Haertel" and he looked at the only grown man among us. Haertel Kolle stepped forward and received his order to join the war. This was too much for Tante Mieze. Quietly she collapsed and cried. Was this the end of Mönchgut? The end of everything? Tante Mieze was elderly and had to run the big estate almost single handed, now all the male servants had gone to the war. Haertel Kolle kept things going as best he could on his own. What was she to do without him? What could anybody do?

Sad, helpless and depressed we went back to Berlin in the New Year, ready for the beginning of the new term at school.

❋❋❋

The raids were an everyday occurrence and had become a routine. I felt little fear and worried less. None of us had time to worry. The raids had become a part of our lives.

Around Easter of 1943, a cold and blustery day, we were all in the sitting room, looking out onto the street and the trees beyond to watch for the first green, and a return to our garden. Mother said:

"I will have to feed the rabbits as soon as it stops raining."

Berliners had been asked to produce something to help beat shortages which occurred everywhere. Mother chose Angora Rabbits because of a lack of space in our garden. The wool they produced, Mother took to a collecting place, where it was spun and a percentage given back to us for our own use. There never was enough to knit a lot. She had unravelled some old pullovers and had a lot of red wool of different hues and thicknesses, which she cleverly knitted into two dresses for Bine and me. The white angora sleeves and collars she knitted, set off the dress beautifully. They were the prettiest things we had.

❋❋❋

8

The raid that followed, after Mother had left to go to the garden to feed the angora rabbits nearly cost her, her life. It cost the lives of many people I knew in our neighbourhood. It also destroyed our garden to a great extent, killed Frau Sauer and Emil, injured Omi Pless. It really brought home to me the merciless horror of the war. There seemed to be no escape.

When I went to school again, almost half the class was missing.

The teacher was reading the names of the missing children to us, and in a remembrance ceremony we sang the song *Ich hat einen Kameraden* (I had a friend). This song was on everybody's lips a lot now, every time somebody died at home or on the front.

We did not return to the garden after Frau Sauer's and Emil's death. We just could not bear it any more. A few days after their death, Mother came to fetch me from school. Normally I walked home on my own. She had Tissi in the big pram and Bine sitting across on a board between the handlebars. She had unhappy news and as we walked home she said:

"You are not going back to school, we are all going to be evacuated."

"What is evacuated?"

"That is when you are being sent somewhere, where it is safe from bombing. No more bombing, isn't that wonderful?"

"Yes that would be nice." and then it struck me:

"But what about our things." I looked at Mother and I was worried. What if everything was bombed while we were away. I worked out, that it was only a matter of a very short time, when our house would be bombed too. Almost everybody else's house was bombed.

"We put everything into our lockup in the cellar. There it will be safe. We will not be a very long time, the war will soon be over"

"Where are we going?" I asked, a little reassured now and started to skip along. I loved to go on a journey by train.

"First we go to Obernigk and you stay with Grandmother and your brother."

"Why can't we go to Mönchgut?" I didn't want to go and stay with my grandmother.

"Tante Mieze has no time for us since Härtel Kolle has gone to war, Onkel Jo is gone too, and Tante Fee is alone on Dornitz and they cannot cope with a woman and three little children. I wouldn't be much help"

"I can help" I said, but Mother shook her head sadly.

"It wouldn't be enough, we would be in the way. Times have changed." Mother cried a little. "No, no it is best you stay with Grandmother, it won't be for long. I shall go and prepare our place in East Prussia. That is where we are going. In the meantime, you have to look after the two little ones. You have to help *Tante Hilde*." Tante Hilde was my father's sister and had never married. I feared her terribly. I could never imagine that anyone could or would ever love her. She was hard and cold, never smiled and always punished me. She seemed to enjoy punishing other people. Her hand was always raised, ready to smack. Mother said she suffered a lot with headaches, and was always in pain. The only people I loved in Obernigk were my father and his brother Onkel Holder. He was also my godfather. I loved him very much and often wondered why, since he was so nice, his mother and his sister were such horrible old women. They were both like the witch in Hänsel und Gretel.

"How long do we have to stay there?" I asked my mother. I dreaded any separation, especially if my Mother had to go back to Berlin. I could not imagine living without Mother and having to look after the two little ones on my own, or even worse to have to live with Father's mother.

"Two or three weeks at the most. It will be exciting in the country, and you will go mushroom picking in the forest. You always enjoyed that." That was true. I remembered earlier occasions when I went mushroom picking. We would always try and compete as to who would find the most mushrooms, and who could tell the good ones from the poisonous ones. My brother, who lived in the country all the time, and was older, was an expert, but too selfish to teach me. He was Grandmother's pet, and always liked it when we were told off and he was praised. I realised too, that he didn't like to share his grandmother with us.

As a result, the only time I learned anything about mushrooms was when Onkel Holder was with us. He would tell me which ones to pick and which not even to touch, or if accidentally put in with the good ones, would make the lot very bitter and only fit to be thrown out. One had to be very careful, but if one had a nice collection of mushrooms in the bucket, the meal afterwards was a delicious treat. The mushroom season was always eagerly awaited in Silesia. Equally the bilberry, raspberry and blackberry season. The forests were so rich with fruits. We also found cranberries, which didn't taste so nice when eaten raw.

Things didn't look quite so gloomy, I decided. I could look forward to some good meals at Grandmother's, she had chickens and eggs. Eggs turned into pancakes, the odd chicken went into the pot for Sundays. Grandmother's relatives had a farm nearby and we would have smoked sausage and ham. She used to bake big sheets of *Streuselkuchen und Bienenstich,* and Silesian poppy seed cake, the delicious smell of baking filled the house. One had to get used to my brother though, being served first, getting the biggest piece and having second helpings. Some time ago Onkel Holder had told me not to be jealous.

"Look at it this way," he said "your brother has to grow up without his mother."

I know, I did feel sorry for my brother, and I resented the whole setup. It made no sense.

We reached our front door just as the *Voralarm*, the warning went off. That might give us 3 minutes to collect things from the apartment before the continuous howl announced the air raid. We raced in, grabbed some bread and a pot of precooked stew from the stove, the potty for Tissi and the first aid box and settled in the basement shelter.

I was listening to the adults, as they were discussing the bombing. They were all arguing, blaming Hitler, Churchill and Stalin. But they were unanimous that the English bombing raids were murderous and merciless. They would wipe out Germany, city by city. Not just factories, airports and railway stations, but everything, not a brick should be left standing. Somebody said that Churchill had vowed to wipe Germany off the map. I didn't quite understand what that meant. What sort of people are the English anyway?

The old air raid warden said that there was a time when wars were never fought with women and children, but the English are going to kill every German regardless.

Bine and I listened in horror as Frau Meier said that it would only be a matter of weeks before Berlin would be flattened. Her sister lived in Lübeck, a historic *Hanse Stadt* on the Baltic Sea with beautiful old buildings mostly of wood, which was partially destroyed. The town was of no importance but it lay at the top of Germany, the top of the map, the top of the list of destruction. Luckily the Swiss Red Cross intervened and insisted that a Red Cross Depot was installed in this town because then it would be protected from further raids. But only because it was historically so important. Other cities were not so lucky. Frau Meier knew all about it, she had relatives living in Lübeck and Stralsund. She said first they would drop firebombs in strategic places, then when the area was well lit up they would drop high explosive bombs.

Frau Pfeiffer knew that Köln was also utterly destroyed, all except the gothic twin towered cathedral. The dead were too many to be buried. God had saved the church. Is it not a miracle that the entire city lay in ruins except for the House of God? Her Cousins had saved themselves into the Sauerland Mountains. But all they saved were their lives.

"How far is Cologne away from here?" I asked my mother.

"Not so very far, my heart." She took my hand into hers and said:

You must not worry about death. You see, when somebody is dead, only his covering is left here on earth, like an old and worn out coat which one doesn't need anymore. The soul of the person that used to live in that old coat has not died."

She looked at me while she held Tissi very close, Bine leant against her knee. We were listening again to what our neighbours had to say. They still had a lot of dreadful things to tell. The shelter warden said:

"The English have become butchers and they enjoy what they are doing." Gravely everybody nodded their heads in agreement.

Already, Berlin looked like a big untidy heap of rubble. I did not recognise the city anymore. It fascinated and saddened me. I tried to adjust to all this chaos, but it filled me with dread. Most of the beautiful buildings were now roofless empty shells. Tears streaming down his face, the warden said shakily: "Never in human history has there been such wilful, wanton destruction, done by one people to another." I shuddered, I did not entirely understand what he said, but I understood the expression on his face.

People lived in holes in the rubble, calling themselves wood lice or voles. It would be good to leave this darkness. But I didn't really want to leave. I loved Berlin, I loved the people who lived here. But for how long would they all survive? I felt a shudder.

Herman Göring had his name changed by the Berliners. He had said in 1939 that if even one enemy plane flew over Germany, his name should be Meier. He became Hermann Meier.

A well-known liqueur manufacturer with the name of Meier and with businesses at every street corner, had a slogan:

"*Keine Feier ohne Meier,* (no celebration without Meier). There were also camouflage nets spread over parts of Berlin, to make the area look like forests; "Hermann Meier's canopy" we called them. And Berliners were saying that if the English kept on bombing like this, they would have to bring their own houses to bomb, as there would be none left here.

Berlin was dying fast. I grieved.

Yes, it would be good to leave for now, but I will return.

✳✳✳

9

I was travelling in the luggage net, my favourite place in the train. The *D-Zug*, the express train which also had a buffet car, was racing east. The train was crowded with soldiers, and in the dining car every table was occupied by officers in black uniform. They remained there, even when they had finished their meal. None of the other passengers could use the restaurant car.

We had brought some potato salad and bread. Mother even had some hard boiled eggs. Those were a farewell present from Onkel Kurt. He was paid in kind rather than money by some of his patients. They had access to things money could not buy. There was no shortage in money and Onkel Kurt preferred food.

The feeling, that our stay away from home, would be a short one, vanished when we saw Onkel Kurt for the last time. He was very grave and sad. So was Tante Guste. Hannele and Bärbel cried, Hermann had been sent to Southern Germany to stay with his mother's sister. I missed him very much. The place was not the same without him. Tante Guste missed him too, but his safety came first.

Kurt was away with the *Hitler Jugend*.

Onkel Kurt took mother to his study and had a long, private talk. When she joined us again she was wiping tears that would not stop running. I felt my throat tighten until it was painful.

In the end, I cried too, because when we said goodbye, it was so very different from all the other times we said goodbye. As we stood outside their lovely house, which was still untouched by war, Tante Guste kept hugging me over and over. Suddenly, I had the feeling that I would never see them again. It just could not be. I told myself that I was being silly. Tall, noble and unselfish Onkel Kurt, caught all of us in a massive hug. To Mother he said:

"Have you heard the latest?"

"No," Mother said, "what?"

"They have arrested Goebbels, accusing him of embezzlement."

Mother laughed through her tears. Typically Onkel Kurt. He would make you laugh no matter what. Mother said:

"No, go on?"

"Yes, he has Victory in his pocket and won't deliver it up." Onkel Kurt gave Mother a last squeeze.

"God keep you."

His chauffeur had driven up the gravel drive to take us home. Public transport had become very complicated, with delays and danger and Onkel Kurt would not let us go home in that chaos anyway. So we got into the black Mercedes with the big star on the bonnet. The luxury of being allowed to sit in this car did not help to dry my tears.

We also went to see Tante Ria for the last time before we left. She was in mourning, because her son had been killed in action, near Moscow. She had only just had the telegram. My heart seemed to kick my stomach.

What did his death mean to me? What did it help me, that his soul wasn't dead? We were left behind without him. It meant, that I would never see him again. This never *was* never, and I felt such a loss, life would be empty without him. I also hated! But who should I hate? This hateful thing had no face. The enemy! But who was the enemy? The English? I had never seen any of them except the planes they came in. I had seen Russian prisoners of war in Berlin, who were helping to clear the bombed streets, putting the twisted tram rails back again and when we passed, or had to wait nearby before we could cross over, they always smiled and looked friendly, they waved and I shyly waved back. How could they be the enemy?

There were Poles in Silesia, who were neighbours of Grandmother's, who spoke German with a strange accent, but were very nice. Yet they too were now the enemy, but not when they lived in Silesia? It was all very strange. There were three names which were in everybody's mouths: Churchill, Stalin and Hitler. One in the east, one in the west and one fighting the two. Listening to the adults, one could think that this war was the fault of those three.

"Why can we not lock them up in a room, first Stalin and Hitler and then Churchill and Hitler, and let them fight it out." I said to Bine in our nest in the luggage rail. Bine thought it would be unfair, two against one. Well that was true, sort of.

Klike-di-klik, klike-di-klak, klike-di-klik, klike-di-klak, Bine and I were copying train noises. There was something else the train was saying as it puffed laboriously: *"Ich schaff es doch, ich schaff es doch"* one could hear it distinctly (I will manage). The train had to climb the beginnings of the *Riesengebirge*, a mountain range separating Silesia from Bohemia.

Frankfurt an der Oder, Guben, Sorau. We were leaving the Mark Brandenburg and entering Silesia. Sagan, Liegnitz. There had been many happy visits in the past, to Mother's school friend, who had a large farm in Kammdorf.

Grandfather had been brought up in Liegnitz where his father taught at the academy for young noblemen. This was familiar home ground to us. Maybe we could stay here and not have to go to Ost Preussen? Mother didn't think so. We had been allocated a place in East Prussia, not here.

"It would only be for a very short time," she reassured us again.

Breslau. The engine stopped with screeching brakes and steam puffing, finally coming to a sighing halt. I loved trains, even though one got covered in soot. Tante Hilde, wearing the funniest hat I had ever seen, my brother Dieter and Grandmother were there to meet us.

We still had to take a local train to Obernigk. This was a small slow train with a big wooden bench running around the walls of the wagon, with a space in the middle for luggage, farm produce and small animals. It was a fourth class compartment.

There was a third class compartment in front of us with seats in rows behind each other, but that was full of soldiers.

At the station in Obernigk was a taxi cab and horse waiting for us to take us to the house. Grandmother lived in the vicarage. Grandfather used to be the vicar. Although he had died, Grandmother chose to live there. It was a lovely big house sitting in its own big garden very close to a large forest.

Mother left the next day and promised not to be very long. We would all be together again soon.

I looked after Bine and Tissi, so that Grandmother did not have to get cross with any of us. I avoided her where ever I could. Dieter was a pain. He did not want to share any of his things in his room, and anything we touched or played with, he said:

"That's mine, you may not touch. I am going to tell Grandmamma."

"I am going to tell Grandmamma." I mimicked. Mama sounded so daft.

I was a Berliner, and in the verbal fights we had, he lost. Crying, he would run to Grandmother and tell tales. She would then hug him and with him hiding halfway behind her, with a stupid grin on his face, she would tell me off, wagging her finger into my face, without even finding out what it was all about. I hated her and I had a love hate relationship with my brother. One never knew when he was nice or when he would run off crying for no reason. There were children in the neighbourhood and I started to play with them and found out they didn't like my brother either nor my grandmother.

Bine had become Father's pet and there must have been a letter, because I overheard Grandmother one day saying to Bine:

"Now when your mother returns, you tell her you don't want to go with her, you want to stay here. Your father wants you to stay here. You will have a wonderful time with us. Much safer to stay here than to go with your mother to this faraway place you don't know." When I came into the room, Grandmother accused me of listening at the door, Bine came running over, and hugging me, cried:

"I don't want to stay here, I want to go with Mother and you and Tissi." Grandmother said:

"What an ungrateful child you are."

I kept my arm around Bine, and we both went into the room where Tissi slept. We stayed there all afternoon, whispering. At supper time, Grandmother was very friendly. Nothing more was said that day. But that was not the end. Whenever she found Bine on her own, she would try to persuade her to stay. Bine started to follow me around everywhere. I told her, that Mother would *NEVER* leave her behind. Bine wasn't so sure:

"She left Dieter" she said.

"That's different, he is a boy" I answered.

***

One morning, about ten days after our arrival, as I changed Tissi's nappies, I heard loud sobbing downstairs. I put Tissi on the pot and rushed to where it came from. Dieter was standing at the bottom of the stairs as if he had been waiting for me, and said:

"Onkel Holder has been killed in action." He said it proudly and without sadness or emotion. I felt shock. My beloved uncle killed in action! In Russia. All my special uncles were now dead.

I went into the kitchen and looked at my grandmother. She was so small and crying so much. Her daughter, Tante Hilde sat at the kitchen table looking at a piece of paper, not really seeing anything, because her eyes were so full of tears. I put my arms around Grandmother, and she hugged me back. It was the first time she showed any emotion towards me. I hugged her and hugged her. My throat was tight and hurt but I could not cry.

I saw Tante Hilde put her arm on the kitchen table, hide her face and begin weeping. I felt very sad, but still there were no tears. I felt ashamed, guilty that I had no tears. I left the kitchen, went into the dining room, and copying Tante Hilde, put my arm on the table, my head into it, and made crying noises. Somehow, I felt better, pretending.

Tissi was completely forgotten by everyone, except Bine. When I didn't come back, Bine picket her up and staggered downstairs with Tissi in her arms. Through the frosted glass of the entrance hall door I saw her teetering on the stairs with her heavy load nearly tripping down. Tissi was far too big for Bine to carry, but Bine was so proud to have managed it all by herself.

In the afternoon, everybody wore black, lots of people came to tell Grandmother how sad they were, and all brought flowers. They had known Onkel Holder all their lives. Two days later, my father arrived.

He had been given special leave to see his mother. I was so happy to see Father, but he had little time for the three of us. He was busy comforting his sister and mother. Everybody cried, except me. I still could not cry. I just held on to Bine and Tissi, the only reality left.

I kept telling Bine, as long as we stuck together, nothing could hurt us or separate us. And that was how it stayed. We were always together in everything that happened from then on, and seldom anybody came into that tight little circle.

We all went to the funeral service without Onkel Holder because he was in Russia and would remain there.

The vicar said he had gone to heaven. Where was heaven? I wanted to speak with Onkel Holder. I remembered all the times we had together. I still loved him. Would I always love him, even though I would never see him again?

Strangely, I felt so very sad, as if nothing nice, beautiful or wonderful would ever happen again. Everybody who shared the times when I was happy, was now gone.

✽✽✽

Mother had gone back to Berlin after she left us in Obernigk, to arrange everything, pack the things she wanted to take to East Prussia, and all the things we had to leave in Berlin, she put into our lockup in the basement.

With as much as she could carry, such as clothes, bedding and cooking utensils she boarded the train which took her on that endless journey, stopping often in the open countryside. She could not find out the reason why. Eventually she got to a little town called *Mehlsack*, (Floursack) so called because it was in the middle of Germany's "Grainstore". The rich soil of East Prussia grew the most and best grain since the crusader knights of St. John tamed, drained and cultivated the land

There was a long row of hay wains, pulled by teams of strong Trakehner horses, onto which Mother put her luggage and herself along with all the other evacuees who had brought their children already. Some of them had their destination in Lichtenau, the same as Mother. There she was given a room in a house owned by 3 spinster sisters. It had its own entrance, and contained two beds, a washstand with a bowl and pitcher with the most beautiful flower design on it, two chairs and a wardrobe. Mother moved in and pushed the two beds together, so that there was more room for the four of us to sleep on. Then she prepared to come back to Silesia to fetch us.

Unannounced, Mother arrived one day. Father had left again, the day before, to go back to the war leaving no message for mother. Grandmother would not let mother come in. When I saw Mother, I was so excited, I ran and fetched Bine and Tissi and then Tante Hilde would not let us through. Mother said:

"I have come to collect the children"

"You are welcome to have Ange and Tissi, Bine stays here." Grandmother's face was ugly. Bine's eyes became huge and black and her little hand squeezed mine. I put my arm around Bine and squeezed back. Tissi started to fret. Mother said quietly:

"The child comes with me."

Tante Hilde and Grandmother were now both talking to Mother.

"The children's father insists, that Bine is to stay, if you do not comply with his wishes, you will be dragged before the courts." Now Mother even managed a smile.

"Why don't you let him try." she pushed passed the two women and came to hug us. Bine said:

"Don't leave me here."

"Quickly, get your things together, we are going right away." Mother said, giving Bine a little push. There was very little to collect.

✻✻✻

10

My brother would not say goodbye to Mother, he stood behind Grandmother and watched us.

There was such a lot of hostility, we were not loved here. I was glad to get away.

I couldn't tell whether my brother was glad or sad to see us go. I had the feeling that his little heart was aching and he was afraid to say so. His small face looked puzzled and scared. I wanted to hug him, but I couldn't. Grandmother looked so hateful, she wouldn't let me near him.

Sad and lonely we walked to the station, and waited for the next train to Breslau and then took the Express to East Prussia.

There was a lot of room and we could spread ourselves on the hard wooden benches. It was a long journey. There were few stops and when we stopped there were ladies from the station mission with hot soup and bread for the few soldiers and the civilian passengers. Eagerly we looked forward to the next stop. Then the train stopped for hours. We looked out and saw no one. Just fields and forest, no farms or houses. Eventually the train rolled on slowly, then gathering speed, it raced on through the open countryside.

Suddenly we stopped at a small station. Lots of soldiers with guns and battle pack came and sealed our train. The windows were boarded up on both sides from the outside. The train became darker and darker, there was no light. We could only see a fraction through the cracks between the boards but we could not make out what was happening. Mother said:

"We are entering the polish corridor. This is a war zone."

"Why is there a war here?" I asked my mother. War had always been so far away.

"It is difficult to explain." Mother said. "There has always been a dispute over the border here. Centuries ago, the people from the east as far away as Mongolia pushed west into our lands, then we had to push them back, and while we were at it we pushed a little further to keep them well out and then they pushed us back again and so on. Over the centuries our people have mixed quite happily, with Poles marrying into Germany and Germans buying land in Poland and intermarrying. Politicians will not give it a rest though. They keep up a senseless tug of war. And then something else happened. Communism started. Many people do not like Communism. It is against their principles. To be a Communist means one is not free. There are lots of people trapped in countries where communism rules, and they need help. It is so bad, that if one does not believe in communism, one might be put into prison, deported to Siberia or even executed. There are many Russians in Germany who would prefer to live in America or Australia, rather than to return to Russia and be forced to become Communists. Most of the German people who live in Russia on the Volga and in Poland and in the Balkans do not want to be Communists either, because it means they have to give up their farms to the state. But you are too young to understand that."

"No I am not" I said. "How did the Germans come to be in Russia?" I asked my mother.

"Well that is a long time ago. When *Katharina die Grosse* (Catharine the Great) was Czar of all the Russians, she invited German farmers to cultivate lands along the river Volga and to show the Russian peasants how to farm so that they could grow enough food to feed all the Russian people and not just the peasants themselves. Katharina was herself a German princess; that is why she picked German farmers. But then a few hundred years later the Russians killed the Czars and started Communism."

Communism. That word again. Stalin and Communism seemed to go together. I was afraid and didn't want to go to East Prussia. Why did we have to go through a war zone? We were supposed to go where it was safe. Mother insisted though, that it was quite safe.

The journey was endless and we were still unhappy about leaving Berlin and I was thinking of my brother in Silesia. The more I thought about it, the more I knew he was unhappy. But if he was, why didn't he decide to come with us? He was older than I was. He could have come with us. Mother would have been so happy if he had.

I usually loved to travel, but sitting in the train now, I felt no excitement at all. Eventually I went to sleep.

We woke up when the shutters came off. It felt as if it had taken the entire night to travel through the Polish Corridor. Tissi slept in Mother's arms throughout. Bine and I had a bed on the benches. Finally, we arrived in Mehlsack and took the bus to Lichtenau.

What a strange and beautiful country this was. So different from home and Silesia. There was so much sky! So much light! It was the middle of summer and the days were long. So green and golden. All the colour of the white houses, the red roofs and the wild flowers were so clear and sparkling. The climate was different too. One minute, it would be sunny and warm, next, even though the sun was still shining, a freezing wind would make you run back for warmer clothing.

The three spinsters, who had given us a room, were very friendly, but we were not allowed to make a noise. Their name was Krause. Even though we were now in the country, surrounded by rich farms, there was very little food. Apparently the food went to the front.

I soon had new friends from school. I learned the East Prussian dialect, which at first sounded like a different language to me. But after a while I realised they were the same words that I used, just pronounced differently. I took pride to speak *ostpreussisch*, and the children soon treated me as one of their own.

The local children had access to more food than was available to the evacuees, and they also knew what one could eat of the fruits that grew free and wild in the country side.

I learned to eat fresh acorns. After peeling them and chewing them and spitting out the bitter juice, they tasted delicious, like hazelnuts and were quite satisfying. We collected beechnuts, they were prized. Mother would ask us not to eat them raw, but to bring them home and she would bake them into a nut cake. There was such a rich harvest though, we didn't need to pick them, we could just scoop them up. We dried them on the *Völkischer Beobachter*, the available newspaper, and then when winter came, we would sit near the stove and crack and peel them ready to be baked into Christmas Cookies. Mother read fairy tales to us. It was cosy and warm, and often children from the village asked to be allowed to listen too.

After the harvest was brought in, women and children went gleaning the fields. We would then sit and rub the ears between our hands, blow the chaff away until we had the clean grain which we would collect in a bag. Ground through the coffee mill, it would turn into rough flour which we could use for pancakes, cake, bread and porridge.

The room in the house of the Krause spinsters was too small for the four of us, Mother went to the Bürgermeister to ask for bigger lodgings. He agreed and found a little cottage for us belonging to a very sweet old Woman, "Little Mother Poschmann" she was called everywhere. We were given the "Best Room" in the cottage, a large room with a white scrubbed wooden floor, containing a very large green *Kachelofen*, a tiled stove. It had a bench running around it, a slow baking oven where one could bake apples, potatoes and chestnuts. It also kept things hot. Lentils and dry peas could be slow cooked. The very top was an area the size of a double bed, where one could sleep and the three of us curled up there for the winter.

Winter arrived early here and we had to see that there would be wood to burn. Going into the forest to collect wood became one of our daily tasks.

Bine had a tough time, because Mother classed her either as one of the two big girls, when it came to collecting wood or fetching potatoes from the cellar, or as the two little girls, when it was time for bed. The two big girls had to go and collect wood. We had to take Little Mother Poschmann's small sparred frame cart and pull it along the wet and empty cobbled village street which would end with the village and lead to the main road which was not surfaced and was muddy with deep grooves from the farm carts. The forest was about a kilometre from the village. There we had to find sticks and fir cones and load the cart so full that we could hardly manage. To keep warm, we needed one cart load a day.

One day, a farm labourer saw Bine and me dragging the laden cart along through the mud, and asked where we were taking it. We explained where we lived, hoping he would help, but he just laughed and cracked his whip over his horse and went on. The next day a huge load of logs had arrived mysteriously at our door with a note saying: "For the two little big girls" Mother had to split the logs, which she happily did and we had it warm for weeks. Then there was another load of logs, when this one had nearly run out.

Because we were evacuees, Mother got separation money from the state, but there was little to buy. No one wanted the money.

The little cottage had no electricity, and we had to use a petroleum lamp. Petroleum was rationed and we sat a lot of the time in the dark. The days up here were very much shorter in the winter than in Berlin or Silesia. Mother told fairy tales in the dark hours by the light of the fire until we could light the oil lamp. She didn't need the book, she knew all the stories by heart. It was so cosy and we liked to listen to the tales, we often delayed lighting the lamp, and only put it on for the evening meal.

The kitchen, which we were allowed to use and share with "Little Mother Poschmann" had an open fireplace to cook on. Mother had to learn fast how to use it. Little Mother Poschmann had fun teaching Mother, and thought her really ignorant not to know how to use such a stove.

I tried to explain to her, what our range looked like in Berlin, with the fire enclosed, and the ash falling into a little drawer, and rings on the top which one could slide back for fast cooking, or replace the rings for slow cooking or simmering. A baking oven, where one could bake cakes from the same heat that did the cooking and that there was a container at the side where one had permanent hot water. All achieved with the same fire. We did not burn wood, we burned briquettes. I explained to her what briquettes were. Little Mother Poschmann nodded her head. She had heard the Bürgermeister had such a clever stove. Personally, she had never seen one and couldn't really believe that there were such things. I tried to explain and describe our gas cooker, where the gas came from a pipe in the wall and if one produced a spark with a gas sparker, it would light up. Puff, just like that. I explained, that we used that cooker in the summer or if we wanted to heat something quickly, without having to light the range. When I told her about the gas heating hot water in the bathroom, she just fell about laughing. A bathroom! Those Berliners could tell stories! Even the children were good at it.

There was no water in the house, just a deep well in the garden. To get the water we had to unwind the rope on which a bucket dangled and let it into the water. Turning the handle, the rope would wind itself around a long piece of wood and the bucket would slowly rise up. There was a little wheel with notches, so that the full bucket would not fall back into the well, if I had to have a rest from winding it up. Pulling the full bucket over to the side was quite difficult and Mother would come out to help. Usually, there was a beautiful creature in the bucket which we looked at and admired. We would throw it back and put our heads over the side of the well and look down into the depths and watch the water settle. Our faces appeared in the still water. We spat into it to see how long it would take to fall down, and then watch the newts gobble it up.

Little Mother Poschmann went to visit a relative, and Mother was left alone in the cottage with us. She thought she would surprise Little Mother Poschmann by giving the kitchen floor a real good scrub. It looked like it needed it. It was always dirty and always dusty when we swept it. She got the scrubbing brush and a bucket of water and a wiping cloth, and soon she was wallowing in deep mud. What she realised only too late, was that the floor was a dirt floor and should never be scrubbed. Carefully, we smoothed the mud with long boards and then put boards down to walk on and left it to dry for about a week. Little Mother Poschmann came back in the middle of the drying process, and had yet another real good giggle. Those Berliners! Did they know anything?

Not being able to buy much with all the money we had, Mother saved most of it in Post Office Savings Account. One day she said, we would be able to buy things again, and catch up with all the clothes we couldn't buy now.

All the evacuated mothers went to Mehlsack once a week to shop for rations. One day, Mother came back with some grey blanket material. This she made into winter coats with hoods for the three of us, with matching muffs. She was also able to get little artificial bunches of violets which she sewed on the front of the muffs for decoration. Tissi was now just over two years old and looked so sweet in her little coat.

In the autumn we collected lots of tufts of wool, which were left by the sheep on the barbed wire. Little bunches of that she knitted into the mittens for us, so that they were warm and fluffy on the inside. On the outside the white stiches showed up in an interesting pattern.

I had never seen so much snow, as we had in that year. More snow than I had experienced in Berlin and Silesia or even Bavaria. It snowed and snowed. Then the wind blew it so that the entire country side was flat. One never knew where the snow was really deep, or where it was shallow. Soon though, from necessity I learned to recognise the signs. A few dried blades of grass meant shallow snow, nothing at all, or a little stump, which could be the top of a fence post, showed deep snow.

We made friends with the mayor's daughter. She was paralysed and could not come out to play with us. Mother had been asked by the mayor to bring us along and talk to his daughter. She wanted to get to know the refugee children. It was difficult at first, because she could not speak and had no control of her limbs.

Her mother put her daily on the kitchen table and then pulled her arms and legs and exercised them. Her name was Inge, she was my age and she made a funny face which her mother said was smiling. Her mother could understand what she said and translated it for us. Soon we understood her too. It was boring though, to play with her and we made excuses not to go. Mother said:

"Imagine it was you, sitting there like this, not being able to move. You would like to have visitors. What if they didn't want to come and see you?" So we continued to go sometimes and I asked some of the village children to come too. They had never been to see her before, which I thought was strange.

Christmas came ever closer.

✺✺✺

11

We prepared for Advent, the time before Christmas, by making little gifts for everybody, and Mother was baking. We needed an *Advents Kranz*, a wreath, and four candles, one for each Sunday before Christmas. We had to have some forest green to make the Advent wreath. Some candle ends which we had saved were turned into thick homemade candles.

Mother took Little Mother Poschmann's sledge, a heavy country pull-push sledge with a footboard at the back to hop onto on downhill slopes. One held onto the backrest of the seat and with twists of the body, could steer the sledge. There were not many downhill slopes in this flat country and Bine and I used to push it along, running, and when we had gathered speed, we would jump onto it, with Tissi sitting in the seat wrapped in a blanket crying: "More, more." Keeping one foot on the board and pushing with the other we could keep it going.

We collected fir branches for the wreath, sacks of fir cones to burn in our stove, and acorns which Mother used instead of nuts in cakes.

The forest was a very old prime forest, with giant trees and big mosses and lichen. It was here that I discovered the realm of the gnomes and elves. There were whole villages for the gnomes and castles with secret passages, towers, courtyards. We could see their orchards where they grew succulent blueberries and sweet strawberries, juicy raspberries and mushrooms. Golden chanterelles glowed in the darkness of roots and pine needles, looking like dancing fairies in swirling skirts. Solidly and squarely, the golden-brown fir bolete and the stone bolete gave shelter to a lot of little creatures, and if one wanted to pick them for food, one had to be quick before the little tenants took over. A host of other mushrooms found their way into our basket. When we picked any of these fruits of the forest in the summer, we made sure that we would leave some for the gnomes, and that we would not damage their land. We tried to be gentle and thoughtful giants. Now we saw their land in deep snow, and imagined that they would be snug and cosy in their beds. We looked very carefully for tiny footprints in the snow, but never found any. Mother said that they would have little tunnels under the snow, which would be much warmer anyway and those tunnels would let the daylight come through so it wouldn't be too dark.

There were other footprints though, and we learned to distinguish between rabbits and hares, fox, dog and cat, deer and the enormous elk, which we encountered several times.

On one such occasion, we came face to face with an elk. Elks are about the size of a cow, except for their enormous antlers, which makes them look much bigger than they are.

We all stood stock still, the animal looked at us and stopped moving its enormous floppy mouth, none of us knowing what to do. We looked at each other for ages, when suddenly the elk turned and sedately walked away. At that time, it was the biggest wild animal I had ever encountered.

With a full load of everything the forest had to offer for Advent and Christmas we returned home.Mother went to the local smith, and explained that she wanted to bake in our stove, but there was no real baking oven. Could he make her a large flat baking sheet, and she gave him the measurements, and a wrought iron stand, where she could rest the tin on? The smith went to work and produced what Mother wanted. A few days later, she tried out her invention. She lit the fire, and filled it with wood and cones. When the roaring fire had died down, she put the stand into the cavity, the tin on top and watched as the cake baked to a beautiful golden brown. We were lying on top of the stove looking down enjoying the warmth. We had a baking oven. Little Mother Poschmann watched, shaking her head. She muttered again:

"Those Berliners!"

We baked many varieties of Christmas cookies with things we had collected in the forest and on the fields with our own flour. We had some real flour from the ration books, but that was used for extra fine and delicate baking. Sugar was rare and we had to be careful, but Mother found, that she didn't need as much sugar as the recipe said and despite that, lost none of the flavour. Nuts, acorns and beechnuts were welcome additions. Fruits were our own dried plums and apples and pears. We had sliced and threaded them to dry in the autumn. Milk and eggs were begged, exchanged or bought. It was going to be a great Christmas. Except that all our decorations were left in Berlin.

Mother made up her mind there and then. She would go back to Berlin and fetch them. She left us with a neighbour and took the train. She was gone four days and returned with the little stable which our Father had built, and the clay figures of Mary, Joseph, Little Jesus in his crib, a donkey and a cow. She also brought our enormous red and blue spheres and lots of little ones, ruby red glass fir cones and the big star for the top. Some of those decorations she had had since her own childhood and they reminded her of her mother.

She came back with our duvets and pillows, covers and cases and bedlinen, clothes, and prudently she thought of bringing the silver cutlery and some bowls and other silver. She couldn't bring it all, but she brought the most beautiful and at the same time, the most useful.

On some of the trips to Mehlsack, Mother met a young farmer, who gave her a lift on his cart, and Mother sold him our cigarette ration coupons for smoked ham and speck.

We were all set for Christmas. It was difficult to be patient. On Christmas Eve at three o clock was a celebration in the village and all the children were invited. It had been dark for most of the day but here we did not have to worry about the blackout as we had to in Berlin, where we had been taught never to show any light in the darkness. It was very festive to see all the little cottage windows lit with candle lights and lanterns and people everywhere getting ready for *Heilig Abend* (Christmas Eve). The children gathered in the village hall to hear the Nazi official give a little speech and then we sang some Christmas songs. They were not the usual Christmas carols, more winter folk songs. I don't believe the man who spoke to us, believed in Jesus or Christmas.

While we were at the village celebrations, all the mothers secretly prepared everything for the giving ceremony in the evening. Little Mother Poschmann celebrated with us. When we came home, we waited in her kitchen for the little bell to ring and she told us of Christmases past in her little cottage. She had a brother, who had inherited the family farm. His son was the farmer there now, with a grown son to take it on. Her sister had lived most of her life on the farm as a helper. She had never married. Little Mother Poschmann had married, but her husband was dead now and her sons, married and with children lived in Königsberg and Braunsberg. They used to come and visit. But the son in Königsberg had fallen in the war. They wouldn't come this Christmas.

Mother opened the door to our room and as we entered we sang *"Ihr Kinderlein kommet"* and *"Oh du fröhliche, oh du selige*. It was a beautiful tree and the burning candles in the tree illuminated the room and made the decorations sparkle. It was good to see the old familiar tree hangings. It felt like home.

Mother read the Christmas story of Christ's birth, how Mary could not find any shelter to have the Baby, and how the angels told the shepherds the wonderful news. When we sang *Stille Nacht Heilige Nacht* we had to bite back the tears. We missed our father, Onkel Kurt and Tante Guste. We remembered the previous Christmas at Mönchgut, Onkel Martin who died in Russia somewhere, place unknown. Tante Ria, Onkel Max Ludwig who died two Christmases ago, and Onkel Holder who had died six month ago.

Finally Mother said:

"Go on, look at your presents." We already knew about the coats, and anyway the presents were not wrapped, just beautifully arranged in three little areas, one for each of us. Mother surprised us with the muffs and mittens which we hadn't known about before. The silver bowls were filled with Christmas cookies.

Mother had a small silver brooch for Little Mother Poschmann and she gave Mother some wool which we had watched her spin. Every afternoon she had been sitting in the corner of her kitchen and combed the wool until it was like silky angels hair. She had some delicately carved wooden cards to do that. Then she would start her spinning wheel with a flick of her wrist and start treadling. The flywheel would turn so fast, one couldn't see it, and she would feed the finely combed fleece into this whirring flywheel where it was twisted into wool.

We decorated fir cones, by opening them in the warmth, stuffing moss and forest green into the openings and then placing them into cold water where they closed up, trapping the green. We used those to decorate the table.

It was a festive, joyful Christmas and Little Mother Poschman thought our tree was so beautiful. She had not seen a better decorated one. She pinned the silver brooch Mother gave her onto her dress and wore it all the time.

Between Christmas and New Year Little Mother Poschmann's sister suddenly arrived and decided to stay with her sister. Now we had to leave, there simply was no room for all of us.

Mother went back to the *Bürgermeister* and asked for another accommodation. He found us a farm labourer's cottage half an hour's walking distance outside the village. There were two rooms, a kitchen, a larder and a big tiled stove like the one at Little Mother Poschmann's, an open stove to cook on, a cellar and a loft. A well in the garden, no loo. The window pane in one room was broken, there was a big crack in the wall where one could see through into the open countryside, there were fleas and mice. We all went to work to make it habitable. I stuffed wet newspaper into the crack with a stick to keep out the freezing wind. Mother put cardboard into the window pane, we swept and scrubbed the wooden floor.

When all that was done the farmer harnessed a horse to a sledge and collected our things. We moved for the third time, decorated Christmas tree and all. Little Mother Poschmann was sad to see us go, she had fallen in love with Tissi, and we had to promise to visit often. As we left, with our few things and the tree, she laughed again, tears running down her wrinkled cheeks: "Those Berliners"

We moved our things into the cottage. It was dark outside and only flickering candle light inside. But when there is snow outside, it is never really dark and the eyes get used to it, so that one can see perfectly well in the dark. Anyway the draught blew the candle out many times and in the end we did not relight it until the door was finally closed.

The first thing Mother did after everything was inside, was to light the fire. It hadn't been lit for a long time, the stove was full of old soot and we choked with the smoke. Our eyes watered and stung. Mother wasn't beaten. She said:

"Come, Ange, help me with these pipes." and we heaved and pulled them off the stove and the wall and carried them carefully out into the back yard. There our new neighbour joined us with a stove brush and helped de- soot our pipes. Herr Kramp, our next door neighbour had gone onto the roof and poked the brush down the chimney while we tried to catch the soot indoors. It wasn't until next morning when we saw the mess we had created in our newly scrubbed little room. But the fire was roaring and very warm.

The man next door was the only remaining farm labourer who lived there with his family, and they were our only neighbours, no other house as far as the eye could see. One could just make out the church tower over the horizon if one knew where to look. The big farm of farmer Graf was over a little hill, about five minutes' walk.

From here I had to go to school, when it began in the New Year. But in the meantime, we tried to get used to this loneliness, and made snowmen, explored the countryside and made friends with the children next door, and even hitched a ride with the farmer into the village to see our old friends again. It was a little difficult to make friends with the children next door, because they had lived in such isolation and were dreadfully shy. Slowly though, we became friends, and they were really nice.

Apart from Herr Krause next door, the only other man was farmer Graf. Everybody else had been called up. There were two Russian prisoners of war, the rest were women who did all the work on the farm.

Robert, one Russian prisoner, came from Georgia. He was friendly, fatherly, tall and very handsome. He had a farm at home, but liked to be in Germany. He often expressed the wish to stay after the war if only he could fetch his wife and small children. He explained to me that when the war was over and he had to return to Russia, his own people would imprison or even kill him.

"But you are a prisoner here." I said, "How can you be also a prisoner in your own country?"

His German was difficult and broken, but he could say all the important things in a roundabout way. "I not communist, I white Russian, I have daughter like you also." I wondered what his daughter was like. Did she miss him as much as I missed my father?

Robert was speaking about red and white Russians. Adults used this expression to mean something I did not understand.

Robert wasn't white, as I imagined white. Here was a real Russian, I talked to him and we had become friends but he was not white! In fact his skin was brown and his moustache was dark, his eyes were a purple-blue. I also noticed, that the other Russian and Robert were not friends. I asked:

"Why don't you like Ilia?"

Robert put his finger to his lip, and looked left and right and over his shoulder. "Pssht, Ilia nix gutt," (no good), "Ilia red." Ilia had not made any friends on the farm, and he always pretended that he could not do the work, because he came from a city.

"I come from a city. Berlin is a big city, and I can work." I said, as I helped Robert put hay down for the horses and cows. Helping Robert with the horses had become my voluntary job. I loved the smell, the horses' noises, when their soft mouths caressed my shoulder and there were rewards. I was allowed to ride the horses.

Ilia wrinkled his nose:" Stink, dirt, nix gutt." In fact, everything with Ilia was 'nix gutt'. The women avoided Ilia. He tried to kiss them and Robert had to intervene. He was "nix gutt" and that became his nick name. "Nixgutt" everybody called him jokingly, but he looked back in hatred.

❋❋❋

12

The day came when I had to go back to school. Early that morning, I started to walk up the lane to the farm. It had snowed again during the night and even the fence posts had disappeared under the snow blanket. Just about halfway between our little house and the farm I got stuck in the snow, luckily this side of the rise. I could not lift my leg high enough to take the next step. I tried and tried, in the end all I could do was to call for help and hope that somebody could hear me. I put my hands to my mouth to form a funnel shape and tried to twist and turn back towards our little house. Even that was difficult, as I was facing away from home.

"Mother!!!" I kept calling over and over. Eventually she came.

"I heard a faint noise in the distance, but thought it was Bine and Tissi playing, until I realised it couldn't be those two. When I looked out of the window, I saw a tiny black spot in all that whiteness, and didn't take much notice, because I couldn't see you were stuck. I kept an eye on the little spot and when it didn't move, I put on my boots and here I am." Mother said laughing. She pulled me out of the snow, put me on her shoulders and took me as far as the farm.

Robert laughed when Mother told him how I had got stuck. He harnessed a horse and put it in front of the wooden snowplough. Two farm children, myself and three Kramp boys who had followed in Mother's footsteps, hopped onto the plough and Robert took us to school.

The plough was V-shaped; two sturdy wooden boards held together with a cross board, which also served as a seating platform for us children. The plough was weighted down with a lot of big rocks. A rigid guiding pole stuck out at the back and Robert held that securely under one arm and the reins in the other hand. We had to hold on to the side and our hands got cold and wet from the snow as it was pushed up on the sides. The horse was harnessed on the front of the V and we sat right behind the horses hooves. Every now and then a big lump of snow would shoot from the hollow in the hoof and we ducked, giggling. The snow crunched under the hoofs and Robert sang a beautiful song, as he walked beside the horse with his breath making white clouds. It was in his own language, and sounded powerful and sad.

He promised to keep the road free, for when we had to walk home, should it snow in the meantime.

From now on, Robert cleared the lane from our cottage to the farm every time there was new snow or the wind had blown the snow into a big drift over the lane.

From the farm, we were either taken by sledge or snowplough every morning along with the milk. It was the only time when I really enjoyed going to school. The air was so fresh and clean, there was no noise, everything was muffled in the snow, and the trees wore thick, white clothing. Everything, even our little house, got an extra thick white wall against the weather side, where the snow had piled up to the roof, which kept the draught out and the warmth in. We carefully carved a little square in the snow where the window was to get the light, and found the snow wall was almost a meter thick.

Our lavatory was just a shed a fair distance from the cottage. It was a hole in the ground with a box over the top and a roughly cut out shape to sit on. It was horrid and smelly and dreadfully cold. We had to time ourselves carefully, not to sit there too long, otherwise we would get painful frostbite.

Mother went to the carpenter in the village and showed him a plan of a chair like construction with a shaped hole in the seat, on the side she had put some measurements with arrows leading to certain points in the drawing. The carpenter built this in beautiful pine wood. Mother paid, took it home, put a big two gallon jam bucket underneath and placed it behind the cellar door. We had an indoor loo now. Bliss! It was still chilly sitting there but not as cold as the shed. Once a day the bucket was emptied.

We had many jam buckets. There was plenty of *Vierfrucht Marmelade* (Fourfruits jam) available. It was thick, sweet, tasted nice, was very red, and contained bits of sawdust and unmistakably potato peels and probably potatoes. It was nice though. The buckets we could keep, and the use of them was unlimited.

After a lot of begging, the farmer finally gave Mother three children- sized beds for us, and one big one for Mother, and access to as much straw as we wanted. We filled our mattresses as full as possible, then we sat on it and worked it into a nice comfortable shape. After pummelling it for a while, we put some more straw into it. We had warm, soft beds which smelled deliciously of fresh straw. The stuffing made a reassuring noise as we wriggled around to get comfortable. Good thing Mother brought our duvets and pillows.

Cleverly, Mother had wrapped the bedding into a carpet in Berlin, to keep it all together in a big bundle, and now we could put the carpet down and stop the draft from the floor boards. Mother also filled old socks with straw and stuffed them into the broken window and cracks in the wall wherever she found cold air coming through.

We had brought our firewood, when we moved, but now we had to find some more. The man who had supplied the wood in the village was too far away now. The forest was a lot closer than it was in the village, but the snow was so deep, we had to dig for the wood. It was hard work.

Mother had invented something else, which was quite useful. We came away from Berlin with only a few things, and in the meantime had collected more, but there was no box or suitcase to put it all in, so she invented a large trunk with a lid which could be turned into shelves inside this trunk. A very useful thing and the carpenter in the village made several, and a lot of other evacuees bought one.

The farmer also gave Mother a large tin bath which looked more like a trough, which we kept in the kitchen, and once a week we had a warm bath, starting with the three of us all at once and then as we dried on top of the stove, Mother would have her bath in the same water.

The water was heated in an open recess in the Stove, which we found was just the size of a jam bucket. We put a bucket of water there all the time, and so had constant hot water.

We had no electricity here either. All the light came from a paraffin lamp and fuel was rationed. I had light to do my homework, and anything else where light was needed, was done during the time I worked; cooking and eating was done by the light of the fire, and so was story telling. The four of us sat cosily together, safe.

The sun was shining often, in this wonderful land, and now covered in snow, it was so light during the day. Even in the night the snow reflected a mysterious light which lit the darkness.

Looking into the distance the snow shone blue or pink, purple or golden, according to what the sun was doing. The days were short, almost non-existent at Christmas, but getting longer each day. The snow glistened like a zillion diamonds. Every morning the windows were thick with wonderful ice flowers, created there for us during the night. They were all different, lilies, tulips and stars, so intricately drawn, I marvelled at their excellence.

In February, the Berlin evacuees met in Braunsberg to discuss the situation and see how everybody was getting on. We walked from Lichtenau to Mehlsack and then took the train. The Mehlsacker road was clean and white and smooth. The snow had been swept clean across the road by the wind. Frozen hard, it made a perfect surface. The telegraph poles marked the road. In many places, there was no indication as to where the road was except for the poles. The wires were thick white with hoar frost, and so were the twigs and branches of the trees. We stomped and skipped hard to keep our feet warm and watched each other's noses. If they were getting white, they had to be rubbed carefully to get the blood back in to stop them from freezing. A nose could freeze, without it being noticed.

It was nearly 20 degrees below zero. We were all glad that there was no wind that day, otherwise it would have been unbearable cold.

In Mehlsack we took the train to Braunsberg and there was a sad meeting of worried mothers. Some had had news of Berlin. Others, who came from different towns told equally desperate stories. Systematically all the towns from Lübeck to Frankfurt, from Hamburg and Köln to Leipzig and Dresden were razed to the ground, burnt, with hundreds and thousands dead. Frau Pfeiffer wiped her eyes:

"I am sure this is the end of Germany. We'll never…" Frau Müller from Leipzig cut in:

"Don't forget Hitler's secret weapons," and some women laughed bitterly.

"The secret is, that there aren't any secret weapons." said Frau Schröder, another Berliner. She sighed: "They are telling some funny jokes in Berlin. I miss that. Here nobody makes any jokes, at least at home they joke about everything, and no matter how grim, one can still laugh about it. I had to laugh about something, one of my neighbours wrote. She turned to the other women and asked:

'Do you know, that in the future, teeth are going to be pulled through the nose?' She looked around expectantly, somebody said: 'No, why is that?' – 'Because nobody dares open his mouth.'

They all laughed. "How true" Frau Pfeiffer said.

We children were getting hungry. The meeting took place in the Station waiting room, and we were huddled around the canon stove, which was red hot. We were restless and bored. Ulla, a girl I had met before and who was as tall as I was, said:

"In our village, where we live they call us *Bomben Gesindel*, (bombed trash), and they tell us to go back where we came from. They call us 'city weeds' and I hate the smell of cows and pigs and horses. Do they say the same in your school?"

I had not heard such an unkind remark. Anyway I loved the smell of pigs and cows and especially horses. But I didn't say so. I just shook my head.

One by one the mothers got up and somebody said:
"Let's find some food in the station's soup kitchen."

A heavy plate filled with thick pea soup and a slice of very black potato bread was what we found. We had to pay dearly with ration coupons but the soup tasted good and there was plenty of it. It was hot and satisfying. The bread was a bit salty but the children were also allowed a mug of free milk, which made the bread taste good. The adults had some smelly Hitler mocha (Roasted barley and chicory).

The result of the meeting was the decision to stay in East Prussia. Going back would mean living in piles of rubble. No one had a home to go back to. All agreed, to keep listening to the news, not to believe everything one heard. It was also strictly forbidden for East Prussians to leave and go west. So we had to be alert. We promised to keep in touch and phone Frau Schröder, who had a room in Braunsberg, and she would keep us all informed. We returned to our beloved Lichtenau, hoping we would never have to leave, that the war would stay away, or at least finish very soon. For now, all the bad news was pushed to the back of our minds. Without noticing it, I had begun to love this country and the people in it. They were a little strange, and hardly ever laughed (not like the Berliners who joked about everything) but were true and sincere.

One day in March, when I came out of school, Mother, Bine and Tissi were there to collect me. Our neighbours were going to slaughter a pig, and, so as not to frighten the two little ones, Mother took them for a walk to collect me. We hurried back to help, but by the time we arrived, the pig was dead.

Peter Kramp, who was 12 years old told me how the pig had tried to escape when the butcher came with his knife. I shuddered at Peter's description of the actual killing. His mother had caught the blood and stirred it first with a wooden spoon and then with her hand, up to her elbow, until it cooled down, to stop it from clotting and put it aside for black pudding. I saw the two buckets with blood, and quickly looked away. I did like black pudding, but never thought about how it started off.

I was glad to have missed the beginning of the *Schlachtfest*, (butchers festival).

When we got back, the pig was already hanging upside down from a ladder which was leaning against the house. It had its belly slit open, and the bowels were hanging out. There was plenty of evidence of the bloody battle between the pig and the butcher; the snow was red all around.

"Oh look, the sausages are already made inside the pig." Bine shouted and everybody laughed. Soon we learned the smelly truth, when Mother was sent to wash and turn the intestines for sausage skins. The various parts of bowels were turned into different size sausages.

A lot of water was needed and we children had many trips to the well, which had no wall around it, as the one at Little Mother Poschmann's had. There was a long pole with which we broke the ice, also we had to pull the bucket up hand over hand which was hard and dangerous work.

I was allowed to help scrape the bristles of the pig's skin. Boiling water was poured over the pig and the bristles came off easily. They were saved to be sold later. I helped mince a lot of meat, which was meant to go into sausages. August Kramp stuffed the meat into the top, careful not to get his fingers caught, and I turned the handle.

The washhouse was used for butchering and the big copper was lit with a lot of water in it, salt, onions and herbs, the empty head, the trotters, the tail, the heart, all pieces one couldn't use for sausage meat or smoking, were chucked into it and boiled. It was a ghastly mixture. The smell which wafted from the kettle was halfway between nice and awful. The taste though was delicious. We all had a bowl full with a slice of bread for lunch. Herr Kramp made sure everybody had a piece of meat floating in it.

Just then, the local Policeman arrived, pushing his ancient bicycle, the 'wire donkey' Mother called it, checking that it was a legal killing, the permitted 3 hundred weight pig per year. Good naturedly, he accepted a glass of Schnapps and a bowl of broth from the big kettle with a slice of bread and a big piece of meat floating in it.

Later, we stripped the bones and chopped the meat, fished out some onions and carrots, chopped that too and then filled the pig's stomach. We added vinegar, juniper berries and green peppercorns and laurel leaf. When it cooled it turned to jelly, and was put with a lot of other cuts of meat and sausages into the chimney to be smoked. We filled some jam buckets with the rest of the mixture for immediate use. Some meat was salted away to be boiled as ham, later on.

In the meantime, Frau Kramp was making liver sausage and black pudding in the kitchen. The liver she stretched with bits from the big pot in the washhouse, bread and herbs and turned that into coarse liver sausage to be smoked.

There was work for everybody and little tasty bits which were popped into my mouth by the people I helped, there was happy chatter. The Schnapps bottle came out often and made the round. Even I, was allowed a mouthful every now and then, which made me feel quite dizzy and tired at the end of the day.

We had some good food for a time after the 'slaughter festival'.

❋ ❋ ❋

As the days grew longer, our cosy times in the evening became less and less. We played more outside. The snow melted, slowly and unevenly. Small, mysterious worlds appeared with icicles hanging down over tiny snow caves where the sun had melted the snow, with little bits of grass growing through the snow. There was excitement when we discovered these green blades, after the long winter.

Then came the day when we found the first snowdrops in an island of green amongst the whiteness. At the edge the snow had turned into crystals, glistening like jewels in the sunlight.

Many little streams appeared, the lane turned into a river of mud, the meadow in front of the house into a treacherous bog which we soon learned to negotiate. The children next door, knew all the tricks. Then we discovered a pond in the meadow close to the cottage. It had been frozen solid all winter, and was hidden under thick snow.

Trips to Mehlsack were always exciting, as one never knew beforehand, what one would find in the shops. On one such a trip, Mother found a lot of second hand balls of wool, all in different colours.

In the attic of the schoolhouse lived two elderly ladies who had come here of their own accord to get away from the bombing, and they offered to knit cardigans for the three of us.

Easter came and Mother managed to haggle eggs for Easter eggs which she dyed with onion skins into a rich ochre colour. She had also baked a large Easter cake out of potatoes and a little flour and one egg.

On Easter Sunday, she went secretly out to hide the eggs and when we had found all of them, she said to go on looking, there might be something else. Sure enough, the Easter Bunny had also hidden a multi coloured, striped cardigan for each of us with matching caps.

Getting out of bed one sunny morning after Easter, and looking out of the window, I saw a newcomer to our world. Almost outside our cottage was a stork, catching frogs. Majestically he stalked around the meadow. By the pond, a little further away was his mate. Excitedly I woke the others, and we all watched these large birds in the rising sun. Every time he caught a frog in his long beak, he lifted it up into the air and with a poking movement he made it slip down into his long neck, where one could watch it wriggle slowly downwards. They became a familiar sight on our meadow. Altogether there were about three pairs in our meadow, keeping their distance from each other. When I went to school I discovered what that wheel on the church roof was for. One pair of storks remade their nest up there, where we were told they had lived for generations in succession. It was their home for the summer. Daily we watched the flight of the storks, which was quite incredible. They were flying aces. Mother said they lived in Africa in the winter.

With the storks, the swallows arrived in hundreds, the wild Geese came through on their way further north. Many more birds came, the cuckoo was heard in the trees nearby, but never seen, and another mysterious bird was heard. The Pirol or Oriole. His song was clearly saying:" Ich bin der Vogel Pirol" and he would sing it over and over. Robert said:

"Eet is golden bird, long feathers in tail and crown of gold on head." I saw this beautiful bird sometimes but only as one sees a golden ray of the sun, and it was black and golden and did not have a long tail nor did it have a crown. One of Robert's beautiful tales, and in one of the stories he told, there was such a bird, which was really a little boy who had been changed into this golden bird by his wicked stepmother.

With the birds returning, Robert put the horses into the fields for grazing after the work was done.

✻✻✻

13

At the beginning of the farming season, the farmer came knocking on our door and asked Mother to come and help in the fields along with all the other labourers. I helped when I came home from school; Bine and Tissi played nearby or stayed at home, when the weather was bad. There was manure to spread, potatoes to plant, beets to be thinned. Extra Russian prisoners of war came to help in the fields.

Grinning, they stood in the farm square and waited to be told what to do. They were good natured and willing workers, but didn't understand any German, Robert could not speak with them either, and his Russian was not their Russian. He explained:

"Many countries make up Russia. Many tongues, many people."

We walked out to the fields, accompanied by one guard for all of them, with his gun pointing down. I didn't like that. Robert didn't need a guard or a gun. The prisoners didn't need to be shown what to do, they just copied us.

I watched them, fascinated. These men were also real Russians, but they were not red either. They said things to me, and I grinned at them. I said something back, and they grinned. In a way I did understand what they said. I discovered that the same facial expressions and hand movements meant the same in Germany as they did in Russia. We could understand, sometimes it took a little longer and then we laughed. I thought it was great to be able to speak with somebody without words.

The time arrived when Lieschen, the farm maid, came with "small lunch" at eleven. The Russians kept wiping their hands on their jackets and stood back in confused embarrassment. I could tell they were hungry, but Lieschen had enough for all the workers. She had to ask them several times to take a piece of bread with Speck. Shyly they helped themselves from the basket. Lieschen whispered to me:

"Don't go too near, because of the lice. They all have lice in the camps."

I watched as they ate, biting into the big wedge of farm bread with a large slice of Speck on top, which is smoke cured pork, salty and delicious.

Slowly they chewed and with great pleasure. When the large jug was handed round, they also drank from the same jug, and they did not finish it, but handed it back, grinning, licking their lips noisily and wiping their moustaches. Long after we had all finished they were still licking their fingers. Later they were all asked to have lunch in the farmer's kitchen. We went home to our little cottage and Mother cooked our lunch in the time we had for our break. I was a little jealous. They were going to have meat and sausage, lots of bread, honey and maybe cake. Coffee afterwards I expected. We were going home to boiled potatoes with salt and gherkins and a tiny bit of bacon.

Even though Mother worked for the farmer, it never occurred to him that we were hungry. Mother would not beg. She had the cottage free, and for that she worked. We had only the food that was available on the ration book. Often, although we had the coupons to buy the things, they just were not available in the shops. We also had tobacco rations, but Mother did not smoke. Others did, and Mother could buy food with tobacco coupons from them. Some preferred tobacco to food. The odd silver spoon went for food as well. One day the farmer came to Mother and said:

"I have heard, Frau Gerret that you receive food and ration coupons from the other women."

"Yes, sometimes, why?" Mother said. "We get hungry."

Why don't you come and ask me?" the farmer said.

"Herr Graf, you know I work for you, and for that I have the cottage, I can't beg", Mother said.

The farmer said nothing, he just touched Mother's shoulder and from now on we had a little bread, or a bit of Speck, potatoes or smoked sausage. Every time I came through the farm from school, I found some extra milk, and Lieschen said to leave the litre bucket on my way to school and she would fill it.

Each morning at four thirty, there was a gentle tap on the window, a signal that Robert was fetching the horses. I slid out of bed and into my clothes and rushed out after him. We collected the horses and then rode them bareback to the farm together. Riding horses was my greatest joy. Robert was a horseman, through and through. He sat on the horse as if he was part of it. Mother said he was like a legendary half horse half man, a centaur from ancient Greece. My legs were not long enough to cling to the horse's sides the way Robert's did, but he showed me how I could sit on the horse without falling off, even though I was only perched on the very top of the horse, and how to tell the horse which way to go by pressing lightly with my knees. It was marvellous to feel the huge horse respond. To feel the warmth of its body, its smell and listen to the neighing, which I felt was like a happy horse laughter.

We even had gallops, and although I did a lot of sliding about, I never fell off. I held on to the mane for dear life and loved every minute.

The farmer laughed: "Not bad for a Berliner." I often felt that the people here in East Prussia thought the Berliners were stupid, unable to do anything. They would call us 'Towns people' or 'Townsies'. All the more reason to show them what we could do.

Robert would wait for me to come in the evening, to take the horses back again. He folded his hands and put them between his knees, I would step into them and hop, and I would be astride the horse. Eagerly, I clicked my tongue and the horses, knowing it was the end of the day and freedom in the field would happily canter off, Robert in front, then the loose horses, and I would bring up the rear. My heart was as light as a feather as I flew along with the horse. Watch out frogs, watch out storks, and watch out geese and ducks and lapwings. But the horses were clever and knew where the lapwing's nests were. A long stride across a draining ditch, a few fleeing ducks quacking. Mosquito swarms cut in half with one or two ending up in my mouth. The sun sitting on the wide horizon, golden. The green wide, far country. I loved it. Forgotten the raids, the bombing, the horror, the war. I had arrived in my paradise.

On the way home, Robert would tell me of his country. He said his land was the home of the ancient legend of "The Golden Fleece" and he told me of Jason and the Argonauts, how they left Greece and travelled through the Dardanelles, which he said was a river between the Greek Sea and the Black Sea, and how they arrived and stole away the golden sheep skin. He said that the way this fleece became golden was that the farmers would put the sheep skins into the river and all the gold dust which comes floating down the river would catch in the wool of the skin and after a while they would fish it out and shake off the gold.

He told me the earth in Georgia was rich, lots of exotic fruits grew there, like oranges and lemons. Russian tea, rich red wine which he carried in goat skins. Tobacco and perfume. It was very warm there, like in Italy, even warmer, and like East Prussia which was on the Baltic Sea, his land was right next to the Black Sea. He said it wasn't called that because the sea was black, but because it was such a wild sea. Unlike East Prussia, which had no mountains at all, his country had very high mountains. I knew about high mountains and told him about the ones in Bavaria. Yes, he said, they are just like the Caucasian mountains at home. He was homesick and felt he would never see his land again. Stalin came from his land, and he whispered:

"Stalin nix gutt", and then he said something which struck me and made me confused. He checked over his shoulder, as if in this wide open expanse of fields anybody could hear us and said:

"Hitler nix gutt" and then he took my hand and said: "End come soon, end of war, end of this,", and his hand made a wide circle pointing at the land all around us. I looked at him and was afraid. I wanted to go home. Everything about Robert was so true, I trusted him and now I was afraid. Quietly, he took my hand and gave it a little squeeze. Slowly, we walked home. It felt like holding a father's hand.

When he tapped on the window next morning, the fear had gone. The sun was shining way below the horizon but his beams already reaching to the very top of the blue sky and making the dew glisten and sparkle in rainbow colours.

Dutifully, the horses gathered at the gate at Roberts whistle, and sedately we walked them to the farm. It wouldn't do to tire them before they had to start work.

When I got back to the cottage, about five thirty, Mother had gone to the pond for a swim. Now that the weather had turned warm, we used the pond as our bathroom. We would swim here every morning, and seeing Mother already in it, I stripped and joined her. Now it was the Kramp's turn to shake their heads and say:

"Those Berliners!"

News reached us that the Americans and the English had landed in France and were pushing our armies back towards Germany. The Russians were in Finland and taking Karelia the home of the Kalewala Saga. Mother had read us a story about it. She said that this is an omen. Ancient civilisations and cultures will die and Communism will take over. She shuddered.

✻✻✻

14

Our pond was small. On the sides, grew reeds and lilies and other greenery which we avoided, there were screams and shudders when our feet touched the water weeds. The Kramp children joined us and told us a number of scary stories, events that happened in the past, and what could happen to us if we were not careful. A farm labourer who had lived there before us, was nearly sucked under, one summer's day, and since then, people were very careful. The lilies could wind themselves around your legs and pull you down.

They said the pond was bottomless, which wasn't strictly true, because I could feel the bottom. We certainly did not like to put our feet to the ground, it was soft with black slimy mud. We never felt firm ground, except on the edge which was slippery clay and quite steep. We had dug foot holes in the side with our toes, and that was the way we climbed out, pulling ourselves up and over by the sedge grass.

We had to watch out for leeches and we looked at each other from time to time to see if any of those creatures had attached themselves onto us. With a firm but gentle twist we could pull them off.

We had large pieces of wood, which floated in the water and we clung to that, nobody among us could swim. Bine and I stole wood from the farm. The Kramp children told us that we had to make sure to dry the wood every time, otherwise it would not float anymore.

In early spring, we found the tadpoles and newts at the edge of the pond and in the small puddles in the meadow. We watched the tadpoles turn into baby frogs, and then big frogs of many different colours. There were thousands of them. No wonder the storks liked it here.

The ones I liked best, were the small green tree frogs. We liked to catch them and keep them in a jar so that they would tell us if it was going to rain by staying at the bottom of the little ladder which Robert had carved. He said:

"No keep frog longer than week." and he put up one finger. "They like be free", and while we had them we had to catch live flies for them. We could hear the frogs sing in the trees at night, and I never guessed that frogs could sing so beautifully, it sounded almost like birdsong.

In the evening we could hear the oink, oink in the ditches and near the pond. We called them Unke; they were big toads. Their 'oink oink' accompanied us on every step and the storks didn't like them much.

There were many narrow foot bridges across the ditches and streams. Often, the Kramp boys, Peter, August and Gustav would play with Bine and I.

We flopped down on the little bridges and let our feet dangle in the crystal clear water, looking at the pebbles which shone like amber on the yellow, sandy ground. The streams were alive with tiny silvery fish, grey newts and lizards with green and yellow lines, toads with warts, water fleas and dragonflies. The dragonflies wings were wide and had colours of the most beautiful iridescent blue and green. Their eyes were amber, like the pebbles, their heads enormous. I fancied them to be elves in disguise. I imagined myself as a giant, sitting on a gnome bridge and dangling my feet into their river, careful not to tip their boats, should they be passing at that moment.

Yellow water lilies and marsh-marigold grew in such abundance, we made garlands with them and put them into our hair and round our necks. I picked the bog bean, water-parsnip and the blue forget-me-not into a pretty bunch for our table. All around us, were the tall grasses with unusual shapes and insects hanging on them, their weight bending them down, bees buzzing, and wild flowers of all colours. I was fascinated with quaking grass, which shivered everywhere. There were white areas with cotton grass wafting silkily in the breeze. The beautifully exquisitely shaped harebell which was always surrounded by these dainty grasses, like flower arrangements made by nature.

Mother taught us to collect herbs, which she dried for tea to use in the winter or when we got ill. She told us what the various herbs were good for. The best one was camomile, because that was good for everything. So I picked lots of that, although I did not enjoy the smell. Mother said, that later in the year, we would have to keep the apple peels and pick rose hips which would be good for chesty coughs. Barberries gave the herb tea a lovely tangy flavour and rosy colour. There were also the leaves of Blackberries, and nettles. Nettles are good for any kind of ailment. For everyday use, we mixed them all up and had a bit of everything. Collecting herbs went on all summer.

In the middle of June, August Kramp, Bine and I were sitting on the little footbridge, halfway between our cottage and the forest, our legs dangling in the water. The sun was quite warm and we had been swimming all morning and playing in the pond, watching the stork's acrobatic flying display, but now we were just sitting and talking.

August Kramp was very proud to belong to the Hitler Youth.

"Yesterday, we started to dig defence ditches over there" and he pointed to where the Mehlsacker road came out of the forest and along the fields.

"Is that to keep the enemy away?" I asked. Everybody was discussing the fighting on the eastern borders, the Russians pushing west. One day the borders were in our hands and then they were not. At the moment, Germany was ours, August said:

"Yes, it's going to be three metres' deep and it goes all along the forest over there, and over there." He pointed to the other side of the road where the forest disappeared over the horizon.

"No tanks are going to get across there, not one." he said. He was so grown up.

As he was pointing to the road we both saw some unusual covered wagons moving along the Mehlsacker Road. Two had emerged from the forest and a third one became visible just as we were watching. Very slowly, the wagons jolted along the unsurfaced road. They had a round canvas roof over the top, small, shaggy horses pulled the wagon in front, a cow or two walked behind. Swinging on the sides, were baskets, tin baths and jam buckets.

We got up and ran across the meadow to the road to have a look. Bine couldn't run as fast as we did, and cried:

"Wait for me." I told her to catch up as August and I were in a hurry. Bine's legs were not yet long enough to jump over some of the ditches and I had to go back to pull her across.

As we reached the road, we watched as one wagon after the other came out of the forest. Many people walked beside them. Under the planes, we saw some sacks. August said:

That is the horse's feed and I suppose flour for cooking." He knew everything.

There were also horse blankets and sheepskins and bedding and children's heads looking out. We walked along with them on the Mehlsacker Road until we reached the village. The children in the wagons were watching us, leaning out of their little nests.

The travellers made camp on the village green. We sat on the edge and watched. The Bügermeister came and talked to a tall man with a carefully twisted moustache and long beard with a smoking pipe hanging out of his mouth. We walked over and listened to what the man said. In hard and broken German he told the Bürgermeister that he came from the other side of the border. He was from Lithuania, a 'White Russian' and he was afraid of the 'Red Army' coming back. He said:

"The borders won't hold." He shook his head and looked back to where he had come from.

"All lost. Russian troops are close to Vilna now, we cannot hold. Many Litauer have become Communists, I will not be red, and I leave. Maybe go America." he said.

The women wore white head scarves knotted at the back and busied themselves with preparing a meal, whilst the men unharnessed the horses and cows and let them graze on the village green. They asked for nothing from the village, they had everything they needed, they said.

There were many barefooted children. We stood facing each other for a long time, and then we played. We could not understand what they were saying. More children from the village joined us. The children from Lithuania knew the same games we played, which I thought was strange, since they spoke another language.

I carried Bine on my back, on the way home. She was tired and had walked for ages. She was so heavy and kept strangling me, because she had her arms crossed around my throat.

The Lithuanian refugees stayed about four days. But one morning, when I came into the village to go to school, they had gone, and new people had arrived overnight. From now on there was a steady trickle of people moving along the Mehlsacker road. Mother had become very anxious and talked a lot with Robert in the evenings. When we asked what the matter was, she said not to worry.

***

One day, Mother decided it would be nice to go to the seaside and so we took the little train from Mehlsack via Braunsberg to Frauenburg.

Getting off the train, I could already smell the sea although I didn't know it was the sea. I took deep delicious breaths through my nose and Mother said:

"That is the sea." She also took a deep breath through her nose: "Wonderful isn't it?"

Outside the station of Frauenburg was a statue of a man, and Mother told us about Nikolaus Koppernigk, whose parents came from Silesia and who was born in Thorn, in the times when East Prussia was ruled by the Teutonic Knights. He moved to Frauenburg and worked as a prebendary at the cathedral, where he became the greatest astrologer in the 15th and 16th Century. Mother told us that he was the first man ever to work out that the sun was the centre of our universe and that everything was spinning around the sun. She also told us that in those days a man who thought the sun stood still, and the earth was round and moved around the sun, was a heretic, and often people like that were burnt at the stake. But the inhabitants of East Prussia were free thinkers, open minded. He changed his name to the Latin sounding Copernicus, and he died in Frauenburg.

His cathedral is right by the sea and we went inside to have a look. It was the first church I entered, which had no tower. Inside, the Church was light, white and golden. On each enormous pillar, was an altar and a huge painting telling the story of Christ. The pillars had painted decorations which carried on over the arches. The altars were covered in the whitest altar cloths, edged with the finest lacework, and on each altar were beautiful flower arrangements.

Frauenburg was a small town. The land was very flat, and this flatness led into the sea, land and sea being at the same level. I asked Mother:

"What if it rained, would it not overflow?" But Mother explained, that it was not really the sea, but a gulf or lagoon, and further out on the horizon was a long strip of sandy land which went from Danzig all the way up to Pillau and the Samland. There was a break at Pillau so that boats could enter to go to Königsberg and up the river Pregel. There were graceful cities along this river like Insterburg, Gumbinnen and Trakehnen were the most beautiful and famous horses came from. That strip of land out there kept the sea here calm.

"Are we going to the real sea then?" I asked, almost disappointed that we hadn't come to the sea yet after all. She promised, but to start with, we stayed here at the beach. The sand was golden and one could walk into the sea here for ages and it would not get any deeper. We played in this flat expanse of water and paddled all day.

We slept at a Youth Hostel and in the morning we went back to the beach. We searched for amber, as somebody had told me they had found some. The way one could tell if it was real and not just a golden pebble was to rub it on some cloth and if it picked up a tiny bit of paper or fluff, it was genuine. I spent a long time picking up golden pebbles and rubbing them. When I did find some, a small lump, it had a tiny spider in it. At first, I didn't recognise it and nearly threw it away, when it suddenly dawned on me, what I had found. In disbelief, I looked at my amber, never had I thought I would actually find any. I ran, calling out to Mother, and we looked at it together, and held it against the sun. One treasure for the four of us. Mother promised to look after it.

The next day, a fisherman gave us a lift across the Haff to the *Frische Nehrung* which was the narrow tongue of land. Here the sea was tidal and there were big waves, much bigger even than in the indoor swimming baths in Berlin. I was afraid to go in. Mother picked up Tissi and took Bine by the hand and walked in. Was I supposed to be the only one that stayed out? I walked in right after Mother, and where she pulled Bine up by the arm when the first big wave came, I got drenched. Water ran down my nose, it hurt, it tasted very salty. When the next wave came, Mother said: "One, two, jump!" And I hopped and kept my head above water. The wind was fresh and cold, but we stayed as long as we could, wave hopping.

The fisherman took us back in the late afternoon. Mother decided to go on to Königsberg and to the *Kurische Nehrung*. Here we found enormous wandering dunes. Over the centuries the knights, farmers and fishermen tried to stop the dunes from shifting and burying villages, fields and meadows by planting pines and other bushy plants that do well by the seaside. The sandy strip between sea and lagoon was thick pine forest. We had lots of fish to eat and we watched fish being caught. There were strange fishing boats with see-through sails. Later, I found out they were the fishing nets, which they had pulled up the mast to dry. At the very top of the mast they had wooden carved pennants. Every boat a different one.

The fisherman explained what type of fish they all were, the funniest was the flounder. But there were also pikes, eels and perch.

It was cold and windy here, and we soon stopped wave jumping and came out of the water, stiff with cold. We dug a deep shelter with a sandy wall against the wind, and there we sat looking out to sea. Mother said:

"Straight up and across to the right where the sea ends is Norway, Sweden and Finland", over here in the east is Russia. Lithuania, Latvia and Estonia is are above and to the East."

Then she told us the tale of the 'Fisherman and his wife'. We were watching all the fishermen casting their nets at the beach, and I imagined the fisherman in the story doing just that. "And then he caught the magic fish who said: 'Set me free. I am not an ordinary fish. It would not be of any advantage to you to kill me.' And so the fisherman set him free. When he told his wife what had happened to him, she was very cross and said: 'You should have asked him to grant you some wishes, you stupid good for nothing. Go back this minute and call him and ask for a favour. I don't like this old hut, I would like a nice little cottage.' So the fisherman went back and asked the favour, and the fish granted it. Returning, he found his wife in a beautiful cottage, sitting in its own garden and chickens scratching away in the earth. A cow in the shed. He thought, what more do I want? And now my wife will be happy. But when he got in, the wife said: 'If the fish can give us this cottage, then he can give us a rich man's house in the town. I don't want to be a fisherman's wife any more. So the fisherman went back to the beach. This he had to do many more times. The wife wanted to be a prince, a king, an emperor and a pope. Finally she wanted to be God, and when the fisherman asked the fish to grant that wish, the fish sends him back saying:

'Go home to your wife, she is back in her original shack'."

"It doesn't pay to be greedy." Mother said. I asked her if the story took place here, and she said as far as she knew.

We strolled through Königsberg, which is a charming town with shops and graceful buildings, which proudly lined the streets. The river Pregel is wide and deep and big ships can actually come right into the centre of town. Gigantic, medieval warehouses are right there by the waterfront, and heavy goods horses pulled wagons, heavily laden across the cobbled roads. It is a busy town and Mother told us that the Teutonic Knights founded this city in the 13th century and built the cathedral and castle in the 14th century. Here was also one of Germany's oldest universities.

It all seemed untouched by war. I watched the big barges, so full with cargo, that the water was only centimetres away from pouring into the holds. It looked dangerous to me.

It was so peaceful here.

But going back to the station to travel to Mehlsack on our last day, we read again the slogans on the wall: *"Räder rollen fuer den Sieg"* and here too, somebody had written in chalk underneath:" *Und Kinderwagen für den nächsten Krieg"* (Wheels roll for victory and prams for the next war).

Happy and content, we arrived back at Mehlsack, and Robert managed to have something important to do in town with the horses and wagon, and he just *happened* to be near the station, when the train arrived, so he could give us a lift. What a coincidence. We all laughed. Good old Robert. I loved him.

15

Two days later, Ilia had disappeared.

Farmer Graf reported it immediately, to the local Gendarme, and was told, that a lot of Russian and Polish prisoners of war had fled east. They wanted to be with their communist comrades.

Robert was serious. He said there were many of his friends who would not go back, they would rather go south and west to meet up with the Americans and English. I said to Robert:

"How can you go to the English? They bombed and destroyed all our houses so that we have nowhere in Berlin to live. They are bombing town after town, until there are no houses left at all. They will kill you." But Robert smiled at me and said, that the war would soon be over, and then the English would not be the enemy anymore, and we would all be friends and fight communists together. I didn't believe it.

"Where will you go?" I asked him. We were on our way back from putting the horses into the field for the night. He stopped, took out some newspaper, which we had smuggled to him, very carefully he tore off a tiny strip and started to roll one of his dreadfully stinking cigarettes. The tobacco he collected and dried himself from herbs, he said made fine smoking. Then, he sat down by the side of the field and with his finger, drew a little map in the sandy lane:

"Here we are, in north, here Posen, here Bohemia, Silesia and here Austria. Here River Danube. Danube goes almost to where I live and his finger wandered down the road, Hungary, Yugoslavia, Romania, and here the sea. Americans come from

Italy and over here," and he drew another little map of France and Belgium.

"Here English come and Americans. Americans will help get my family. Then we go America. No good stay here. Deutschland kaputt."

He frightened me again, I didn't understand. I knew where the Danube was, because we had been to Regensburg on our way to the Chiemsee. Mother was born there and lived there as a child until her mother died. I looked at Robert, and I sensed an end to the peace we found here. I felt so at home here. We had made many friends, and even hoped that we would stay here forever, or at least, until we could go back to Berlin, if there was anybody left alive.

"Why can't we all stay here? Here is no war, no bombing and no enemy?" Robert got up and started walking back. He took my hand and said:

"Enemy from east very close. Ilia know, he listen on secret radio. Very bad. You big girl, brave, help Mother like you help me, you promise?" I looked up at Robert, and asked:

"Couldn't we at least stay together?" Robert squeezed my hand and said:

"Is no permitted, I prisoner, but be patient, maybe change come. On the wind it is written what becomes of you and me."

But the worries were soon forgotten, my birthday was near and Mother had promised a party. All the Kramp children would be invited. I asked if Robert could come too, but it was not allowed. He could not come until the evening and I promised to keep him a piece of cake. He said he would play for us on Mother's accordion. Mother had brought that too when she went to get the Christmas things and our beds from Berlin, and Robert played many times for us. He was much better at playing the accordion than Mother.

When we worked in the fields, and the monotony of working from one end of the field to the other, thinning beets or cutting thistles or whatever, and it was too boring to bear, Robert would tell stories and poems in Russian or sing some of his songs.

There were melancholic songs of the tow boats on the Volga, songs from the River Don and from the Tatar Steppes, of Stenka Rasin, who was a Russian hero. Robert could sing the highest and the lowest notes, he could sound like two people singing together. When extra prisoners were sent to the farm in the busy season, they would also sing, and even the Polish POWs would join in. It was like organ music in a cathedral. To me, it was so beautiful, it almost hurt.

Very early on my birthday, Robert knocked on the window and I dashed out to get the horses as usual. He gave me a present. It was a tiny wooden doll he had carved, and it had moving arms and legs, blond hair which he had made from bits of untwisted rope. It was small enough to put into a pocket. Robert picked me up and twirled me around, laughed and said:

"You like?" I felt such love for Robert and wished we would never be parted.

"Thank you, it is so beautiful. Please wait while I put it into my bed." I ran into the cottage and put my doll into bed and carefully tucked her in.

I rushed out again and caught up with Robert and we rounded up the horses and rode them back to the farm.

The summer holidays had started early, because of the hay and barley harvest. We were filled with the strange feeling that everything had to be hurried because time was running out. People were talking about the end of the world. They had talked about the end of the world in Berlin too and it still hadn't come.

In the village, lived a very old man, Franz Stekuhn, and he could tell the future. He told a story and it sounded like this:

"And then a man will rise from the people and come among us and he will give false witness. He will be as a king and create a mighty empire. Beware though of his teaching, as he is the Antichrist. And a great war will come and make the heavens red with fire in the East and in the West and in the South. And where the horses hoof beat sounded and man's foot once walked, rows and rows of graves will grow and the villages will be deserted and at the end of that time, at the end, the German People will gather under the Linden-tree, their numbers few and scattered."

He would end his prophecy with a whisper, his eyes round and dark, and I always walked away with a shudder.

There was an extra surprise for me in store, and I think Bine knew about it but would not tell. Robert had something to do in Mehlsack, and often when he had to go into that town for farmer Graf, I was allowed to come too, if I didn't have to go to school. This time he said: "No."

At about eleven, in late morning a woman came walking down the lane from the farm. I watched her carefully, wondering who it could be.

Here in the country, one knew everybody, if one saw a person walking anywhere one usually knew who it was and greeted them. The Kramps had also noticed her and came up and discussed who it could be.

Suddenly, I recognised her. I gave a yell and started to run. Halfway up the lane she spread her arms wide and I ran into them. It was Ta-Echen, Mother's aunt. She was my Grandmother's youngest sister and a spinster, Tante Edith von Tielemann. After my Grandmother had died, Tante Edith had taken a special interest in Mother, and had been a guardian to her. She lived in Halle in Saxony and had come on that long trip to see us. What a wonderful surprise. Bine and Tissi could not remember her. They were too small when she had last visited us in Berlin, and now the two looked shyly at Ta-Echen, but very soon she had them sitting on her lap. She had gifts for all of us.

Mother had made a birthday crown from wild flowers, and it was lying in a soup plate of water for me to put on later in the afternoon.

She spread a table cloth on the meadow in front of the cottage, we had to shoo the ducks and geese and chickens, who constantly wanted to eat the delicious things Mother had prepared. *Frau Kramp* had also made some open sandwiches with homemade bread and *Schinken* from her own smoking chamber. There were gherkins too. Little Mother Poschmann couldn't come, but sent some oat cookies with the children who I had invited from the village.

Kramp's entire fowl population would not give us any peace, so *Frau Kramp* decided to feed them early that day behind the cottage. The Stork pair came closer to have a look, and majestically paced up and down on the meadow, every now and then stopping to swallow a frog.

We were not allowed to go swimming in the pond with a full stomach and Mother fetched her Zeiss Box Camera and carefully aimed. Everybody wanted to be in the picture.

Ta-Echen had news from Mönchgut. She had heard from Tante Fee, a niece. We sat around and listened to her. Tante Mieze had had a very difficult time, but had been allocated some Russian workers. I hoped for Tante Mieze's sake, that they were as nice as Robert, and not like Ilia.

After that we children went to the pond.

During the afternoon, a thunderstorm gathered. On the eastern horizon heavy black-purple clouds appeared and a strong gust of wind made us look up. The people here were still very superstitious and would not venture outside during a thunderstorm.

The children from the village looked at the sky and hastily got dressed and ran across the field towards the village.

Thunderstorms had primeval powers that man would bow to. "God is angry" the people would say. The heavens turn black as it was at Golgatha. The steam that could be seen coming from the earth after the first drops fell, would be as the original fear man felt in the beginning of time. To sit near the window during a thunderstorm would be sheer sacrilege. No fire on the stove, it was forbidden to touch iron or to watch the lightning. The thing to do was to go indoors, read the hymn book with meek humility. To all of us who came here from Berlin, this sounded very strange. Often in our garden, in Berlin, we would listen to the thunder. Or when we were in our boat on the Wannsee, and too far out to get back in time, we would watch the lightening. But here, we had to go along with the local people.

While we were gathered in our cottage, waiting for the summer storm to pass, Robert suddenly appeared.

"Come quick, fire in farm. Lightning struck, lots burning." He also knocked on the KraMPs door, and every able person was rushing up the lane to the farm. There we found the cowshed and a barn in flames. The horses were neighing and screaming. A man I had not seen before was leading the horses.

"This Nikita from Kasan, he knew help and my friend," Robert said and then he grabbed me and chucked me onto the back of one of the horses and handed me a lot of lines and said:

"You take into field over there, not far. Close gate. Come back and help with bucket."

When I got back, the line from the well to the fire had long gaps, I grabbed a bucket and put myself in line. Ta-Echen was here too passing bucket after bucket. I remembered what to do. Berlin came back into my mind and Mother helping with the great fire, at our block of flats. Mother gave me a proud look. I was "die Große" now (the grown up one) Frau Kramp had stayed at home with all her little children and Tissi and Bine. Frau Kramp was very pregnant.

We saved the cowshed partly, but not the barn and most of the winter hay was burnt.

"I wonder if the Führer has any hay for me" the farmer shouted. He was very red in his face.

That was the end of my birthday on July the first nineteen-hundred and forty-four. What would this New Year bring for me? Would we all go home soon?

Tante Edith only stayed a few days. She had to go back to Halle. We were sad to see her go but promised to visit just as soon as possible.

Tante Guste had written a letter to Mother which we received a few days after my birthday. The US Air Force had broken the back of Berlin with a massive air raid on the 21st of June, a day after Mother's birthday. Berlin was dead, she wrote. No water, no electricity, gas leaks everywhere and explosions out of the blue, unexploded bombs and fires that would not stop. Dead people under the ruins and no one to help dig them up. The smell was terrible. The entire city smelled of death. There were only women, a few children and old and sick people in Berlin. Onkel Kurt seemed to be the only doctor around. He was overworked and very ill, and had no time to look after his health. Tante Guste with Hannele and Bärbel did what they could to help him look after the injured and sick, but it was more than they could cope with. On top of that, she wrote, there were thousands of refugees from Lithuania, Poland and the Ukraine now arriving in Berlin with nowhere to go. They had arrived in time to be killed. And there is no food. There is no coal for cooking. Never before was there such carnage.

Mother kept wiping her eyes. She could not stop crying, whilst reading Tante Guste's letter. Sobbing, she said:

"What are we to do? What can I do?" she said.

✳✳✳

16

Mother looked out of the window, into nowhere, deep in thought. She dried her eyes, looked up and said:

"Children, what do you want to eat? You must be hungry?" Relieved, I got up and went over to our larder to have a look.

"Mashed potato and bacon!"

Mother lit the fire in the stove and sliced the bacon and put it in a pan. Bine and I scrubbed the potatoes, and Tissi played with the water.

Mother sliced the bacon and put it into the frying pan. Fat gathered and a delicious smell filled the room. We mashed the potatoes and poured milk into it and creamed it all up. Mother put a dollop on to our plates, made a hole in the middle and filled it with bacon fat, a slice of bacon on the top. To drink we all had a glass of sour milk. It was so good.

In the days that followed my birthday, we listened to the rumours about the Russian Advance. They were in Vilna, they were not in Vilna. A tug of war. Thousands and thousands of German soldiers surrendered in Minsk. Many people shed tears. They had fathers, brothers and husbands there.

"We will never see them again. They will be shot, or worse, transported to Siberia. We will never see them again, ever."

Mother continued to work for Farmer Graf as usual, I helped too, and it was no different from any other beautiful sunny warm July. It was summer, the swallows and house martins were soaring and screaming, the telegraph wires were humming in harmony, the frogs were singing, the storks majestically pacing around our pond and the farmer's geese were grazing in the meadow, the chickens scratching. The pigs snorting contentedly.

Then one morning, as Robert and I rode up with the horses for work, uniformed men drove into the farm court. They strutted over to Robert and me, looked at the horses, opened their mouths, inspected their teeth, felt them all over, gave a sign, and then they led them away. Our horses were gone.

In a total panic, Farmer Graf threw up his arms, screamed and ran around.

"You can use the cows from now on," the officer said, "and this old nag you can keep, it wouldn't last a minute where these are going." and he waved the horses away. I was stunned. Robert too. He was speechless. I went over and took his hand. After a while he said:

"My horses, what I do now?" I sat down on the stable block and watched. The soldiers left again, and the farm was very quiet. With his head hanging low, Farmer Graf came up to Robert, and put a hand on his shoulder. The two men looked at each other.

"Do you know how to handle cows?" Robert shook his head.

"Njet" he said "but I try. Will cow know what to do?" Farmer Graf went over to the harness room and rummaged and came back with some very old oxen harness. And the work continued. But everything slowed down so much. The cows walked so slowly and awkwardly, I had no patience. This was not for me. It wasn't for Robert either, but he had no choice. Poor Farmer Graf.

The same day in the afternoon, there was another visit by officers in black uniform.

This time they were accompanied with soldiers who carried guns. They herded all the people into the farmyard. Slowly, everybody arrived from the stables, the fields and the house.

"Who else lives here? Anybody on leave from the front? *Los raus mit der Sprache*" (speak up) one of the officers said. He was wearing a *Ritter Kreuz* (Iron Cross order) around his neck. Another strutting officer! I thought he looked stupid.

Farmer Graf shouted from where he stood with his back against the burnt out barn:" What is the matter now? This morning you came and took our horses and now this? What is the meaning of it all, ha? How are we supposed to feed the army with all this harassment, ha?"

One of the Gestapo officers came over and stood there in front of Farmer Graf.

"The entire area is sealed off. No one can escape. Should you harbour any of the assassins, you will be shot, with anybody who helped you." Farmer Graf was quiet, thinking, then he said:

"What assassins, what has happened?" But the officer didn't tell him. Many soldiers were searching in all the buildings and others had ugly looking dogs which they let loose and then ran after them and disappeared in the countryside. Mother went over to one of the officers and said:

"I have two little children in our cottage over that rise, they are by themselves, and if this takes long, I had better go and fetch them." The officer nodded and asked for another soldier to go with Mother. Mother pointed to where I stood and said:

"That is my other daughter, she comes too." The man nodded and we went back to our home. On the way, Mother and the soldier started to talk. Mother asked him which part of Berlin he was from. He said Tempelhof, and I said:

"That's where we live. We had a garden in the Colony, did you have a garden too?" The soldier laughed and said, yes he had, but he hadn't seen the garden in three years, and his house in the Manfred von Richthofen Strasse was bombed, but his family was safe in Silesia. Mother asked:

"What is all the fuss about? We have no assassins here. Apart from the men who came this morning, taking our farm horses, we had no visitors. What has happened?" The soldiers face became very serious, and he looked at Mother.

"They tried to kill the Führer in his bunker today. The assassins escaped but they will be caught, and anybody who had anything to do with it."

"Mein Gott" was all Mother said. When we reached the cottage, Mother invited the soldier in, for a cup of *Hitler Mocha,* which was what we called the *Ersatz Kaffee*. Grinning the soldier accepted. Mother said:

"The Wolfschanze is at Rastenburg, that's a long way from here, about eighty kilometres." The soldier said:

"They will not rest, they take no chances. They will find the people who are responsible. This search for the assassins goes on throughout the fatherland. Nobody is safe. They will find all of them. "Heaven help them!"

We all sat down with a cup of 'H.M' on the little green bench outside our cottage.

Twenty minutes later, a man appeared at the top of the rise and let off one shot. The soldier got up, thanked Mother for the coffee, shook hands and bowed his head and at the same time clicking his heels and said:

"Seems to be all over, I didn't think there was anything here. But you should not stay here." He leaned over, looked left and right, saw there was no one anywhere except Mother and the three of us and whispered:

"Go west, Madame, the Russians will be here any day now", turned on his heel and left quickly.

Life returned almost to normal, and again, war seemed a long way away.

The berries were ripe in the forest and we wandered off with jugs to collect raspberries, forest strawberries and bilberries. We had sour milk ripening on the windowsill, and fresh berries with sour milk and a tiny bit of sugar, mmmm!

It was shortly before the grain harvest, and Mother could have a little rest from the fields. For the moment there were the four of us picking berries in the forest, swimming and picking some more berries, either into the jugs or straight into our mouths. Bine and Tissi had berry moustaches, purple tongues and blue teeth. I laughed. Then they pointed at me, but I couldn't see myself. Mother said:

"You can laugh, just look at yourself, and looking at my fingers and at Bine and Tissi, I could imagine what I looked like.

✳✳✳

On the sandy soft forest road, we could hear the hollow sound of horses pulling a wagon, klop-klop-klop-klop. The horses looked thin and old but were contented to work on this beautiful day and happy to have missed confiscation for war. The wind was hardly noticeable, the snowy white clouds were sailing gracefully under the sun. The grain was ripening, and the larks were rising ever upwards, singing their song of happiness.

From the endless meadows the beautiful scent of freshly cut hay hung in the air, the storks were stalking after frogs, a heron stood without moving, at the edge of the forest, drenched in the sun a deer with two fawns was resting. Nothing disturbed this peaceful scene. We were all totally at peace.

With all our jugs full to the brim we returned home. Frau Kramp was outside her cottage and when she saw us, she came walking slowly towards us. She was heavily pregnant, but August Kramp came running up and yelled:

"You all have to leave, immediately. The Bürgermeister was here." Mother dropped her jug, borrowed Frau KraMPs bicycle and rode into the village. But there was nothing the Bürgermeister could do.

"Orders from the *Gauleiter*" (District manager) he said and Mother rode back. Farmer Graf came walking up to the cottage and asked Mother not to leave. "You are such a good worker. You can't leave with harvest time coming up." Mother didn't want to go, but she explained that it had nothing to do with her, she, and all the other evacuees had to go. That evening, we went to the village to say goodbye. Goodbye Little Mother Poschmann and the Krause sisters, the Bürgermeister and the friends at school.

Mother said, that Onkel Stupps, before he went to Russia, and his death, stopped here with his regiment. In a letter to Mother, he wrote that when the war finished he would buy a farm in East Prussia. The only place for him. 'The Land of Light' he had called it.

My heart felt as if there was a knife in it. There was such an ache in my chest. The tears were running and I could not stop them. I could not speak, and Mother took us home.

"Oh beautiful and beloved land."

Next morning, Robert was outside with a cart and the one remaining horse harnessed to it. He put our things on it and we left to go to Mehlsack. Frau Kramp waved, weeping. She had to have her baby without Mother's help.

Robert said nothing. He just walked in front, leading the horse, I walked behind with Mother. Bine and Tissi sat in the cart on top of the bedding. As we reached the village, other evacuees joined us on this way to the station in Mehlsack. No one knew where we were going. Nobody was happy to leave. Slowly, quietly, heads bowed we walked along the well-trodden road to Mehlsack.

✳✳✳

17

There was no train at the station. Evacuees without homes to go back to stood around amidst bundles, boxes suitcases and snivelling children. I felt wretched. Robert came over with our things. The bed bundle, tightly rolled up in the carpet, a suitcase with clothes and the box the carpenter had made for Mother containing some pots and the silver carefully wrapped, in fact all we owned. Our indoor jam-bucket-loo Mother had given to Frau Kramp who was so happy and grateful.

I carried my leather satchel with my school books, and the doll Robert had made on my back. Bine had put some things into it for safe keeping. She wasn't really quite sure what was happening, and her huge eyes looked at everybody quietly. Her hand in mine, we stood there while Robert shook hands with Mother and bowed. He came over and put his big hand on my shoulder and came down onto one knee:

"You too big to cry. I count on you to help Mother and sisters. War not long now. I find you after. You meet my children." But he too cried, tears were running down his face and the pain in my chest got unbearable. He got up and walked away. Bine held my hand tightly as she watched him disappear. Mother was cuddling Tissi.

Lost, all lost. Like the fine amber sand on the beach at the *Kurische Nehrung*. No matter how hard I closed my fist, the sand always escaped.

For many hours we waited for the train. It was well into the summer night, when the train could be heard in the distance. I watched it grow from a small dot into a huge monster as it puffed towards us. Slowly it came to a screaming halt. It was already full of people, and at first it looked as if we would not get on. But the people in the train quietly made room and helped.

The train looked like a centipede, as many arms stretched from the windows. We were heaved into the train through the windows, first the baggage then the children and then the mothers. This time it was a struggle and nobody laughed. There was no help from the outside. Our box was used as a table, seats and foot rests. The suitcase ended up under the bench, and the luggage shelves took the bedding, Bine, Tissi and myself. We had to share the racks with other children. It was all very cramped and we had to let our feet dangle down. There was no room to lie down.

All the windows were open, to let in the July night. It was all very dark, but we could see enough to settle in. Nobody spoke. Everything was done routinely. The waiting continued. The train did not move. Eventually we went to sleep, and around four in the morning, when the sun was just above the horizon, the train started to move very slowly. We looked out of the window in the direction of Lichtenau. Would we be able to see it once more? We all knew we couldn't. It was far too distant.

I looked around at the women and children in our compartment. They too had been quietly weeping. Nobody spoke. Mother looked at the woman opposite, she was holding a little boy on her lap.

"Where are you from?" she asked and the woman replied:

"We are Berliners and were evacuated to Königsberg. Two days ago we had to leave. We don't know where we are going. We are not going to Berlin, they won't let us." Mother said:

"Two days ago, but Königsberg is not that far. What happened?"

"We just halted on the open railway line. No houses or people. We were hoping to get some food at Mehlsack, but there was nothing. Have you some food? It looks as if it will be a long journey."

Mother said she had some salted bacon and some bread. Dried peas and lentils, but nowhere to cook it.

The little boy on the woman's lap wanted to pee, and the woman pulled down his trousers and held him out of the window. He did more than pee. Nobody took any notice, as if that was the most natural thing to do. I whispered to Bine:

"Do we all have to go to the loo that way? I couldn't." Please let there be a loo. I tried to get Mother to look up. I couldn't ask her aloud in front of those people. Mother guessed what I wanted to ask, and also knew that none of us could 'go' like the little boy.

She got up and climbed over luggage and people to get to the door of the compartment, and over her shoulder she said:

"I am going to find out."

Right below me, a mother said:

"You'll never get through, we go whenever the train stops, and it will stop often. You can then go *bei Mutter Grün*, (at mother greens), everyone does."

"How do we know the train stops long enough?" Mother asked.

"It just does, you'll see." Mother came back and sat down. I didn't tell her that I needed to go now, it would have to wait. The hours went by, the train rolled so slowly, one could have walked by its side. By seven in the morning, I was very hungry, Bine too, I could hear her tummy rumbling. Tissi was still asleep, thank goodness. We all knew what would happen when she woke up. She would cry for food until she got it, whether there was any or not. I pressed my knees into my tummy, a trick I had learned long ago, only it would have been more effective to be able to lie on my tummy. It made the hunger pains go away.

The train had gone through the stations of Wormditt and Liebstadt without stopping. Somebody said that Mohrungen would be the next stop. A big town, that will be a soup stop, surely, I thought to myself. People were full of anticipation. I was hopeful, that we would get a slice of bread and some soup.

But the train stopped between stations in the open countryside before we got to Mohrungen. We could see some people in the fields, cutting rye and bundling it together into sheaves and stacking it into a corner. Why can they stay, and we have to leave? After a while the woman by the door said:

"This looks to me like a loo stop." Sure enough, looking out through the window, the train was emptying and the people walking into the field, crouching down and disappearing in the tall rye.

After half an hour, somebody walked up to the engine to find out how long the train would stop, but the engine driver didn't know either. He just sat there waiting for the signal to change.

Someone else suggested to cook some food, start a fire, but there was no wood, and anyway what if the train leaves before the stuff was cooked? Mother handed each of us some dry bread. When she saw our outstretched hands, she shook her head. She put the bread down again and rummaged in her bag, which was filled with useful things. Out came the talcum powder, and she rubbed some into our faces and hands. Now they looked nice and clean, covering the black dirt. She sighed:

"I wonder when we can wash ourselves again."

The bread was hard, but it tasted good. If only we had something to drink.

Two trains passed east on the opposite rail, whistling but not stopping. We all settled back into the train and waited. Some time during the afternoon, the train gave a sharp whistle and a little later jerked hard and rolled on, slowly gathering speed, our spirits rose. We raced through Mohrungen and finally, in the evening, we stopped at Thorn. Here, Red Cross nurses waited at the platform with soup. They had waited since midday, and the soup was cold, but tasted good. There was a slice of soft chewy bread, milk and enough soup to have a second helping. Mother had managed to secure an army canteen, a kidney shaped container with a lid. The container could be used as a saucepan and the lid as a frying pan. This, she now filled, with cold soup, explaining that she had three children to feed. When she got back, she said:

"This is for our next meal. Heaven knows when that will be. Ange, take the little ones and find a tap and wash them, wash your hands well." I went, holding on to my little sister's hands. Bine, two years younger, was almost as tall as I. We found the tap and the first thing we did was to drink and drink the water. Until then we weren't aware just how thirsty we were.

Thorn was the border town between East Prussia and Posen, which was now enemy country. During the night the train rolled slowly through the Province of Posen. Inowroclaw and many names I could not pronounce. Mother told us of the times when she was a child of seven and Grandfather had bought a farm near the town of Posen. He bred horses there during the First World War, but only came to live here when he was injured in the war. His own father was buried at Nierwiercz, and she said it was very close, so Silesia wasn't that far away.

Grandfather lost the farm, without compensation, when Posen was given to the Poles after the Versailles Treaty.

Silesia!! We were making plans. We would go to Mönchgut. We would live with Tante Mieze and help on the estate. Tante Fee and Onkel Jo were also close in Dorniz. Since Onkel Jo was in the war, Tante Fee coped with POWs. We would wait for the end of the war with our cousins. We would have a home. Things were not so bad. Quietly and contently, we settled down and waited.

The train slowed again, and crawled through the countryside. So slowly, and then it stopped. We all got out, stretched our legs and did the usual, and chatted. We met people from other compartments whom we had met before during the many stops. Everybody was guessing as to where we would end up. Mother said we were not going any further than Breslau. From there, we would make our way to relatives we had near Wohlau. Yes, some people nodded, they too had relatives in Silesia. Which Berliner hadn't. Each child born in Silesia was lifted out of the cradle first thing and pointed in the direction of Berlin, so they knew where they would end up eventually.

We were all covered in awful sores. Mosquitoes were everywhere and we could not close the windows to keep them out, because of the heat. Everyone was scratching and suffering. Mother had a big bottle of peroxide in her Rucksack, and we put that neat onto the sores. When it stopped foaming, all the bacteria were dead. It took a long time for the foaming to stop but the stinging sensation relieved the itching. The bottle was passed around in the compartment.

We couldn't remember what day it was, when we got onto the train. I worked out that it was about four days after they took farmer Graf's horses, which was the same day as they were hunting the assassins, and that was the 20th of July. So how long had we been on the train? This was our third night. Somebody said:

"We were here two days before you, so we have been here five days. *Du lieber Gott* and how far have we come? Barely even one good day's journey." We were still stopping and starting, not making any headway.

Mother gave us each a hard bit of bread. I crawled into my nest in the luggage rack and settled down to suck on it. One good thing, it took a long time to eat. Eventually I fell asleep with some of the bread still in my hand. When I woke up, I was still clutching it.

Thundering noise had woken me up. We all listened. The sky lit up every time there was the thunder in the distance. But it wasn't like the thunderstorms we had in East Prussia.

Suddenly, the train started to move again, then stopped and started again clanking and jerking. Stragglers outside racing to catch the handrail and pull themselves up. The train gathered speed rather quickly.

We raced through Kosten. Darkness, no lights anywhere. No people on the platform. Lissa. The same. Someone said we must be crossing into Silesia any minute now. Then we were back in Germany. In the darkness somebody sighed. What will become of us?

Eventually, at Fraustadt, the train stopped. Here we had Red Cross people with milk and bread. But the train did not stop for long. The whistle went and everybody hurried back. No time to find out anything.

Glogau. Mother was happy. All these places were familiar. There was one or another relative in almost all the towns here, Grandfather's people, Grandmothers people, cousins, aunts and uncles.

Raudten, Lüben.

Liegnitz. Grandfather was a boy here. His father taught at the Academy near this town. Grandfather himself later studied at the same Academy.

The train stopped. Men in uniform and battle gear walked up and down yelling for everybody to get off the train with all their luggage. We would find accommodation here and around Liegnitz. We would have to report at such and such authority and there, we would learn where we were going to be taken from here. Mother said:

"We have not far to go from here to Mönchgut where we have relatives." Mother smiled happily at the officer. He just nodded and walked away. All would be well from now on. We were home again with dear people.

✳✳✳

18

It was late in the afternoon when we arrived in Liegnitz. There were no telephones, no local transport. No way to travel to Mönchgut other than walk.

For the moment, until Mother had worked out what best to do, we joined the endless queue and waited. Then our names were called out, and when it was our turn, Mother received instructions as to where our quarters were. We left our things at the station and only took the suitcase and went in search of the local Vicarage, which was our address. The vicar received us at the door, and when Mother asked how she could get her things from the station, he took her to a shed and pointed to a little cart. No words. Mother thanked him. As we walked back to the station Mother said:

"A vicar! Where is his charity?" When we returned with all our things, a maid took us to our tiny room in the attic three storeys up. There were no beds, and Mother went out to see what she could arrange at the *Bürgermeister's* office.

All the doors to the vicar's flat were tightly shut.

The *Bürgermeister* was a kindly old man and somehow found a bed for Tissi. He also gave us some empty straw sacks and told us where we could find straw. We filled our straw sacks with clean smelling straw, put them onto our cart and left again for the vicarage.

We put them onto the floor, put up Tissi's bed and went in search of the loo. We found it on the second floor. There was a note telling us to use the kitchen in the basement.

Attached to the vicarage, was a school which was now used as a field hospital and was crowded with wounded soldiers from the eastern front. Water for everything, even the loo, came from the pump in the courtyard. Big brown enamel jugs were everywhere, one in the loo, and every time we used water to wash down the loo, we had to go and fill the jug in the yard for the next user. Bine and I made it a habit to go together, thus saving one trip.

Mother tried to arrange a visit to Mönchgut but again there was no transport. She wrote a letter to Tante Mieze, telling her where we had landed. She also took us to Wahlstatt. Grandfather had taken her to this place when she was a child. Now she was taking us and telling us what Grandfather had told her then.

"In 1241 there was a great battle here. The Mongols had come to Europe from the other side of Russia. A place called Mongolia. They had invaded Europe regularly, killing and raping and destroying. They came riding on small, very fast horses, eating and sleeping whilst riding, changing horses in mid-gallop and thus seeming to be everywhere at the same time. Also, although they were many thousands, they rode and fought as one. They left dead people like stones in a quarry, leaves in autumn, killing everyone and everything. Where ever they rode, they left empty waste-land. This time they came through Poland's plains, intending to ride into Germany. They were in sight of Breslau, when Heinrich von Schlesien called on the Teutonic Knights to make a united stand. He rallied every soldier and knight of his own Silesia, the nobility of Poland, the Templars, the Hospitallers, the Knights of St. John from East Prussia; the very core of northern European chivalry united under his banner. His brother in law, Wenceslas of Bohemia came with fifty thousand men. A united and Christian Europe stopped the Mongols at Wahlstatt near Liegnitz. They would never return."

Later, a monastery was built on this site which, centuries later, was turned into an academy for dragoons. Great grandfather was an instructor here and Grandfather came here too as a young cadet.

The new church at Wahlstatt was so beautiful. A baroque building decorated with the most delicate illuminating colours.

I was fascinated. It was like a miracle, that something so beautiful could exist.

"You are standing on German soil." Mother said. I didn't quite understand what she meant, but I had a good feeling in my heart.

Tante Mieze sent a Landauer to take us to Mönchgut.

Things had changed so much in the last two years since all the sons and cousins had died in the war. Tante Mieze had moved into the foreman's villa in the park. Her rooms and all her surrounding, was as it had always been. Calm and elegant, she received us warmly and led us into a beautiful room. She had selected some beautiful pieces of furniture from the *Schloss* (Manor House) and also some paintings, the rest she said was in storage.

"The war, you know." she apologised.

"Unfortunately, there will be quite a change here." she pointed through the window towards the estate.

Most of the horses had been confiscated for the war, the estate was on the market since there was no one alive to take it over. She was keeping the villa some land and forest, part of the garden and park. She offered Mother the hunters lodge in the forest.

"It would be wonderful if we could all be together now, we need a host of young ones. Tante Gretel will come with her troop too." Tante Mieze gave Mother a friendly and encouraging nod.

The hunters lodge was very remote and needed some repair. It was a long way to school too. But Mother liked the idea of living here on her beloved Mönchgut!

It was distressing to see the state of the place. We all walked over the estate, looked at everything. Mother's cousin, Tante Gretel quietly led us to the well in the big square and she drank from the crystal clear water, saying:

"No matter what, the water is always good here."

Most men were in the war except old Hertel Kolle the foreman, who had been injured and had then been sent back because he could not hold a gun anymore. He came towards us with outstretched arms, one dangling a little loosely. I ran towards him and told him that we might live here. Hertel Kolle, who had known Mother since she was a small child, said:

"It would be nice to have you in the hunters lodge, will you come?" Then he whispered:

"The war will soon be over and we can start fresh, bring the children, we need them." Mother told everyone she would think it over.

"In the meantime," Tante Mieze said, "come and live here. It would be better than the vicarage in Liegnitz." We returned to Liegnitz the next day in the Landauer to fetch our things.

That night, Mother got ill with dysentery. The district nurse came to help and gave Mother some medicine. Mother gave strict orders to me, to keep the children away and always wash everything very carefully, and not to touch anything of hers. She was hoping we would not infect ourselves. For a while, I thought Mother would die. She was almost in a coma and very weak. Then came the letter, telling us that Father was missing.

"Does that mean he is dead?" I asked Mother. But she just shook her head.

"It means he is missing, we will find him after the war, *Unkraut vergeht nicht*" was a saying we often used. Weeds are everlasting. She turned her face to the wall, and I left quietly. I knew she was crying.

I took our ration cards and went in search of food. I had to feed the two little ones. Mother needed oats for a thin porridge, the nurse had told me. I collected the daily milk ration, and a quarter litre for Tissi of unskimmed milk. Our milk was watery and blue, hers thick and creamy. But it was Tissi's. She was still classed as an infant.

The vicarage and school cum field hospital made a horse shoe shape, and a wall completed the fourth side. A big gate, mostly open, led into the inner court. As I came with the shopping, Bine and Tissi were waiting by the gate. As they saw me they came running up.

"What have you got?" Their little hands feeling into the bag. I had been lucky. For the meat coupon I managed to get salt herrings. We could fry those. I got Mother's oats. The milk. Some bread. Some margarine and small amount of jam. Going shopping with various containers and bottles was an absolute must. If I had no containers, I would not be able to carry the oats for which I had a little sack, the same for the flour, herrings in a glass, and jam in glass. Margarine was wrapped in some grease proof paper in the shop, the only thing which came wrapped. I had two more containers with me and luckily, I could fill them with pickled gherkins and the other one with Sauerkraut.

Mother was pleased.

"Eat the Sauerkraut raw." she said, "it's good for you." I also bought some yeast. We used to suck it like sweets. I now divided the yeast into two equal halves, the first half into three equal bits. We popped it into our mouths and let it dissolve on our tongues.

Slowly, Mother got better.

Early one morning, the vicar came up the stairs and knocked on our door.

"I hear you are ill *Frau Gerret*. The Russians are at Warsaw, and they will soon be here. You had better get well soon." Majestically he went down the stairs again, his good deed done for the day.

The last days of September were a blaze of orange and yellow, and almost overnight the leaves dropped as we entered October of 1944.

The Americans were in Aachen.

An officer delivered a letter to Mother by hand. It had been to Mehlsack in East Prussia and in Berlin and now it had finally found us here in a suburb of Liegnitz. It was like a miracle. I studied the envelope. It had come from Lichtenau. One of the postmarks said so.

Mother hastily opened the letter. It was written by a *Frau Vasner* and it read:

"Your father has been arrested by the Gestapo. He is accused of undermining the fighting spirit and the will to serve, impairing military discipline. A most terrible accusation. It is a matter of life or death. Please come at once and help your father."

Mother was still very weak, thin and pale. She packed two suitcases with the things we needed most urgently and asked a fellow evacuee to look after the rest of our things. If we should not return, would she please send them on? Mother wrote to Tante Mieze, explaining the sudden change of plan, but promising to be back just as soon as Grandfather was safe. Sadly she could not wait for an answer. We took the train that same evening.

We had been in Silesia two months, and most of that time, Mother had been most dreadfully ill. I had to do the providing and looking after the two little ones. Now, getting ready for yet another journey, was only routine. I had learned how to travel under any circumstance. There was a special spirit among our fellow travellers. A grim humour prevailed. A unity, which somehow expressed:

"We are all suffering the same trauma, let's stick together."

Off course the three of us ended up in the luggage rack again. Our fellow travellers were not evacuees this time, but refugees from Upper Silesia and Poland. Those Polish people spoke a hard and broken German. They were all running away from the Soviets. They said it was quite clear that the war was lost and the Russians would get through. No one can hold them back now, and once they are there, no one will escape with their lives.

The train raced through the night. In Dresden we had to change trains. There we had to turn south. Most of our fellow travellers were going on to the west. We had to get around Czechoslovakia. As we waited on the platform, we had our first air raid since Berlin. We had re-joined the war.

✷✷✷

19

Mother got up from the bench where we were sitting and looked around. There were no lights. The blackout was complete.

"I wonder if there is a shelter here." she said. Soon we realised, that even if there was, only a fraction of the people in the Dresden Railway Station, would find refuge there. Within seconds of the first bomb falling, people were milling around in panic. Mother said:

"These poor people! They have never been in a raid." I could see what she meant. If they were refugees from places like East Prussia, then they would never have been in a raid.

"The Russians don't drop any bombs, and the English can't fly that far east, mother said, and then added:

"I hope they will not bomb the tracks. We have to get to Regensburg very quickly."

Suddenly, the sky lit up as if it was daytime. The planes roared above. The daylight sank slowly down onto the town, and seconds later there was a circle of explosions around the station and fires were burning everywhere.

We were blown off the bench and landed on the platform floor, with Tissi on Mother's lap and Bine and myself hanging on to her arms. The four of us clinging at each other in a tight bundle. Tissi was screaming, Bine cried without a sound, at least I couldn't hear her. I just felt her wet and snotty face. She was forever snotty. I hated it.

My head was bursting, people were falling over us, screaming. Dust, stench and smoke everywhere and where there had been a building at the end of the platforms, there was now a burning inferno. I could feel the heat.

More screaming. The people settled around us, huddling against each other making a tight ball with us in the middle somewhere. The whistling bombs and shattering explosions were never ending.

I closed my eyes. Shining East Prussia, Lichtenau, the horses, the pond, Robert. If only Robert were here, I would feel safe. Someone knocked me hard on the head and I cried. I couldn't bear it any longer. I heard Robert's voice in my heart.

"You big girl now, help Mother." I tried to stop crying. A train arrived at the station. A Miracle. A voice was heard, loud and clear. *Alle einsteigen, schnell, schnell. Alle einsteigen."* A frantic scramble started, but luckily the train had stopped with a door near us. We were one of the first to get in. But we lost the suitcases. Mother said:

"They are not important, but you are. Would I take a suitcase instead of one of you?" She gave us a tight squeeze.

"I am sure, God looks after us. We are still alive. It is a miracle."

The train left the platform and raced out of the station, but soon it slowed down almost to a halt. Many trains had come into the station, to take the people to safety. But then there was a jam. Worse still, we had to travel through fire. Things were burning either side of the tracks, but the miracle was still with us. Very slowly but steadily we travelled on, choking in the thick smoke, leaving the chaos behind.

We had no idea where we were going. Then the burning around us stopped and we travelled in utter darkness. In the distance the bombing continued. People were sobbing and looking back, out of the broken and blackened windows. The sky was crimson, we could still see the flames. They seemed to reach for the stars, lighting up the dark silhouettes of the planes as they dropped more bombs. I imagined Sodom and Gomorrah to be like this. We pulled into a small station and stopped. It was a tiny village station, and the platform was not long enough for the train.

Alle aussteigen, alle austeigen (everybody out). So we queued to get off the train. As we came near the door, I saw two suitcases standing in the passage. Our suitcases!

"Mother look, our suitcases!" Yes, I believed in miracles. Who, in that chaos, would have put the suitcases on the train, and into our carriage? Any other carriage, and we would not have found them again, surely.

We settled on the platform, and watched the burning in the distance. When the train had left, we were in complete darkness. We could hear the crackling of the fire, the constant explosions and new bursts of fire. Nobody spoke. It was as if nobody would ever speak again. Mother rummaged in her Rucksack, which she always carried with her on her back. Even Tissi had travelled in it before now. It contained bandages, salves, the peroxide, the talcum powder and some bread. She gave us each a small hard piece and we started to chew it slowly. She also had some of the oats I had bought not so long ago. She gave us a little. We were careful not to spill any. We popped small bits into our mouths and chewed. I was very thirsty, but I said nothing. Where would she have got something to drink anyway?

Still nobody spoke. It was very cold. The temperature went down to freezing. After all it was October.

We sat and waited and watched the fire. After a while, Mother handed us each a couple of dried peas and whispered;

"Suck these, they will stop you being thirsty." We sucked the peas until they were soft, then chewed and swallowed them and asked for more. Mother gave us a little handful to put into our coat pockets.

Suddenly somebody started to sing a song quietly, and slowly everybody joined in. It's something people do, to relieve their emotion. This was a song about the native homeland of Silesia.

Riesengebirge, Deutsches Gebirge-/Riesengebirge, German Highlands
Blaue Berge, grüne Täler/Blue Mountains, green valleys
Mittendrin ein Häuschen klein/surround a little house
Herrlich ist dies Stückchen Erde/glorious is this piece of earth

Denn ich bin ja dort daheim./because this is my home
Riesengebirge, Deutsches Gebirge, Du meine liebe Heimat Du./Riesengebirge, German Highlands, my beloved homeland.
Ist's mir gut und schlecht ergangen/I had good times and bad times
Hab gesungen und gelacht/I sang and I laughed
In manchen bangen Stunden/In many anxious hours
Hat mein Herz ganz still bepocht/my heart beat quietly
Und es zog mich nach Jahr und Stunden/and after many years of wandering
Wieder heim in's Elternhaus…/it took me home into the house of my fathers.
Oh mein liebes Riesengebirge/Oh, my beloved Riesengebirge
Wo die Elbe so heimlich rinnt/where the Elbe-river quietly flows.
Wo der Rübezahl mit seinen Zwergen/Where Rübezahl with his gnomes
Immer noch Sagen und Märchen spinnt/tells legends for ever more.

It was the first time I had heard this beautiful, yet sad song. The Riesengebirge, Mother pointed out was just over there in the distance to the left. I could make out blue hills on the horizon in the pale dawn. They cradled Schlesien. Most of the people around us were from Upper Silesia, and this song told of their home.

My feet were cold and hurting, so I got up and hopped from one foot to the other, something we always did automatically when it was freezing. I also had to throw my hands around my shoulders to keep them warm. The children around me also got up and started hopping and we made it into a game. Slowly it became light and the crimson glow turned black in the distance. What was bright red in the darkness was now billowing black smoke. The planes had gone. People slowly came out of their shock and started to wonder what was to become of us.

One old woman got up and walked over to the station office and other people joined her. There were timetables on the wall, and with a little luck, we could make our way via many little country lines to Chemnitz. Surely from there, we could catch a train to Nürnberg and Regensburg.

Around midday, it started to snow and in the afternoon a good strain arrived. It went in the only direction we could go; away from Dresden. We climbed on, but some people actually walked back to Dresden on the tracks. Mother gathered us into a corner of the wagon, there was a little straw and we propped our suitcases up to keep the draught from hitting us through the boards, which made a fairly comfortable nest. To pass the time, Mother told stories of Rübezahl, the mountain spirit of the Riesengebirge, who played many tricks on people, but somehow, always helped the poor and helpless. Why won't he help us now? We are so close to him here, but a woman next to us said sadly:

"He cannot help anyone outside his domain. His kingdom is only in the Riesengebirge." She wiped her eyes with the back of her hands.

"We are lost forever." she said. Mother stopped telling stories. It became very quiet. I tried to look out through the crack in the door. The draught was icy through the floorboards and we huddled together into a tight ball. We arrived in Chemnitz, climbed down from the cattle waggon, and walked on the tracks from the shunting station to the proper station. Bine and I dragged a suitcase between us and Mother led Tissi with one hand and carried the other suitcase.

Another miracle occurred. There were people from the Red Cross with milk, soup and bread. We formed a long queue and waited patiently. An official walked down the line and told us of possible trains that would leave Chemnitz that night. It was still bitterly cold and snowing. I could smell the food, and it gave me a reassuring happy feeling. People around us, were laughing and telling grim jokes. The horror of the night before seemed to be forgotten for the moment.

Tissi got some milk in our milk container and Mother had the battle canteen filled to the brim with soup, a woman counted our heads and handed us four thick slices of delicious soft bread with a crisp crust. We got our spoons out and started to dip into the common pot. I saved as much of my bread as I could for later. The soup tasted good and even had bits of meat in it, it was hot and we had lots.

Satisfied, with a warm belly, we waited for the train. Tissi went to sleep on Mother's lap. Bine and I hopped around to keep warm. Mother kept telling us to stay near. Finally, sometime during the night, a train arrived. It was totally empty, very cold and dirty. It was black inside and out and smelled of stale smoke. Everything we touched was sooty. We were too frozen and too tired, to care. We were told this train would take us to the south.

We settled in, and found it wasn't as full as the trains we had travelled in previously. But as we stood in the station and waited to leave, the train filled slowly. In the end, people even sat on the steps outside, in the open. They would freeze to death, I worried, but there was nothing any of us could do. Eventually, we left, and travelled through the night, shunting backwards and forwards, in the end we didn't know where we were headed. People tried to orientate themselves, but most just resigned themselves to being shunted. Somebody said:

"Glauchau." After a while somebody else said

"Zwickau", then "Plauen." Mother said:

"Not far from Hof", and sure enough, Hof was next. The train did not stop until we were near Nürnberg. We could not enter that city, because there was a bombing raid going on. We stopped and watched the raid. It was getting light now, how many days since Liegnitz? When was the raid in Dresden? Yesterday, the day before? I could not work it out. Somebody said:

"They are starting at dawn now, soon they will go on twenty four hours a day."

Suddenly, all hell broke loose, as some planes attacked the train… People ran in panic from the train as they thought the train would be bombed, but were shot at in the fields. Mother told us to lie down under the train. "Heads down" somebody yelled. Thankfully, the raid was very short and the planes disappeared. A woman said:

"They are playing a grim game and having fun with us." But some people were dead. It wasn't fun. It was very real.

We had to wait because the rails had been hit. A gang of workers arrived later and straightened them. Very very slowly, we travelled into Nürnberg. I could have walked faster. At the station a man paced up and down the train and shouted through a speaking tube:

"First three carriages to München, the last four to Köln."

Mother looked out of the window, and counted the carriages in front of us. We were in the fourth, so we had to get out and get into the next one. We squeezed and pushed, and nearly didn't get on. We couldn't get into a compartment, but had to stay just inside the door leading to the entrance platform, resembling a balcony, at the rear of the carriage. It was very cold, the door could not be closed because that platform was also full of people.

A soldier sat on the floor in a corner, where the corridor started. He only had one leg, and he said:

"Come over here, little one, you can sit on my lap. It's not so cold here." Bine said:

"Can I come too?" and the soldier nodded and grinned. So Bine and I rode the rest of the journey from Nürnberg to Regensburg on the lap of a soldier, cuddling up to his scratchy, smelly grey coat for warmth, afraid to be trodden on by dozens and dozens of feet, which were stomping around to keep warm.

✹✹✹

20

We entered Regensburg from the north on the 29th of October 1944. A bridge was down and we had to be rerouted via Amberg and Schwandorf. The rail bridge across the Danube, at the docks area, was miraculously, still intact. But there had been a raid just before we got there and some large warehouses in the docks area were smouldering, some actually still burning. The impressive looking *Stadtlagerhaus* of Regensburg was a black hulk. There was a nauseating stench of rotting burnt fish in the air and mingled with the smell of burning rubber. It made me retch. I could not breathe through my nose or my mouth without wanting to vomit. Looking out of the windows, we saw big ocean going ships in the river, which had been bombed and sunk. I loved ships and to see them on their sides was depressing. I could make out some words and thought maybe it was the name of the ships, it said 'Bayrischer Lloyd' which Mother explained was the name of the company, which had existed even when she was little. She also explained, that boats from all over the world can come as far as Regensburg. From the Atlantic into the Middle Sea, past Italy, rounding Greece and past Turkey into the Black Sea.

"That's where Robert comes from." I said. Mother nodded her agreement and continued to tell how they work their way up the Danube through all the countries like Rumania, then along the border of Bulgaria, into Yugoslavia, Hungary, Austria and finally Germany, where the *Donau* is born. Because of a bridge, which was built in the 12th century, the ships cannot go any further than Regensburg. Just then, I spotted this wonderful bridge, called the *Steinerne Brücke* and squatting nearby, the twin spires of the gothic *Regensburger Dom*. The Dom dominated the city, dwarfing the red tiled, ancient houses around it. I liked this place already. It was beautiful, apart from destruction we had just seen, and that dreadful smell.

We rounded into the town and entered the station. Everything was graceful and almost untouched by bombing. Outside trams were busily ringing their bells, going into so many different directions, disappearing amongst the many trees everywhere. I was thrilled. Mother took a taxi to Frau Vasner's house.

Frau Vasner had been expecting us for at least four weeks. She didn't know exactly where we were or, once we had received the letter, how long it would take us to get to Regensburg. She was very nervous and ran around in circles.

An elderly lady came into the hall and took the three of us into the kitchen and sat us around a table. She offered us white bread with raisins inside and jam on the top. We ate and ate, until there was no more bread on the table. We had cocoa to drink. I thought at the time, that no matter how much I ate, I would never ever be satisfied. I thought I was still hungry when the bread was finished but pretended I had had enough. Bine whispered to me, that she was still hungry, but I gave her a nudge under the table. And when the lady asked if she wanted more, Bine said "No thank you."

The old lady, who was Frau Varner's mother, had fed Tissi and then took us all into the bathroom and washed us. Later that day when Frau Vasner had finished talking to Mother, we were taken to Grandfather's apartment in the Von Stauss Strasse 8.

It was a very pretty villa, sitting in its own garden. Everything was covered with a thin layer of snow. A little lockup gate at the side led into the back garden. There were fruit trees and some leeks sticking out through the snow in the vegetable section. A Bavarian mountain cottage sitting on top of a huge rockery among fir trees. At the very end of the garden, there was a chicken run with chickens in it. To hide the chicken run, Grandfather had planted berry bushes, which were now bare of leaves.

There was an old man, Father Rappel, who looked after all the things in the garden, the chickens, the wood and anything that Grandfather needed doing. Father Rappel had no teeth at all.

The villa had a downstairs apartment, where a coal merchant lived, the first floor was occupied by Grandfather. It was reached by a sweeping, highly polished wooden staircase with mahogany banisters. Ideal for sliding down. A very wide entree door, half wood half decorated glass, led into Grandfather's apartment. Above that was only the loft with a two roomed flat which faced the loft where he stored things and dried the laundry. There was also a cellar, which, we found out later, was also the air raid shelter. It housed a coal cellar, wash house and storage area etc.

Grandfather's apartment started off with a cloakroom next to the entrance on the left, followed by the kitchen, the bathroom, a bedroom where his cook lived, another bedroom and at the end of the corridor a door led into the *Bauernzimmer*. That end bedroom and the *Bauernzimmer* was going to be our new home.

Next was Grandfather's bedroom and his living room, a study and a larder which brought us back to the entrance hall. What a wonderful place! He had lived here since he moved from the Chiemsee in spring of 1940. The furniture in his rooms were all covered with white dust sheets. Huge sheets were hanging off the crystal chandeliers which I remembered from the house at the Chiemsee. None of his beautiful things were visible. Grandfather's particular smell of good cigars and lavender lingered though.

We moved in that evening, and then Mother got an extra bed from the loft, because our bedroom had only one black iron- with golden brass nobs- double bed in it. Mother arranged it so, that the three of us slept sideways on the double bed, and she had a bed to herself. There was a large golden ball at each end of the bed and I was disappointed when Mother explained that it was brass and not gold.

The Bauernzimmer was so called because of the built in painted Bavarian style peasant furniture. I thought it was absolutely beautiful, mainly olive green and yellow with colourful painted panelled walls, and a shelf running right round the room at the top of the panelling. Beautiful plates and mugs, vases and beer glasses with brass lids, were displayed there. The window was also painted green and had coloured bull's eye window panes. All the windows in the house had green shutters on the outside.

At the end of the room, a glass door opened up onto a carved wooden balcony with a roof and double glazed windows on three sides and exotic plants growing in pots. It seemed to reach into the trees like a treehouse.

Grandfather, we found out from Frau Vasner, was at a Concentration Camp near Munich. Mother explained that it was a prison.

Frau Vasner told us not, under any circumstances, to talk to the man who lived in the downstairs apartment. It was he who had denounced my grandfather. Apparently he had overheard him as he was talking to a friend in the well of the staircase. This friend had a name, which a week later appeared on the list of persons wanted for the attempted assassination of Hitler in East Prussia, or so it was claimed. Grandfather had no comment.

Grandfather's attitude was a constant cause for alarm and argument within the family. Onkel Kurt felt that his uncle should be more diplomatic. The family felt, that as Captain of the Royal Horse, retired, for the Prince of Regensburg, Grandfather had a certain security. But Hitler had no fondness for the German aristocracy, and Grandfather's open loyalty to the Kaiser didn't help either. This and a lot of other circumstances, which seemed suspicious, finally condemned him.

"The man downstairs will not rest, until he has Father's life. Heaven knows why. It seems any lie would do to condemn people today. If Father is found guilty, he will be executed. There is no doubt. What does the wretch downstairs get out of it?" Frau Vasner said. It was strange to hear her call my grandfather, father. Mother still hadn't worked out what relationship Frau Vasner and her father had, but she decided it didn't matter, as long as she was on her father's side.

I could not imagine, how Grandfather must feel, knowing that he would die, that somebody would come up to him and kill

him, and Grandfather would have to let him, we would have to let them kill Grandfather.

"Mother you must save him, can you save him?" I asked, and Frau Vasner also looked at Mother and said:

"You are his last hope. You arrived almost too late, because next week he is transferred from Munich to Berlin for trial. You must go with him. There are his relatives, his nephew." Mother said:

"Kurt, he will help, is the telephone working?" Frau Vasner picked up the receiver and dialled a number. She said:

"Connect me with Berlin, Kurt von Stückerodt, Wilmersdorf," she gave our telephone number and hung up.

I was fascinated. Grandfather had his own telephone! After a while the telephone rang and Frau Vasner picked it up. She handed the receiver to Mother, who started to cry.

"Kurt, Oh Kurt" she cried and then she briefly told him what was happening, but he already knew. She also told him that she was coming to Berlin next week, didn't know what day, but hopefully with her father and could Kurt help. After a long silence Mother said:

"Thank you Kurt, you are my only hope", and then she hung up the telephone. She wiped her tears. I hadn't seen her cry in many weeks, and now she couldn't stop.

Next morning, Mother and I went to seek out the *Ortsgruppenleiter* (Local branch leader). When we entered the building of the Local Branch Office there was nobody there. All the rooms were empty, so she kept on knocking on various doors, waiting and then looking in. Finally we came to a door and after knocking somebody said:

"Come in." Mother entered and found the exalted gentleman, seated behind the desk in his socks and feet up. His feet came down smartly, and he hissed:

"How did you get in here?" Mother's arm shot up, she snapped "Heil Hitler", and then she said:

"I came to speak with you, but there seems to be nobody in the entire building, so I finally came to this door. I am here on behalf of my father, Baron von Stückerodt, who has been arrested some time ago. I would like to know, why this man, who has only the best intentions for our beloved Germany at heart, has to suffer in this way. After all, he has brought me up. My father is not a common criminal."

The man's face became friendly and he told Mother to go to the *Alte Rathaus* (ancient town hall) room number five, and there we would find the men who could help. We ran. We got to the *Alte Rathaus* and straight into the claws of the Gestapo. No help here!

As we left the *Alte Rathaus*, a man who had seen us go into number five, whispered:

"Go and see Vicar Käppel in the *Silberne Fischgasse*. He will help people like you" and then he vanished. We went straight to this address and this dear man instantly became the go-between for Mother and her father in prison. He smuggled letters and food to Grandfather. He was Mother's first new friend in this city where she was born, where her mother had been so happy. Now there seemed only hostile people, people who looked upon her as a foreigner, people Mother did not understand anymore.

❋❋❋

Mother thought to seek out the Princess of Thurn und Taxis, who was her godmother. Could she help? But there was no time to lose. It would take too long to get an audience.

As we raced home again, Mother told me a silly little story she remembered. When she was about seven, her mother had sent her through the adjoining gardens and park, to the palace with a basket of red cheeked apples to give to her godmother, the princess. They looked so delicious on the way over, she took a bite out of every apple, just where the red was, and put them back into the basket, with the missing bit facing down. On a day out riding, the princess laughingly told Grandfather about the apples, but Grandfather gave Mother a week's house arrest as punishment. Years later, Grandfather had reminded Mother about the little episode and had said at the time, he laughed so much about it with Grandmother, but still felt, Mother had to be punished.

Mother sighed. That was so long ago. Too much water had gone down the Danube since then. Mother was not a baroness anymore, she was plain Frau Gerret. We hurried home.

A few days later, the bell rang and I went to open the door. Three men stood outside, the one in the middle was my grandfather. He was happy to see me and opened his arms. We hugged and the men led him into the apartment. He was not allowed to go into any of his rooms. He was only permitted to sit in the hall. I stayed with him, and one of the men stood a little to one side. The other man had gone with Mother into Grandfather's rooms to collect some clothes and put them into a suitcase. The man who had stayed with Grandfather took out some biscuits and offered me one. I looked at Grandfather. He nodded in agreement, so I accepted one and asked if I could also have one for Bine and Tissi, who were playing in the Bauernzimmer. The man gave me all the biscuits and I thanked him with a curtsy, something Grandfather had always insisted upon, and now I remembered it in time. Grandfather gave me a proud nod.

I leaned against his knees. I wanted to ask him so many questions, but I said nothing. I think he was grateful for that. He just held my hand and we stayed like that until Mother and the other man came into the hall, and Grandfather was led away. He was so erect, proud and dignified. He would never show how he felt, no matter what. If he was afraid, nobody would ever know. I knew. I would not show it either, in front of these men.

When we were quite alone again in the hall, Mother and I held onto each other and cried. But there was no time. She ran into our bedroom and packed a bag, got some money and rang Frau Vasner. She was ready to leave for Berlin. Frau Vasner arrived and Mother told her of Grandfather's visit. "Grandfather is travelling up by military transport." Mother would follow by train on her own. Hopefully all went well.

There was just the question of what to do with us. Grandfather's cook had left some weeks earlier, and Frau Vasner was working in a shop she managed at the Domplatz.

"My mother will cook for them." she said, and turning to me she said:

"Breakfast you can do yourself, lunch at one and evening meal at six at my house. You are grown up enough to bring your sisters over" and she explained how I could find her house. It wasn't that far.

Mother looked at me but said nothing. I knew. I wouldn't let her down. Trouble was, how to get Bine and Tissi to behave. Mother hugged us tightly and told Bine and Tissi to do as they are told by their grown sister. They promised solemnly. Then, Mother and Frau Vasner left.

The three of us were quite alone in Grandfather's apartment. Now it was up to me. Mother had left money and the ration cards. "We will manage. We will not let Mother down." I looked at the other two, and I knew, that in turn, they would not let me down.

Suddenly, I heard a key turn in the entree door and we all looked in that direction, wondering who it was. Quietly, Father Rappel let himself into the apartment and with a dear, reassuring nod started to make a fire in the Bauernzimmer, so that we could sit cosily on the bench by the *Kachelofen* (green tiled stove).

I had difficulty understanding him. First he had no teeth to make his words sound properly and then he spoke with the broadest Bavarian dialect. But, with a twinkle in his eye he said:

"Come with me, I have something for you." and we followed him up to the loft, Tissi, climbing the stairs on all fours. He produced the sledge I remembered from the Chiemsee. We wanted to go sledging right away, but he shook his head and said it was already too dark. He said he would be back the next day and to keep the fire going and was there anything else we needed. He would keep an eye on us.

Frau Vasner came over later that evening and told me, that I had to go to school, and she showed me through the kitchen window in what direction and how far that would be and at what time I would have to be there. It was a convent school and she told me the name of the nun I had to report to.

My heart sank. School. I preferred to go sledging.

At six o' clock the next morning, Father Rappel let himself into the apartment again, and busied himself with the fire. I dressed myself and went into the kitchen to cook the flour soup for breakfast, cut a slice of bread for each of us and laid the table. Bine meanwhile dressed herself and Tissi.

Father Rappel sat down with us and tore his slice of bread into little bits and put it into his soup to soak. I didn't eat my slice of bread. I saved it for the break at school. After breakfast, Father Rappel said:

"*Der Herr Baron* would like me to look after you while your mother is away. You go to school, I shall be here with your sisters." I was so grateful. I told him that we would have lunch at Frau Vasner's at one o clock and he said:

"I will take your sisters, you find your way?" I nodded. It wasn't far. This old city was so homely with its narrow streets and beautiful to look at. I liked it and strangely I did not feel like an outsider. Not yet anyway.

We all went down stairs together, Father Rappel took the sledge, Bine and Tissi sat on it and Father Rappel pulled. We went up the street passing two villas on the left towards the *Ostentor* (East Gate) and the *Bayerischer Lloyd* and there on the corner of the Gabelsberger Strasse I had to leave them. They turned left into the park, sledging, and I went straight on through the *Ostentor* and up the Ostengasse to the school of St. Clara.

✸✸✸

21

I entered a very quiet, large building. A tall statue of Mary stood in a recess in the side of the wall opposite. An enormous crucifix hung high up on the wall at the end of the corridor. There was no one in sight. I was too early. I stood in the stairwell and waited. Eventually, a nun appeared, walking up the corridor. She looked at me and walked past. I waited. Then some children came and I followed them. At the classroom door a nun stood and handed pretty little pictures to the girls as they entered. I waited next to her and when she did not take any notice I said:

"Excuse me, I am the new girl, which class do I have to go to?" All heads turned in my direction and the nun said:

"Wait your turn."

When no more children came, she turned to me and said:

"What is your name?"

"Angela Gerret" I replied, looking up to her. The nun turned to go and said: "No one by this name has been reported to me." Turning back, she added:

"How old are you?"

"Nine years." I said.

"What is your religion? Are you a Catholic?" I shook my head.

"I am protestant"

"Take the last desk by the window" and she walked away down the corridor.

It was all very strange here. It was difficult to understand what they were saying, and the children were unfriendly. They looked at me as if there was something funny about me.

They had a strange religion too. They constantly crossed themselves, said their prayers very fast without forming words. When entering or leaving the classroom, they dipped their fingers into a little bowl hanging on the wall by the door, curtseyed and crossed themselves again. I didn't know what they were doing but after a few days there I copied them. It seemed the right thing to do.

All the teachers were nuns and wore black habits over their heads and shoulders reaching down to the ground. A white band went across the forehead and the side of their faces. All one could see, was the very front of the face. They hitched their hands into their sleeves. When they had to write something on the blackboard, they pulled out one hand, wrote, and then tucked it back into the sleeve.

I sat at the very back and when the hour came for religious instructions, I had to leave the classroom, and wait in the yard. It was very cold out there, no one to talk to, nothing to eat except my slice of bread, which was in my satchel in class. Later, I found that religious instructions were three times a week lasting an hour.

I occupied the time in making a huge snowman and wondering how Mother got on in Berlin. Were the trains very full? Would she be bombed on the way? Would she come back? Would anybody ever come back? Would we have to live here forever? Would we be able to go home soon? Would we ever see our relatives again? Tante Fee, Tante Mieze, Onkel Kurt and Tante Guste, Bärbel und Hannele, their daughters, Hermann and Kurt their brothers? Tante Ria? I wouldn't see my uncles again, they were dead, except one, who was missing in Russia, presumed dead. Was my father alive? Would these people here in Bavaria always be unfriendly? Did I still like this beautiful, ancient city?

The bell finally rang and I went inside. My feet and hands hurt with cold. I tried to make friends, but there was no one who wanted to speak with me.

I started to learn the Bavarian dialect from Father Rappel, hoping it would help to make friends. But it didn't seem to work.

After school we went into the park, sledging, until six in the evening, and then we went to Frau Vasner's house for supper which was literally across the street from the park. We thanked her for supper, and left straight after washing up. That had become Bine's and my job. I stood on a foot stool in front of the sink, and handed the washed plates and cutlery into a bowl of clean water on a stool next to me. Bine would fish them out, dry them and put them on the table. Tissi would sit quietly all that time, on a chair nearby, not moving at all, just watching.

As soon as we were finished, we quickly put on our coats and left. Back in the park we went on sledging until after eight, when I was so troubled with a guilty conscience, that I took my sister's home.

We managed very well with Father Rappel's devoted help. He seemed to know always what had to be done, and did it quietly. I told Father Rappel of my trouble in school, and the very next day, instead of going with Bine and Tissi into the park, he came to school with me. He sent the two on and promised to join them very soon.

At school, he ushered me in and then led the way down the corridor and knocked onto a door. At the word "Enter" he took his hat off and went in alone, and after a while when the door opened, a nun came out and smiled. Father Rappel followed, shyly squeezing his hat and giving me an encouraging nod before he walked away. The nun led me into the classroom and I sat down. She said something to the nun at the desk, who looked at me, and then also smiled. I was given a seat nearer the front, next to a girl with plaits like mine.

Dear Father Rappel! Whatever did he tell them? From now on things were different, the other girls spoke with me, even came over and admired the snowman in the school yard, who had been untouched and ignored until now.

When I saw Father Rappel after school, I asked him what he had said to the nun, and he answered simply:

"Nothing much, just told them who you are." I had never thought about who I was. I was I. I was always accepted as being myself. I never had to make an effort about telling anyone who I was. I could not work out why it should be important.

About twice a week, there would be an air raid, but nothing severe. I even said to Father Rappel, that it was hardly worth it to go into the cellar for that.

But two weeks after Mother had gone to Berlin with Grandfather, there was a heavy air raid where residential areas were badly hit. Up to now, they had bombed the Messerschmitt Assembly Works and the docks, the goods station, the sugar factory and other works, but not the city. People in Regensburg were convinced, that because it was an ancient gothic city, perfectly preserved in its medieval state, it would not be bombed. It was an open air museum in its entirety.

Things altered rapidly though, the air raids became more frequent, and we were told that the shelter in our house was inadequate. We had to go to the *Bayrischer Lloyd* and use their shelter, which was deep, large, and had secure iron doors and we could sit at opposite ends of the cellar and not have to see the coal merchant's family, who had harmed Grandfather. They sat stony faced in a far corner.

There was even a deeper storey, where, we were told, we would have to go to, should the building itself be bombed.

Whenever the sirens howled, we were back in the old Berlin routine, as if we had never left it. Grab the first aid case, food, blankets and be off. It was as if the peaceful year in East Prussia had never existed. The three of us were old hands at this game, and Father Rappel shook his head in amazement and followed us like a lamb, picking up Tissi as he went. Down the stairs, out the front door and along the street two houses up, round the corner and into the big door of the Bayerischer Lloyd, down a flight of stairs, through some steel doors into a large room with many benches. There were rows and rows of people already sitting down there. These were the employees of the Bayerischer Lloyd and people from the neighbouring area.

People here, were not used to heavy raids. They worried and were terribly frightened, made the sign of the cross at every bang.

They looked at the three of us, sitting there with Father Rappel, clutching our bags and waiting for it to finish. In our family we did not make the sign of the cross. Doing it now, because everybody else was doing it, felt wrong. I felt uneasy. On the way home Father Rappel said:

"Have you no fear?" I lifted my shoulders and looked at him. I had not really thought about it. Yes, I was afraid in Berlin, in Dresden, when the train was shot at. But it depended on what was happening at the time. Air raids were unpredictable, and one should never take a chance. But why be afraid until one had to. I said:

"Yes and no. These raids aren't heavy, only a few planes. In Berlin and in Dresden, they were really bad raids with hundreds of planes and lots and lots of bombs and people dying." Father Rappel shook his head:

"You should show humility, pride comes before the fall." He was still shaking his head and muttering. I was confused. What did he mean? I looked at him, wondering. Then Bine said:

"It's true what Ange just said. She doesn't tell tales, and we don't cross ourselves either and there *were* dead people." Father Rappel stopped walking and put Tissi down. He looked at us and said:

"No. No, of course not!" I felt that there was something which I had missed. I still did not understand what Father Rappel really meant or why Bine had this outburst. But I let it be. Times and people were strange.

The weeks went by and it felt as if Father Rappel had always been with us. How would we have managed without him while Mother was in Berlin?

It was in the second week of Advent when Mother and Grandfather came home. The door opened one late afternoon, we were all busy making things for Christmas, when they walked in. I was so happy to see them, Bine and Tissi ran into Mother's arms, and she cuddled them, looking at me all the time. In my mind I said to her "Yes Mother, we managed ok." Aloud I asked:

"How was it?"

"First let's have some food, we are both very hungry." Grandfather said.

"Onkel Kurt and Tante Guste send their love, and Tante Ria and everybody", Mother said, while she busied herself with hanging up the coats and putting the bags somewhere where weren't in the way for the moment.

In my mind, I could see my aunt's and uncle's dear faces, so very far away. When would I see them again? I pushed these thoughts aside, no time for that now. First things first.

Grandfather said to Father Rappel:

"Take the key to the larder and fetch some smoked ham and some bottled cherries." Turning to me, he said: "Have you some bread or potatoes or both?" I nodded:

"Yes, there is some bread. But that has to last until Monday." Grandfather nodded and said secretively:

"I have some flour in the larder, we can bake some more." In a very short time, Grandfather, Mother and the three of us were gathered in the Bauernzimmer around the beautifully carved and painted table, getting ready to have a rare feast. Merely to have food on the table and some dear faces around, already made it into a feast.

After helping to lay the table and get things from the larder, Father Rappel was about to leave the room, when Grandfather said:

"Rappel, you may sit with us today," and shyly, Father Rappel sat next to me on the bench. I wondered why he hadn't in the first place, it would have been the natural thing to do but I sensed somehow, that this was the first time Grandfather and Father Rappel shared a table.

Mother had managed to find two candles in Grandfather's larder, and we lit those to mark the second of Advent. Two more weeks before Christmas. Mother said:

"I wonder, if the vicar in Liegnitz has sent our things on. I wrote to him, saying we would not come back. That is a fair while ago. All our Christmas things are there, the bedding and clothes and books. But then suddenly, Mother threw her arms up and laughed aloud:

"What am I worried about? I have you three and Father. We are all alive and healthy. We have a roof over our heads. There is nothing more for the moment that I want." Grandfather gave her one of his wonderful golden smiles. He was back. He was safe. He was alive!

"Mother tell us, how was it, please tell!" and in the candle light, the tiled stove emitting cosy warmth, Mother told us what happened in Berlin.

Grandfather's face became serious and sad, as Mother told of somebody else, who was accused at the same time as Grandfather, somebody he didn't know personally. It was a young aristocratic woman, a girl really, no more than twenty two years old, Mother said. This young woman stood in front of all those 'black beasts' at the *Berliner Voklksgerichtshof in Moabit* (People's Court) so elegant, unblinking, dignified and poised. Her mother and teenage brothers were there too. She was caught handing out leaflets in München and she was sentenced to be shot for that. Mother said, she never cried or gave any indication of how she felt. She walked away, unaided, after the sentence was passed, with her mother and brothers following, a truly heroic family. Noble beyond question. We were all stunned." Grandfather said:

"My case in comparison, was so unimportant. I wish I could have helped that child."

"You didn't even know she was being tried, how could you have helped?" Mother took Grandfather's hand.

Onkel Kurt, Tante Guste, Tante Ria, Tante Ella, Grandfather's sister who spent her life as a Sister of Mercy in a convent near Berlin, all had gathered in Berlin to be with him, while he was on trial for his life, and all were deeply shocked and disturbed by the trial of this young aristocrat and felt for the mother with her young sons, who seemed to stand alone against a wall of silence. Nobody could get in touch with them afterwards. It was as if the earth had swallowed them up.

It was a shortly after that, when Grandfather was led in by two men of the secret police. He walked in slowly and erect, feeling his way with his walking stick. He was immaculately dressed in hunting tweed from England, which he had bought between the wars, while travelling in that country, a hand embroidered chamois leather waistcoat, his first wife had embroidered and handmade brogue light brown shoes. A silk shirt and green tie, which was fastened with a golden pin, completed his dress.

Tante Ella, who had not seen her brother in many years, whispered:

"The poor boy, he has become blind in prison."

Grandfather defended himself in court, not trusting anybody in uniform, and he never looked at a single sheet of paper throughout the trial. The man who had denounced him, the coal merchant, tried to trip Grandfather, bring him down, but did not succeed.

Grandfather answered all questions put to him by his accusers without hesitation, and in a clear voice.

Three hours later, Mother and Onkel Kurt stood as a guarantee for Grandfather. In other words, if he was accused again, Mother and Onkel Kurt would be answerable for his actions.

Grandfather was free, and Mother could take him home. They led him out of the court in Moabit and into Onkel Kurt's car and as they drove away, Grandfather said:

"I can see a lot better now." Everybody was astonished, but he explained:

"I would never give them the satisfaction of taking my life. I am still needed around here. I would die for Germany but not for them."

✳✳✳

22

Onkel Kurt laughed sadly:

"The important thing is to stay alive and outwit these people. You are no good to anybody, dead." Grandfather had wondered what to do with that wretch downstairs, but Onkel Kurt reasoned that the war will not last long and that miserable man, the coal merchant, would then be dealt with. Then he said something that would be discussed within the family for a long time afterwards:

"There is an important issue that worries me very much. I listen to the radio daily. The Americans are getting close, but they are wasting precious time. They could be our salvation, if only they moved faster. It looks as though the Americans will allow the Russians to get to Berlin first. Churchill wants Germany and every German dead, wiped off the map, and if they let the Russians advance into our land, then that would be the end of a peaceful Europe. Berlin would be dead. Germany will probably not survive. The Russians would see to that. As much as they hate us, they can't do without us. The Americans and the English do not know the Soviets, do not want to know what they are really like. It does not suit their politics at this particular point in history. Why are they so blind?" Everybody looked at Onkel Kurt, in silence, then Grandfather said:

"Only the English, particularly Churchill and his hangers on, are seemingly blind. The Americans cannot assert themselves because they entered the war late, they have to abide by the wishes of Churchill. Many brave men have tried to speak to that cigar smoking blockhead, putting their lives on the line, have even died for it. But can those idiots across the channel ever admit they were wrong? Can anybody admit they are wrong? It takes a certain nobility to be able to do that. The tragedy is, that Europe, as it has stood for a thousand years, is finished. The English will regret bitterly, that they allowed that warmonger to run things these past years. In the years to come, they will be ashamed of his actions, just as we are ashamed of Hitler's actions." Grandfather lifted up his hands in defeat and sighed deeply. He looked at us and said:

"And what do you understand of it all?" He ruffled my hair and smiled.

Mother mentioned that Onkel Kurt had lost so much weight, he must be dreadfully ill, he was only a shadow of his former self, had asthma and carried an inhaler where ever he went. It was less than two years since we had seen him and she was very shocked at the state of his health.

We were still sitting around the table in the Bauernzimmer, the candles had burned down quite a lot, but there was no electricity, and Grandfather said not to worry, there were more candles in the larder.

"You know me, Gittel, I am an old hoarder." he grinned at Mother.

"And Tante Guste?" I asked, and Mother said she had grown old, her black shining hair had become white and dull and her face was thin but she was still very beautiful. I could not imagine Tante Guste old.

"When the war is over, Onkel Kurt will get better." I said confidently.

"Kurt, their oldest son is now a prisoner of war in France" Mother said, "Hermann is still with Tante Guste's brother near München, the girls are at home." After a short silence, Mother said:

"What Kurt said, about the western allies allowing the Russians to advance into Germany. I don't believe they can be so naïve, as to allow that, Father. I simply cannot believe it."

Recently, Grandfather had taken Mother's hand into his, so many times, giving her such looks of deep love and affection.

Mother often remarked on that later, that never ever before had he openly shown her that sort of love. She had spent years in her childhood and in later years, thinking her father did not love her. Grandfather had felt, that showing affection openly, was not the thing to do. But it was great to see father and daughter, so very happy to be together, especially when he had once disinherited her and sent her away, because she had married my father, against his wishes. Grandfather answered:

"Unfortunately, that is so. There is such jealousy and hatred aimed towards Germany since the First World War and before that. There is nothing we can do right at this stage. Sadly, one day the allies will regret not listening to some brave and conscientious German voices. We will have to survive, that is all we can do now. These men and women must not have died in vain. Even if it takes a hundred years to put right." Grandfather said.

We were still cosily gathered around the table, lost in silence. Only Father Rappel had got up to see to the fire. I thought to myself, that it must all be Hitler's fault. But we still had to say "Heil Hitler" in the street as a greeting, or at school when the nuns came into the classroom. It had been the same in East Prussia and Silesia. It didn't add up.

Grandfather turned to Father Rappel:

"Rappel, we will have to find some more chickens. We have a family to feed now and need eggs and maybe the odd chicken for the pot." and Father Rappel promised to do something about it. He had a sister in the country who had a farm. He would ask her.

Chickens and eggs! Happily I asked:

"Can I look after them and feed them?"

"You can, but you also have to keep the chicken house clean." Grandfather said, laughing at me, and then he turned to Mother:

"What about some Christmas baking, Gittel? See what there is in the larder, we are going to have a wonderful Christmas."

A week before Christmas, a huge pile appeared outside the entree door. There was no ring at the door. The only indication was a shadowy mount visible through the frosted glass in the door. Mother opened and looked out into the stairwell. On top of the pile was Tissi's glass potty, which had accompanied us since Berlin. We looked closely at the pile, which was held together by Tissi's cot bed, badly damaged, and recognised our things, which the Vicar had sent on from Liegnitz. Everything was loose in the cot but nothing was missing. Mother shook her head over and over. She kept walking round the pile, in amazement, picking things up.

"How did it get here? Loose like this? I don't understand! Who brought it?" But there was no answer. It could have been Rübezahl (Silesian Mountain Spirit) himself it was such a miracle only he can't work miracles outside the Riesengebirge.

Life, apart from the very occasional mild air raid, was almost normal. We were all fairly happy, except that we were a little homesick for Berlin.

We had to watch the blackout and we had to arrange our lives according to the many power cuts. Best of all, the Christmas holidays had started, and there was no school.

The other thing we enjoyed very much, was the use of the bathroom. Since Berlin, we had not had a bathroom, or running hot water or even a shower. There was also a loo in the bathroom and in the cloakroom and there was central heating, which was on for a few hours in the day. It was such bliss, and bath time on Saturday did not come round fast enough. We spent at least two hours in the bath, sneaking more hot water into the tub.

Christmas Eve came, the excitement was unbearable. We spent the day sledging, and Mother told us after lunch, not to be back until six. She had spent many evenings making things in secret, for us and Grandfather. The days were spent baking. She was happy.

Secretly, we had been creating little presents too in Grandfather's study.

We would remember the twenty-fourth of December 1944 forever. It was a special day for us in the park that day. We had begun to make a row of snowmen, all different, and that led to making snow castles. Many children were working together, picking leaders who knew how to make the castle. Robert had taught me in East Prussia, and now, a year later, I was building a castle in Regensburg.

Suddenly, men appeared from the Von der Tann Schule just around the corner, (local grammar school) which had been turned into a field hospital. They began to give us a hand lifting the big ice blocks up as the walls grew taller. It had become difficult for us to reach. All these men had been badly wounded, some had an arm missing, or a leg, a bandage around the head, one had no face, and it was all bandaged up, except for one eye. Their clothes were worn and torn. Some had only Dutch clogs on their feet. At first, when they joined us, we felt strangely afraid because of the ghastly injuries.

One of them, wearing a huge bandage turban which also wound round his neck, asked for big snow rolls, and some of the children started to roll them and he piled them up expertly. Then, with a kind of bayonet, he started to carve and scrape the snow, and gradually he produced a most beautiful princess, larger than life size. She was so clean, white and shiny. She sparkled!

Our castle was almost finished. There were other soldiers, who had built a castle nearby, and the soldier who had carved the princess, now created dwarf after dwarf, while many children rolled snow rolls and set them up, ready to be carved into more dwarfs. It was fascinating to watch him. Every cut, scrape or chisel mark was always right. He was so absorbed in what he did, so alive, so nimble with his hands.

At four o' clock, night was complete but we did not notice it. We were so engrossed with what we were doing, that we forgot the time and what day it was.

Suddenly, Mother stood there, admiring the beautiful scene. Other mothers had come, wondering where the children were and following the noise. Some children, whose home was very near, went to get some candles. I too, raced home, to get some candles and matches, and we put a candle into the castle. Lit like that, it made the castle glow orangey pink, from the inside and the snow which was in the shade was deep purply blue.

People stood and admired the exquisitely carved Snow White and the Four Dwarfs, because there had not been time for all seven. But the soldier promised to finish them in the morning. Somebody started to sing: "Stille Nacht, Heilige Nacht," and we all joined in. *Oh du fröhliche, oh du selige* was another carol we sang. A single, beautiful voice started to sing *Es ist ein Ros' entsprungen* (A rose grew from a tender root). It was the soldier with the bandage over his face, but his one eye looked so alive and happy. He might have lost his face, but not his voice.

We used to sing this song in Mönchgut. The memory choked me.

Mother said it was time to go home. There is always another day. We said good night to our new friends and promised to be back. When we got there in the morning, St. Niklaus and an angel had joined Snow White and there were Seven Dwarfs. A photo appeared in the local paper, telling of Christmas togetherness, in the midst of war.

But for now, everybody was eager to get home to start celebrating.

When we arrived home, we could smell potato salad. There was a power cut, but soon we had many candles burning. We changed our shoes and put some thick socks on, we had no slippers. We had no best dresses either. Our clothes were almost non-existent, and for me, as I grew out of things, there were no new ones. Bine got my clothes and Tissi got Bine's. But we were not very clothes conscious.

Mother disappeared, and shortly afterwards a small bell tinkled. Grandfather came out of his living room, and smiled happily. We all went into the Christmas room. There was a tree, little piles of presents for all of us and something that I noticed immediately, and could not take my eyes off. It was a Wendy house under the table. Cardboard walls with windows and doors cut out. The windows had shutters and curtains. The door opened and closed. Inside was a doll's bed, made from a carton, and a doll in it! A doll! I saw all that while we were singing a Christmas song, I also saw two more dolls in similar carton beds. After the song, Mother read the Christmas Story, then we remembered all our relatives, our father and brother. We remembered our last Christmas and told Grandfather how it was. He laughed as he visualized us sitting on the sledge, holding onto the Christmas tree, when we had to move from Little Mother Poschmann's cottage into our little house in the fields. I remembered Robert. So much had happened since that last Christmas. My thoughts went back to the Christmas before that at Mönchgut, and even further back in Berlin with Father. Mother sensed that we were getting sad and she pointed to the various piles of presents and said:

"Bine, this is yours, and this is yours, Tissi," pointing to the next one, she said "Ange, yours is in there," and she pointed to the little house. "The house itself is for all of you to play with, of course, but it's mostly Ange's Christmas present."

Bine and Tissi picked up their presents and joined me under the table. It was just big enough to squeeze in happily. We looked out of the window, closed the door. There was a stove, made of a carton, a table similarly made, a clock on the wall made out of a round cheese carton, pictures on the wall. It was fabulous. Mother knocked on the door and handed us a plate full of homemade cookies. She looked so very happy. Could this have been the best ever Christmas? Almost. We went to bed very late that night, clutching our dolls. Somewhere I had lost the doll which I had made in East Prussia from a piece of firewood, but I still had Robert's doll.

Mother came and read two of Grimm's fairy tales, Tissi went to sleep during the second one, Bine and I wanted a third one, but Mother said two were plenty. She wanted to sit a little with Grandfather and talk.

Father Rappel came the next morning, and we had a little present each for him. He was so humble and so grateful. Grandfather said:

"When you have finished downstairs, Rappel, we will have a glass of wine together. My daughter will join us." Father Rappel thanked him and went into the garden, to see to the chickens. I went down with him. It had snowed again overnight, and all the old tracks were covered in a beautiful soft, clean, white blanket. There were tiny little bird prints in the snow.

I stood there in a thin dress, shivering. The garden was peaceful, quiet and beautiful. It felt just like Christmas should feel like. Everything was thickly covered in the whitest, fluffiest snow. I could smell the snow. I had to be part of it and so I plopped down carefully onto the untouched snow blanket and made an angel, by gently sliding my legs apart, to give the angel the shape of a wide skirt, and then starting with the arms down by the hips, lifting them up and pressing them down several times until they came up to the head, making the angel's wings and halo. The difficulty then, is to get up without ruining the shape. But Father Rappel, was already there with an outstretched hand:

"In that thin dress, you silly girl, you'll catch a cold." and he pulled me up.

Among our presents were new slippers, and I was wearing mine in the snow now. They felt elegant and the rubber soles left neat prints in the snow. Father Rappel said:

"Did you bring something to collect the eggs?" Eggs! I lifted my skirt and Father Rappel put two eggs into it. Two! Oh so carefully I carried them upstairs.

❋❋❋

23

January 1945. The Christmas holidays were over. I had to go back to school.

For some reason, Frau Vasner set Grandfather against us. Suddenly, we could do nothing right. Grandfather would not join us anymore in our rooms, he would not eat with us anymore. Frau Vasner was for ever with him and when we saw her in the corridor she gave us looks of contempt. It was very puzzling and I did not understand it. Mother called her 'The Blond Poison'.

On our short visits to her house, during Grandfather's trial, I felt, that although she gave us food, she'd rather we were not there. She was openly hostile, unfriendly and unkind. She had never said anything personal and never wondered how we coped on our own, even though she knew that we were complete strangers in Regensburg. We didn't know our way around town. If it hadn't been for Father Rappel, we would have had a very difficult time.

She was a strange person. Mother thought she behaved like that because she never had children of her own and didn't know how to handle them.

She must have told Grandfather all sorts of stories. He called me into his rooms and questioned me about things we were supposed to have done during Mother's absence.

I defended the three of us and explained to him, that we only went to her house for the meals she had invited us for. We would wait outside until it was exactly the time she said we were to come and took our shoes off before we came in. We ate and then waited until she allowed us to get off the table, thanked her for the meal, always did the dishes afterwards, thanked her again, and left. We had never made a mess or broken a plate, not even Tissi. I could not see what we had done wrong. I felt that Grandfather should know us better than that. I had a feeling he did not believe me. I was sad and felt dreadfully embarrassed and let down.

I didn't want to tell Mother about it. What if Mother didn't believe us either?

The three of us avoided Frau Vasner and Grandfather and kept to our rooms. We started to tiptoe down the corridor when we had to go to the kitchen or the bathroom. Bine and I discussed this, and Bine said:

"They don't want us here anymore. Grandfather has forgotten that we are only here because Frau Vasner asked Mother to come." Mother overheard this and wanted to know what was going on. Reluctantly, we told her. She was sad.

"Just like in the old days. Father will always listen to women, no matter what they tell him. How can men be so weak? Father is one of the worst." She sighed:

"I shouldn't have said that. Keep out of their way and don't take it too seriously. I will find a flat for us somewhere else," and she went flat hunting. An impossible task, as it turned out. No sooner had she found somewhere, when it wasn't available the next day, because it was bombed or confiscated for people who had become homeless. She kept on trying but the housing department told her she wasn't homeless, and could not expect to find a flat.

Towards the end of January, the raids suddenly became very severe. At school the nuns had prepared us for raids during school hours. All of us knew where to go. Since I lived only about five hundred metres from the school, I had to go home, or in my case to the *Bayerische Lloyd*. Everybody who had further to go than that, could go to the school shelter. Usually there was plenty of time to get to my shelter.

There was the 'warning alarm', the 'full alarm' and the 'end of the raid alarm'. These alarms were the same throughout Germany. It felt strange, that this horrible noise should sound the same in Berlin, Dresden and Regensburg. Regensburg seemed to be so very far away from everything that was home, and this dreadful noise reminded me of home. Here, I felt less and less at home, as the days passed. At school, although the girls were friendly now, I was not really one of them. Their religion kept us apart too. The catholic people had an ongoing ritual, and I was totally excluded.

My day started with the normal routine of getting up, cook the flour soup, hopefully without lumps, dishing out the daily bread ration and going to school.

School started at seven thirty in the morning. That morning, at ten thirty, the alarm sounded without the warning, straight into the 'full alarm'.

I galloped downstairs and out of the school building. As I charged up the *Ostengasse* towards the *Ostentor*, the first bombs started to fall. All I could think of, was to reach the Ostentor in time. It had stood there in its splendour since the 13th century, solid and honest, it would keep me safe. The strange thing was, there was no one else on the street racing for shelter. I got to the *Ostentor* and let myself fall on my tummy. There was a big gate, for vehicle traffic, even the tramline went through it now, and there was a side gate for pedestrians on either side. It had a bend inside the little gate, so one could not see through the little tunnel. On my tummy, I crept through, until I could see out at the other end. Only across the street would be the *Bayerische Lloyd*. Sixty, seventy Meters? Should I risk it? I waited for a chance. Mother and the children would be in there. Grandfather still refused to go to the shelter. Always stubborn.

As I looked out, a little petrol station this side of the road was hit. There were only two pumps, a little kiosk, no bigger than a telephone booth and it was only about 25 Meters away. The bang seemed to squeeze my head together, my eardrums went into my head, and the fireball was incredible. I could feel the searing heat and smell my hair as it got singed. The fire went in one enormous

whoosh, and when it had gone, the trees in the park, which stood close to the petrol pumps were totally alight and crackling away, one had fallen across the road, broken off halfway up the trunk.

I could hear a voice above the din, and I tried to look up, but my eyes were burning and watering as if I had cut onions. Another bomb went down somewhere close. Bits of bricks were falling onto the road in front of me. Again I heard the voice. I could hear what it said:

"On the word go, you come running." It was the air raid warden from the *Bayerische Lloyd*. He sounded very cross. But it wasn't my fault, that I was here, was it? I looked up, explosions and bits of debris flying around, I wasn't going out in this! I yelled back that I was okay. But his furious voice reached me again:

"You come over here when I tell you." "Okay" I shouted back and waited for the signal. Eventually, there was a lull, and I raced across without waiting for his command. Another bomb had fallen very close into the road, leaving a deep crater, and that must have caught the warden, because he was on the ground, moaning. I opened the outer door and ran downstairs and banged on the door which led into the shelter and asked the people to let me in, and as the door opened, I pointed up to where the warden was lying. He had been knocked unconscious, but he had no visible wounds.

I looked odd, because I had no lashes and no eyebrows left. When I told them what had happened, somebody said, I shouldn't have been so nosey. Nobody laughed, and Mother said:

"You should know by now, first rule is to tuck your head away. You can live without legs, or arms, but without a head you are dead." She took me in her arms and held me tight. Bine and Tissi held onto her skirt, they had been crying. Mother said they had been worried about me.

"You must promise us to be more careful." and I promised.

The raid lasted many hours, and I did not go back to school that day. There was another raid in the night.

Then the snow started to melt, huge blocks of ice came down the Danube. People in the shelter, which Mother called the 'centre for social gatherings', were worried that it might damage the Bridges across the Danube, and somebody said that the *Steinerne Brücke* had spanned the river for eight hundred years, it would also survive this ice floe but presumably they will blow up the bridges soon in any case, so why worry. Another voice was heard: "That is defeatist talk." and again another one: "Halt die Fotzen," which is Bavarian for 'keep your mouth shut'.

The Danube flooded in no time, because the embankment had been badly damaged by bombs, and we had severe floods. The cellar in our house turned into black water canals and we paddled up and down these canals in the wooden wash trough, using the wooden snow shovel as a paddle. It was great fun until Grandfather found out. The 'Blond Poison' probably told him.

The nuns at school said they were sorry, when they heard what had happened to me, but I still had to go home during a raid. Their shelter was overcrowded as it was. There were a few similar occasions, where the race to the shelter was hazardous, but nothing as bad as that one particular time. The authorities put a trained spotter with special equipment up onto the *Winzerer Höhen*, (ancient vineyard heights surrounding the town,) to give advance warnings.

Vicar Käppel and Mother had become good friends, and he asked for her help with his relief work. There were already so many refugees and homeless people in Regensburg. Schools were requisitioned and turned into refugee camps. Cinemas and theatres became refugee camps too. We met many people who came from Baltic lands in the east, Lithuanians, Latvians and Estonians, but also from the Balkan countries. We asked the Lithuanians for news and they said that it was a very close thing for them; The Russians had been literally, on their heels. Coming in from the south, they were cutting off the fleeing people in the north. When that happened, the only way out was the Baltic Sea, and only if there were any ships. "We made it on the land route just in time." one man said.

I was thinking of the Kramp family, Farmer Graf. Little Mother Poschmann, she would never be able to flee. Would she still be alive? Robert, had he managed to get away to the west as he had planned or had the Russians caught up with him. Ilia would have informed on him. That's what Robert had told me Ilia would do. People in Russia spied on one another, so one could never do what one felt was right, only what the party thought was right. One never knew if the person next to you was friend or spy.

Where were they? Not knowing was such a burden. I had to make myself forget about it. After all, things so far, had turned out all right for us, it would for them too.

While Mother was working for the Protestant Relief Work, she met a lady by the name of von Schwarzenbaer. She had a manor house and lands with a brewery, in fact, a whole village outside Regensburg, was her domain.

Frau von Schwarzenbaer asked Mother to visit her at her home, and Mother accepted gladly, as soon as things turned back to normal. Frau von Schwarzenbaer often came to Regensburg, and I liked her a lot. Her village was called Eichhofen.

Mother came home from work with Frau von Schwarzenbaer one day in the very beginning of February, and started to lay the table for tea. It was a Saturday, there was no school, hardly any snow to go sledging, and I played happily in the Wendy house under the table. Mother laid the table on my roof, as it were. Frau von Schwarzenbaer talked to me through the window, and admired the house and the inside of the little house, when the alarm went again. Oh no!

Mother said: "We will just leave it, and have tea and cake when we come back. Something to look forward to. Anyway, it's Saturday and they won't stay long, they want to get back to start their own weekend." Mother joked.

Frau von Schwarzenbaer and the four of us went off to the shelter. We had just left our front door, when the 'full alarm' sounded and we had to run. Up the road past the two houses, round the corner. I could see the great double entrance doors. We were rushing down the stairs, with a lot of other people, heading for the big iron doors, when the first bomb hit the *Bayerische Lloyd*. There were four blocks of eight steps each, ending on a platform and taking one quarter turn to the left, we raced down the next block. We had reached the third block, which was covered by the stairs going up, when the section of the entrance door collapsed and fell down the stairs behind us. We could hear screams, yells and moaning cries, but we didn't turn around. We reached the shelter, and everybody streamed down into the deeper shelter. It was so crowded, nothing seemed to move. There was shouting, pushing and shoving. The four of us instinctively took care of Frau von Schwarzenbaer. She had told us on the way to the shelter, that this was the first time that she was actually caught up in a raid.

We were still queuing to go deeper into the shelter, when the *Bayerischer Lloyd* was hit again. This time the ceiling opened up into a big crack. Choking cement dust filled the room. The queue moved frantically and we reached safety at last. When everybody was in, the iron door was closed and the warden turned a big lever up to ensure the room was airtight in case of a gas attack. Then he turned on the filter system.

People sat under the benches for extra safety. Even though we were so deep down, we could hear the bombs, whistling and exploding all around us. One blue bulb lit up the faces in an eerie way. Somebody in the gloom said that there weren't as many houses in the area as exploding bombs he had counted. Everybody in the cellar, except Frau von Schwarzenbaer and the four of us, said the rosary. That was something I had never seen before. People holding a necklace, with a cross at the end, and taking bead after bead between their fingers, and mumbling something. It was fascinating. Mother explained what they were doing, and Frau von Schwarzenbaer said, that there were different size beads and each size was for a different prayer.

I asked why everybody here in this town was catholic. Frau von Schwarzenbaer, whispered something about a war many years ago, the thirty year war, which was fought between people who felt they wanted to be protestant, and people who wanted to stick with the old faith. The Catholics are of the old faith, but the Protestants were against the way the Catholics used the faith and Martin Luther protested against it. The thirty year war was a war of faith against faith, neighbour against neighbour. After thirty years, nobody had won and it was decided that both faiths could exist and this is how the new faith was established.

In a way, I wished I could pray like these people. I prayed, but it was quite different from the way they prayed here. Was their prayer more effective?

Maybe I should pray too, now. I prayed, asking for Him to look after us down here, and then I remembered all the people in Germany. In Berlin, in Silesia, in East Prussia, here now in Regensburg. Could he look after all these people at the same time? And what about the enemy, did they pray to God? I turned to Frau von Schwarzenbaer, who sat next to me. Bine and Tissi sat on my other side and Mother at the end.

"Frau von Schwarzenbaer, does the enemy pray to God?"

"Yes she said, and it is the same God that we pray to."

I thought that was very strange. Hadn't God forbidden people to kill? How can people kill each other like that and still pray to God. I thought this was sanctimonious, two faced.

I stopped praying. It came to me that if God is what He is, He would know what to do, without my prayer.

The raid went on and on. When, after many hours, the 'end alarm' sounded, nobody moved. Everybody in the shelter was too stunned, too tired.

The warden busied himself at the door, and soon found he could not shift it. People came to help, they could turn the locking arm but were unable to push open the door.

Eventually the warden said:

"We are buried alive."

✹✹✹

24

Buried alive. What did that mean for us? I looked up at the adults' faces to read their reaction. Frau von Schwarzenbaer was very worried. Everybody was talking at once. The warden lifted up his hands and tried to speak. Eventually, people became quiet and listened to what he had to say.

"We will very likely be down here a little while. The clearing gang will be here. But nobody can say how much damage there is in the area, and how many people need rescuing. Is there anybody hurt in here?"

Miraculously, nobody in the cellar was hurt, but there were the people in the staircase, the people who had been hit just as we were racing into the cellar. I had seen people behind us, but they had not all made it to the shelter. When the Red Cross Nurse and the warden finally came in and closed the iron doors, it was obvious to all of us, that the people out there needed no more help. I had tried not to think about it. It felt better not to think, but now I could hear their screams again, their whimpering and then, the silence. They were buried too, but dead.

Everybody settled down and waited in total silence. I was shaking, as if I was very cold, but I wasn't cold. I could not control the shaking, even when I spoke my voice was shaking. Some children nearby, huddled together and started whispering conversations. I moved up a little and joined them. We felt, that it was wrong to speak aloud. I felt guilty about the fact that I was not hurt. We were discussing this feeling among the other children. They too, knew that there were people out there, who had not made it into the shelter. Some were looking around, trying to think who, among the regulars, was missing. But it was difficult to tell, because there was such a dim light in the cellar, and anyway, I didn't really know anybody that well, and certainly not by name. Strangely though, although they were unknown to me, they were still close. I could not explain it. We had seen people killed when the train stopped and we had to hide underneath. They had panicked and run in the wrong direction. I felt at the time, that it was their own fault. But now I thought, they hadn't known which was the right direction.

War was a grim game. A game adults played. There were hardly any men here. Only very old ones, like the warden, or wounded and disabled soldiers. Was it a game men played? Pretending that we didn't matter? A game where some lost, some won? But who could win this game? I looked around into people's faces. They knew nothing.

I remembered Ali. Ali. Where was he? Mother had told me a long time ago, that he would not be in Germany anymore, he would have gone back to Africa soon after the war started. Hitler didn't like black people. I never asked why. Ali had said that wars were fought, rightly or wrongly and that the stronger would win. But while these people fought the war, what had it to do with any of the people in this cellar? Or in any shelter, or the people that died on the train? What if nobody found us in time and we would eventually die down here?

I heard one girl say:

"And when they opened up the grave again, one could tell, that she wasn't dead when they buried her, only seemingly dead. She had dug at the coffin lid from the inside with her fingernails, until there were hardly any nails left." How dreadful. I felt sick. The girl looked around, enjoying the effect this story had on us all.

"I don't believe a word of it." I whispered, crossly. I remembered a similar story that went round in the school in East Prussia. The school there was only small, and all the classes were in one room, the little ones in the front row, and the sixteen year old pupils in the last row. And while teacher would talk with one class, the rest were supposed to work on something. But often we would talk, or send paper messages. That was where I had heard a similar story. But I also knew, that one kept people for three days before one would bury them. Surely, anybody who was 'seemingly dead', would wake up before then. I whispered that to the girl, but she insisted the story was true.

I moved back to my seat. I didn't want to hear anymore. Mother thought it was a good time to tell a fairy tale and some of the children left that girl and came and joined us.

The warden and Red Cross helpers started to bang onto the iron doors. A steady rhythmic bang. Mother stopped her story for the moment and explained:

"Just to make sure the rescuers know we are down here, and alive. If they hear us banging, they will help us out more quickly. If there are big blocks, big bits of wall blocking our way, they will need a crane to lift it off."

I snuggled down and listened to the story again. I was sure, that we would soon be out again. It must be night outside. I was tired too. It would be after midnight at least.

I had been to the lavatory before, but it was so blocked, it was overflowing. It was horrible. People, in desperation had been using the loo anyway. It was unbearable. Tissi had wet her pants. Poor little thing, she had such a sore bottom too. She could hardly sit. Bine suffered quietly, her big eyes everywhere watching everybody. She would never let you down, one could take her anywhere.

We must have slept a little, but the whistling of the bombs woke me up again. One shattering explosion, very close. People screamed hysterically. And then complete silence. I couldn't even hear anybody breathe. That was worse. There were noises outside. Suddenly, the door jerked open a little, daylight flooded in and blinded us, and a voice through the crack said:

"Careful, take your time, one after the other, slowly, slowly."

People rushed towards the door like maniacs, squeezing and pushing, gasping for fresh air. I wanted to go too, but Frau von Schwarzenbaer held on to me and said:

"Wait until they have gone, and then we go. I would much rather be the last, than squeeze around in that." And her head made a movement in the direction of the door and the heaving crowd.

Slowly the shelter emptied. When there were only a few people left, we joined them and waited our turn. We squeezed through the door, which could not open any further because of all the rubble on the other side, and then we had to start climbing up and down over huge blocks of concrete which had once been the upper shelter or whatever. Sometimes we had to crawl on our bellies. Polish POWs were helping to clear a path. Eventually we reached the outside. The *Bayerischer Lloyd* was badly damaged, but it still stood there, defying everything. We walked around the building into our street, and found the two houses between the *Bayerischer Lloyd* and our house, gone. Completely gone. There wasn't even a heap of rubble. Where had the houses gone? Our house! The front was partially missing. The loo in the cloakroom was entirely exposed, clinging to the wall, sitting on one joist which jutted out into space. The brush holder was still attached to the wall with the brush inside. On a hook above it, fluttering in the wind, was a neatly cut block of newspaper, threaded onto a bit of string. A bomb had gone into the garden, about two metres from the house and created a crater about as big as the pond in East Prussia. The crater extended into the road. We had to climb over a heap of rubble to get to the front door, which had gone and the steps leading to it were just a heap. Grandfather, looking worried and dirty, one arm in a sling, was sweeping the stairs with his good arm, struggling with big bits of masonry. Father Rappel tried to clear the entrance. The banisters had gone. There was splintered wood everywhere.

"I made sure they got you out of that shelter. I arranged for a gang of prisoners from the local prison to be sent. I have special connections there." He said with a grin. Grandfather was very tired. His connections were from the time when he was first imprisoned, before he went to Munich.

"Good thing I didn't go into the shelter. You'd still be stuck down there." he grinned again.

"I was worried sick about you, Father. Wherever were you hiding in that hell? I will not allow you to avoid the shelter again." Mother said firmly.

The door into the apartment was gone. All the windows in the house were gone, frames and everything. All the doors to all the rooms were gone, they were lying crisscross and splintered everywhere. The Wendy house was crushed, the table broken, the tea things, the cupboards... Everything was broken, smashed. Nothing could be used. The ceiling had collapsed in the bedroom and the bed was buried. We went from room to room. Our side of the flat was unusable. Grandfather's side, because it faced to the back, was not so bad. The bomb had gone down just outside our bedroom. We stood in all that chaos, looking around. I knelt down to see if I could get into the Wendy house somehow. But too much weight was on top. My dolls were crushed. Even Robert's. Bine and Tissi cried. I felt totally numb.

Frau von Schwarzenbaer said:

"It is quite impossible for you to stay here with the children. It is winter. There are no windows, no doors, and no loo. You must come with me." Grandfather had stood in the background and now he said:

"Yes, yes of course. It is very kind of you to offer my daughter shelter. I must stay here to repair the house. Rappel will look after me. When it is ready again I will send for you. You take the little cart, see what you can rescue here and take it with you. Now off you go. You had better hurry, if you want to get to Eichhofen before night."

"Oh Grandfather, you'll get killed." I said. I ran to him, and he winced. He was hurt more than he admitted. He looked at me, and I understood. He did not want me to say anything. I understood too, that he would not come with us. He had to face things here. With his good hand he fished a pocket watch from his waistcoat, which hung on a thick gold chain, flicked open the lid and said:

"It is now nearly midday." He looked at Father Rappel:

"Rappel, find the little cart." Turning to my mother:

"Gittel, you must have bedding for yourselves. What about clothes. Let's find what there is." They busied themselves to get some things together. I didn't want to look anymore. Bine took my hand and said she needed to go to the lavatory. Tissi said she needed to go too.

"Come on let's find somewhere" I said. Our loo was useless. The way it sat by itself without floor or walls, and looking at it, I decided that balancing on a joist was too dangerous and open to the public. The loo in the bathroom also looked too dangerous, there was a big hole in the wall and the loo itself was cracked and full of glass from the window which had fallen into it.

I took my sister's hands and we climbed carefully down the stairs again into the garden. We found a hiding place behind the little 'Swiss Cottage', but Bine had trouble with getting clean afterwards.

"Use snow, don't be so helpless." I was cross and very tired and most of all I was so hungry, my stomach hurt and rumbled. I was helping Tissi and I could hear her little tummy making noises. I gave her a kiss. Little thing! She was so brave. I could tell she wanted to grizzle, but tried so hard not to. We came back to the side of the house and what used to be the entrance. We caught Frau von Schwarzenbaer, doing what we had just done. Poor thing. She wasn't used to things like this. She was very embarrassed, and the three of us turned back and pretended we hadn't seen her.

Father Rappel and Mother had finished packing the cart, Tissi's glass potty had survived the raid, as usual. Mother joked and said:

"It is Jena glass, fire-and break proof. They make cooking pots out of this." Now it had become a "war proof potty". Mother lifted up Tissi and put her on top of everything in the cart. Tissi, for the moment was happy. Mother and Frau von Schwarzenbaer took the cart handle and pulled together, Bine and I held on to the back of the cart and pushed.

Does no one else think of food? I thought. I didn't want to say anything, in case there was nothing to eat. If there was food, Mother would give it to us. I could not remember the last time

I had had any food. Nor could I work out when it was that we had gone into the shelter. Was it yesterday or the day before? According to my hunger, it could have been last week. Bine and I followed the little cart in a trance. Nobody spoke.

We had to pass from one end of the city to the other to get to the right road which would eventually take us to Eichhofen. I had no idea how far that would be. Mother and Frau von Schwarzenbaer pulled in silence at the front. I wouldn't ask how far, not yet. I just put my feet into motion.

We walked through big middle gate of the Ostentor, into the Ostengasse and past my school.

Again, we left a home behind. Would I ever live anywhere long enough to belong? Where would we end up this time? When were we in East Prussia? A lifetime ago? A few months ago? When did we arrive here? It all seemed so unreal.

But seeing the houses around us, was real. Every house was damaged. Houses which had stood there, proudly withstanding many wars, even Napoleons canons, and had survived for nearly a thousand years. Like the *Brauerei Brandl* with the ancient mural of the 'Bear on the chain' on the side of the house.

When I first came to this town, I had wandered around a little and just past the school on the other side I discovered this beautiful house with gothic windows. It had an inscription also. Very old and difficult to decipher. It took me some time, but it said: *"Dies Haus steht in Gottes Hand, Zum Bärn an der Ketten ist's benannt"* (this house is in God's hand, and named after the chained bear). Grandfather, when I had asked him, explained, that hundreds of years ago and as recent as the thirty years war, there were wolves and bears still roaming in Bohemia and the Upper Palatinate. Regensburg is in the Upper Palatinate which is northern Bavaria. A man with a dancing bear stayed the night at the old inn, and the bear stopped brigands from robbing the landlord and his guests. I had marvelled at the ancient story. Everything in this town had survived centuries and was still alive. It was a wonderful place really.

The mural had a big crack. It saddened me to see such beautiful buildings damaged or destroyed.

At the end of the Ostengasse, we turned left into the Schwanen Platz and onto the *Alte Korn Markt* (old grain market). Here, the twin spires of the cathedral of St. Peter came into full view. Something huge had gone through the very top of the latticed spire. In at one side and out at the other. We all stopped and looked. Eight hundred years the cathedral had stood there. The miracle now was, that it had not collapsed. If it would still fall, the falling masonry would hurt the cathedral below. I could not bear to think about it. I hated this destruction. I wanted no more of it. No more.

✹✹✹

25

We walked past heaps of rubble and gangs of men clearing it. They were POWs. I wondered again for the thousandth time where Robert and his friends might be. We had difficulty with the cart getting around the piles on the street but there were helping hands from the POWs who needed no bidding. We crossed the *Domplatz*. The cathedral was overwhelming. I turned my head up and followed the spires until I thought the very tip reached heaven. I had a sensation as if the spires were moving, but it must have been a wandering cloud. I had never seen anything more sublime. It rose so nobly up, in straight and true lines. Heavenly beings looking down upon this destruction indifferently, and hellish creatures grinning evilly, seemingly enjoying what they saw.

I felt compelled to enter, and be kept from harm, but Frau von Schwarzenbaer urged us to continue, time was short, and she did not want to be caught in town in another raid.

We left the Domplatz via the Residenzstrasse and came to the *Neupfarr Platz*, into the *Gesandten Strasse*, (The Street of Ambassadors) and finally out through the opposite city gate of the *Ostentor*, the *Jakobs Tor*, past the ancient church of St. Jakob.

Mother used to go past this church, on her way to school and explained that a wandering Irish monk by the name of Marianus came here in Anno Domini 1067. Although this area needed no converting into the Christian faith, he stayed anyway with his fellows, and built a monastery and church. Even though it is now called *Die alte Schottenkirche* (Scots church)

We left the city behind us now, as we headed down the endless *Prüfeninger Strasse*, along the tramline, but the trams were no longer running. There were people like us, pulling little carts and moving in the same direction. I heard the Bavarian greeting all the time. They were saying:

"Grüss Gott, miteinand" (God's greeting to all of you). Frau von Schwarzenbaer and Mother greeted back the same way. Bine and I wondered what had happened to "Heil Hitler". But it felt so much better to say *"Grüss Gott"*. It turned out that all those people had relatives in the country, and that was where they were headed. They had either already been bombed, or afraid that they would be, and didn't want to be caught up in another raid.

We marched and marched, just putting one foot before the other. Nobody spoke anymore. Everybody seemed busy with their own thoughts. Suddenly the cart stopped. I looked up. There was a small shop and it was open! Mother and Frau von Schwarzenbaer walked over and went in. After a little while they came back with milk and bread.

Mother carried the army canteen carefully. Frau von Schwarzenbaer had the bread. Two loaves! We were so hungry! Frau von Schwarzenbaer said, breaking big lumps of bread off the loaf:

"Take this for now. You'll have more when we arrive home. There is no shortage in Eichhofen yet. So eat!" We all drank directly from the canteen. The bread was fresh and so was the milk. It was delicious. We finished the lot. Refreshed but very tired, we continued. Frau von Schwarzenbaer said that we had, so far, only walked about five kilometres, and there were about fifteen to go. I didn't quite take it in, but I worked out it would be three times as far again as we had just walked! I might as well try to reach the moon! I just continued to put one foot before the other, hanging on to the back of the cart. Bine and I were not pushing anymore, we were being pulled. In the distance we could see a big bridge, which would lead across the Danube, the *Mariaorter Brücke*. The bridge had been bombed, and two of the tall arches were missing. The church below the bridge was a well-known place of pilgrimage.

The bridge was very tall and spanned the river from one hill this side to another hill on the opposite side. The River Naab entered the Danube on the other side making a wedge of land for the little church. Both rivers had carved their way deep into the earth, creating a small canyon with white limestone rocks sticking up like fingers.

We were not sure if we could still cross the bridge, but we had to try. Some people had got this far, but were not going on. They were arguing, whether or not it was safe to cross. Some said there was a ferry across the Danube, but Frau von Schwarzenbaer said it would be a long way round. Let's first find out about the bridge. The trains are still using this bridge, so it must be alright.

We walked onto the bridge until we got to the damaged bit; a makeshift wooden structure had been put down for people to cross. We had to go carefully and place the cart accurately to get all the wheels on. The wood moved underfoot. Way down, the river flowed. It was so very deep. I had never been so high up anywhere, and nowhere to hold on to except the back of the cart or a handrail either side. Tissi was screaming. She was terrified. She hated heights and open spaces. If Bine was terrified, I couldn'tt tell. Bravely, she followed the cart. Mother kept saying:

"Don't look down, hold on tight, don't look left or right. Just hold on tight. Not far now." There were no people in front of us, but I could feel them behind me now. Their weight was bending the wood, and it gave me a very sick feeling in my stomach. Why couldn't they wait a little? Why did they have to be so close? It was difficult to hear Mother, because of Tissi's crying. I tried to talk to her, but she was too terrified. There was no getting through to her. I closed my ears to it.

There was a scream behind me, which made me jump and from the corner of my eye I saw a little object like a shoe or something disappear into the depths. It made a wide arch, and the splash, when it hit the water, was hardly more than a tiny white dot. Eventually, we reached the other side.

We were all badly shaken. I was exhausted. The people behind us were equally in a state. They walked over to where the church tower of "Our Holy Mother of God" reached up from below and knelt down. The entire group was praying, which looked comforting. I wanted to pray too, but Mother and Frau von Schwarzenbaer pressed on.

The countryside was strangely peaceful here. The River Naub was so tranquil and clear. We were heading up the hill, towards Allerzhausen, when there was another raid over Regensburg. We looked back. The entire City with the cathedral in the middle, hundreds of towers of the ancient churches and patrician houses, spread proudly out along the River Danube in the winter sun. It looked majestic.

Above, the bombers circled like a swarm of angry vultures, constantly dropping chains of bombs. I suddenly realised, that the people who flew these aircraft, could see this beautiful city just as we could see it from up here. They could see its beauty too. Surely, they must feel that it was so wrong to destroy something so rare and precious, so old. The city had lived so long, and now it was being blown to bits. We could actually watch buildings disappearing in clouds of dust and smoke.

There was no resistance from fighter planes, no ak ak. They had a free for all. This is what it looks like, when one is not in the cellar, I thought. Previously we only heard what was going on, now we watched the grim spectacle. Would all this ever end?

As I turned away from this awful scene, I discovered some snowdrops. The snow had melted only where the little flowers grew. Everywhere else, old, grey dusty snow still covered the earth. What power these little white flowers had, to come out when everywhere else it was so cold, too cold for anything else to grow. Their power must have melted the snow. I could hear the distant rumbling, the horror, but here was peace. The snowdrops looked so beautiful. I remembered the snowdrops a year ago in East Prussia. There was peace and beauty too. Bine saw them as well and joined me. We both knelt down to have a closer look. It was Bine who said:

"It would be a pity to pluck them. They would only die, and they are much more beautiful here." Gently, she touched them with her finger and made their little heads rock.

Tissi had gone to sleep in the cart. The poor little thing looked so small and thin. Her legs had no flesh on them, they looked like matchsticks. Mother carefully pulled up the old horse blanket Grandfather had given us, and covered her. It was so cold and the wind was so icy. Slowly we moved on.

One foot before the other, left, right, left, right. Walking, walking. Mother had come to her last resort again. She was telling Grimm's Fairy Tales. It was taking our minds off this endless walking. No resting. Just walking. I was hanging on to the back of the cart with Bine, and watching my feet come up and disappear. The left one, the right one.

My shoes were skiing boots, about four or five sizes too large. I had grown out of my shoes, there were no new shoes, and the only ones available were Grandfather's skiing boots.

Every time I lifted my feet, the shoes stayed behind until my feet got to the neck of the boot, then I had to give an extra tug and slide the boot forward. I learned to use the weight of the boot to my advantage, so that by giving it a tug with a twist it would throw my foot forward with the weight of the boot. But now the boots felt like blocks of lead. I wasn't going to say anything though because Bine was smaller than I and bravely carried on without complaining. She was wearing my old shoes. If I started, she might too, and we would never get to Eichhofen, wherever that was!

Night had fallen, it was pitch black. The stars were brilliant. The Milky Way was clearly visible. I remembered that Robert had pointed out some stars to me, and he had explained how they came to be there. Greek gods and goddesses and heroes were up there. I could distinguish Orion the hunter quite easily. Robert had outlined him to me. I found him by his sword which pointed directly to his dog with bright Sirius blazing in the black void. I could not find the bull which Robert had tried to show me, only part of him which he called the seven stars or Pleiades. But I found the great bear and Cassiopeia with the polar star in the centre. Cassiopeia, Robert had told me, was a goddess lounging on a sofa. I was proud to find the polar star and imagined what the earth would look like right underneath this star.

The stars were a great wonder to me. They were usually visible, even if we travelled for days and days to completely different parts of Germany, the stars were exactly the same. They hadn't moved at all. Their picture was the very same shape. I thought that Germany must be a very small place, compared with the world up there. Was heaven past the stars? Where did the stars go in the daytime? That thought had never occurred to me before. I wanted to know but now I was too tired to ask. I would have to wait.

How many hours since we left Regensburg? How many days since I slept in a bed? If I went to sleep now, I would never wake up. Bine was crying. Mother stopped, picked her up and made Tissi move over. They snuggled up together. I plodded on behind, on my own.

What seemed hours' later, Frau von Schwarzenbaer said to Mother:

"There is a station over there. Stay there with the children. I am going on alone. I shall send the coach for you." She disappeared in the blackness of the night.

Mother took us into the waiting room and I walked over to the wooden bench and lay down. I was asleep immediately. All I noticed before I dropped off was Mother putting Bine next to me and going out to fetch Tissi. They did not wake up while she carried them in.

I woke up suddenly, cold and shivering, as we were being carried from the waiting room to a black coach, pulled by two horses. We entered through a little door and sank onto soft upholstered seats and cosily snuggled down. I was too tired to enjoy the luxury. The cart was put at the back somewhere, the coachman climbed up on the high seat in front and clicked his tongue. The horses were off and I went promptly back to sleep. I did not wake up when they put me to bed.

❋❋❋

26

When I finally woke up, it was because I was so hungry and I could smell food. I looked around and through the open door I saw some children sitting around a table. They were eating in a room across a dark hall.

Bine and Tissi were still asleep next to me. I turned round and woke them up. As I got up, and a woman came in and smiled.

"I suppose you are hungry? Come, there is some food for you. First you must get yourselves dressed." I put on my clothes. They were smelly and dirty. When had I last put on clean clothes? In fact how many days had I worn these clothes without even taking them off once? I could not remember, without thinking of the last days. I did not want to remember them.

Bine got dressed and together we dressed Tissi. Sometime in the past, Tissi had wet her pants and they were smelly. I looked around, but there was no sign of any clean clothes we might have had. Tissi was embarrassed and I gave her a reassuring kiss. It will have to do.

We arrived at the table in record time. The children had been watching us getting dressed and that was embarrassing too, but for now I didn't care. I wondered briefly, where Mother was, but that could wait until after we had eaten.

The table was laid with napkins, knife on the right, fork on the left, two spoons at the top. I sat down and put my hands into my lap and waited. Bine and Tissi copied me. The other children were eating already. The woman came over.

"I am Lisa Hirsauer, I do the cooking here." It was then that I realised that this room was an enormous kitchen, with a huge black and gold stove with many cooking pots steaming away on top. The ceiling was vaulted. It was all white and clean. The table was scrubbed wood and spotless. The floor was paved with rich yellow, natural stone flags.

Lisa filled our plates to the brim with soup and bits of fried bread sizzling in it. I picked up the outer spoon to eat the soup. Bine and Tissi watched me, and did the same. It had been a long time, since we had been eating at a properly laid table. Bine and Tissi, especially Tissi could not remember what to do.

Next, we had stew with meat, potatoes, carrots, peas, onions, cabbage and leeks. So many vegetables all at the same time! The meat was tasty, it could only have been cooked once. The stew also contained white semolina dumplings. We used our knife and fork to eat this.

There was a spoon left. What would we eat with the remaining spoon?

When we came to scrape the plate clean, Lisa was standing by, smiling: "Would you like some more?" Politely the three of us said: "No, thank you."

"Oh", Lisa said, "it is not worth keeping", and put some more onto our plates. Happily, we ate that too. I was still wondering what we would eat with the remaining spoon. The other children waited, watching us eat, and now we all were waiting.

Lisa put a huge bowl of something brown into the middle of the table. I could smell it, and it was chocolate. I waited for my turn with the most willpower I could muster. I looked at Bine. She grinned back happily. Tissi wasn't quite sure what was happening. Lisa filled bowl after bowl with a generous helping and all the children sat and waited until all the bowls were filled. Then we all tucked in together. Slowly I put the spoon into my mouth and let the chocolate pudding melt on my tongue. I could sit here all day and eat my pudding, making it last. Bine and Tissi had finished theirs. Everybody had finished and they were all watching me. Lisa said:

"It looks as if you don't want anymore. We are all ready for another helping." I started to spoon my pudding, to catch up and Lisa laughed, giving us all a second helping.

I thought we had arrived in the land of milk and honey.

A bell rang, and Lisa went over to the wall and opened a door, which at first I thought was a built in cupboard. She emptied it of dirty dishes, and then put some bowls of steaming food into it and closed the doors. I wondered what she was doing. After a little while there was another bell, and Lisa went over again, opened the door and the bowls were now empty and she took them out, put a large coffee-pot and milk into it and closed the doors again. What magic!

When we were allowed to get off the table, the five children came over and introduced themselves. Three were Frau von Schwarzenbaer's children, and two were their cousins. There was Hannes, Gottfried and Bärbel von Schwarzenbaer, Beate and Marianne von Hallfeld. Bärbel and Beate were Bine's age, Gottfried a little older than myself, Marianne maybe a little older than Tissi and Hannes was a big boy of at least twelve or even thirteen years old.

Bärbel said:

"Come on, I'll show you around." She took us out of the kitchen and into the hall. The walls here were covered with antlers, even the hall chandelier was a gigantic twelve ender with a carved figure in the middle and imitation candles as bulbs. It shed a dim light, but looked very pretty. Grandfather too, had some of antlers in his apartment. He had a swaggering hunting story to tell about each one.

The floor was the same as in the kitchen, ochre coloured stones and so were the stairs, which led to another hall. A number of coats of armour were on display here, along with old weapons and beautiful banners, arranged in intricate patterns on the wall.

A medieval chair, which seemed just right for an ancient knight in his castle, stood in a recess. Different carpets and rugs covered the floor.

Bärbel raced up another flight of stairs. This time they were of polished wood. There was a long corridor and many doors that led into as many rooms. We entered the playroom, where there were dolls, cradles, a large dollhouse and a beautiful rocking horse. Many toys were stored in a big box. There were also many books. I wanted to have a closer look, but Bärbel and her brothers and cousins were eager to show us the rest:

"We can play here when it is raining. Let's go outside." I took Bine and Tissi's hand and we all stormed out of the room and ran downstairs. As we came back into the hall with the coats of armour, a door opened and a lot of people walked into the hall, among them our mother. We ran towards her.

"Where have you been?" we asked and she laughed.

"This is the dining room. The adults eat here. Apparently lunchtime is for adults only. Breakfast and vesper (their name for the evening meal) is with the children."

"What did you have?" Bine asked, but didn't wait for Mother's answer. "We had chocolate pudding, and we had two helpings." Mother said:

"Well then you had the same as we did, except we didn't have two helpings of chocolate pudding." Tissi said: "Oh" and we all laughed.

"We are going to play outside" I said, but first, we introduced the children around us to Mother.

Bärbel led us past the dining room into a little lobby and out into a park. The *Schloss* was built into a hill, with the main entrance at the bottom, where we came in the night before, and then this entrance into the park. There was a path leading around the house down a long flight of outside stairs which led back onto the front of the house. On the opposite side of the stairs was another door into the anteroom which led into the kitchen. The park rose further up the hill and at the back of the park was forest. I was interested in a strange building which stood between park and forest. I asked what it was and Gottfried explained, that they made ice in that for the brewery and the cooler in the kitchen, even in the summer. I was impressed, but couldn't work out how it was made.

We had reached the point in the park which was level with the roof of the Schloss, and looking across it we saw another hill and a tower jutting out of some rocks. Just behind the tower was a huge cave.

"What's that over there?" I asked and Gottfried said:

"That is *Burg Loch* the oldest castle in Europe." Again I was impressed but couldn't help the feeling that Gottfried might be showing off. There was something about these children. They were very nice but were full of their own importance all the time. Maybe I was wrong. I suppose they had a right since they were the barons of this village and lived in a real live *Schloss*.

Later, I learned, that he was right about the Loch castle. All the rooms in that castle were inside the mountain and the only man made structure was the wall and tower. Large natural caves with walls which had been panelled with beautifully carved and decorated wood, a hole in the soaring ceiling was used as a chimney, where the smoke could escape undetected into dense forest high up on a cliff and one could still make out the fireplace below. The cave-rooms funnelled off in the gloomy rear into natural tunnels of several kilometres through the mountain, which eventually were supposed to have led to Allerzhausen. Now they had partly fallen in.

The village of Eichhofen was in a very narrow valley which had been carved by the river Laaber. Opposite the Schloss was a brewery and a flour mill with a granary and storehouse for barley and hops. Adjoining, there were large houses, where the workers lived. In between a path led onto a narrow bridge across the Laaber. The river divided here into two canals which fed the mill and the brewery and there was also a weir and a lock. Huge waterwheels worked hard outside both buildings and I could hear busy clanking noises from within.

The narrow bridge led over the lock and then turned sharply left and extended across the weir into the village, which was called Loch, the same as the castle. It had only one row of houses deep and right behind the houses the hill rose steeply up to the castle. From here, we had the opposite view of our Schloss. The road ran right through the *Schloss Hof* (The castle court) on either side were huge gates, which were always open.

Eichhofen continued along the road outside the gates, which ran parallel with the river Laaber. About two hundred metres from the gate, we came to a small cluster of houses, hugging the river. First a longhouse, with a lot of children and chickens playing outside, then a derelict flourmill and almost touching that, a building with a huge roof and a big green double door.

We entered and found a woodworking shop, and to the right a smithy, where a couple of horses waited to be shod. Separating the two, was a wide wooden staircase which led upstairs onto a huge loft.

We watched, fascinated, as the smith made iron shoes for a waiting horse.

He took a piece of straight iron, put it into a blazing fire, sparks flying everywhere. A small girl with shaggy dark hair and hazel eyes pumped the bellows and the fire flared up, making the coals glow. When the iron turned into almost white hot metal, the smith grabbed it with some very long tongs and start beating it on an enormous anvil. Did Siegfried work in a place like this when he learned to forge his sword? I wondered.

The smith had strong, muscular arms. He was naked from the waist up, even now in February. His body was covered in soot and he wore a large black leather apron almost down to the ground. He hit the horseshoe hard three or four times, and then the anvil, gently, which made it ring out softly: ling ling ling. During that time, he turned the iron into a new position and his hammer would then be ready to strike again at the iron to shape it. The anvil was wide and square at one end, and from about the centre it turned into a cone shape, round and getting quite thin at the other end. Cleverly, the smith placed his piece of iron first on the square end, then shape it around the round end. Both ends of the iron were turned up into heels for the horseshoe. Endlessly, his hammer sounded "bang, bang, bang, lingeling ling. The lingelings varied according to how long it took him to get the iron into the right position. He worked with a regular rhythm until he decided to put the iron back into the fire, or, as he later explained, for metal strengthening, into a big trough, filled with black water, where it steamed and hissed and made the water boil.

During the time the iron was heating in the fire, the smith would go to the horse and trim the horse's foot, which rested on the smith's knee. The horses were huge, much bigger than the ones in East Prussia. Big chunks flew off as he moved from foot to foot. When he took a still red hot iron and placed it on the horses hoof, I let out a gasp and immediately put my hand on my mouth. The horse did not seem to mind, it hissed and sizzled and smelled awful, the kind of smell my hair smelled when it got burnt, but much stronger.

It was magical. This was a place for me. With every sense in my body I watched and felt that more than anything, I would like to work here too. But the von Schwarzenbaer children urged me to come away. Reluctantly I followed them.

"It is nearly time for vesper", said Gottfried, and that made me move faster.

We cleaned our hands and tidied up. I felt very self-conscious about my dirty clothes, but there was nothing we could do, right now. Mother had nothing else for us to weir.

We entered the large dining room. It seemed much bigger than the one at Mönchgut, but Mother said it wasn't. There were about fifteen people around the table, including the children. A large white cloth covered the table, there were several baskets of bread, several plates with slices of different sausage and cold meats like ham and *Schinken*, cheese and butter! I could not remember seeing such a rich table, except at home in Berlin, and even then there would not be such a variety. And of course, I remembered, Christmas at Mönchgut, how could I forget that.

We were told where we would sit by Frau von Schwarzenbaer, who seemed so distant now. I had not seen her since she left us at that station, yesterday? The day before? Or was it only this morning? I could not work it out. It was as if she and I were strangers, which I could not believe, after all the trauma we had been through together. I had no sign of recognition from her, no friendly nod, nothing. It was strange.

We had to stand behind our chairs, until Frau von Schwarzenbaer sat down, then we all followed.

First the bread was handed round, then the butter, which was cut into small, round portions and I took one, then the meat. I took a slice, which was big enough to cover the piece of bread. The children had cocoa to drink. I had finished my bread quickly. Would they pass the bread and things again? Would I have to ask?

A man next to me, with the most beautiful hands and the longest fingers I had ever seen, handed me some more bread, and bit by bit, the other things arrived too. Bine was sitting on her own at the other end of the table, but Tissi was next to Mother. So Bine and I had to fend for ourselves. Did Bine have somebody who passed her things? She was sitting beside an attractive lady wearing a Russian blouse with exquisite colourful embroidery and a high neck. She wore her hair in a big black bun low at the back of her head. Her eyes were large, dark with very long lashes and her face looked like a beautiful carving. I saw that this lady looked after Bine and she was talking to Bine now.

Suddenly, I heard the familiar deep drone of enemy aircraft overhead. Slowly they crossed the valley, but nobody stirred. I wanted to go to the cellar, but the man next to me said reassuringly:

"They don't drop their precious bombs onto this insignificant little village. They cross here to go to Regensburg. They come back soon, empty." They crossed the valley, in intervals, back and forth, squadron after squadron, laden going southeast, empty going north west. Poor Grandfather! I did not want to eat anymore. I felt sick inside. The man next to me touched my hand with his fingers and it made me feel strange.

"You must eat. You never know where the next meal is coming from." he said.

✹✹✹

27

Later that evening I heard beautiful, haunting piano music in one of the upstairs rooms. I followed the sound and stopped outside a door near the dining room. I had been listening for a few minutes, when the door opened and the lady, who had been sitting next to Bine, came out.

I was embarrassed to have been caught listening at the door and fumbled for an excuse, when she said with a hard but beautiful accent:

"Do you like music?" Her lips formed the words in a most unusual way. I felt strangely drawn to her. I answered, yes. No one in our family played an instrument, not counting the *Knautsche*, the squeezebox as Mother called her accordion. There was a piano at Mönchgut, but it was never used, and its lid was permanently shut, after all my uncles had perished in the war. I had never thought about playing the piano myself. Maybe it just wasn't the time.

"Come in and sit down," she said and led me near the enormous black winged piano. The man, who had sat next to me at vesper, was playing it. Immediately I realised why his hands were that shape, and that long. I was fascinated to see him find all the right keys and so fast and without looking, his fingers knew where to go. The music was beautiful. I had only heard this sort of music in the radio, when Mother was listening to a concert. Now for the first time, I saw real music, not just heard it.

I had laughed at some evacuated children in East Prussia, who did not know, milk came from cows. Now I felt ashamed.

I never knew, real music was created like this! I had thought the radio or the black discs on Grandfather's gramophone made the music. But how did they get it into the radio, or onto the black discs? There was so much I wanted to know. For the moment I was quite content though to just sit and listen.

I suddenly realised, the man was playing for me. He kept looking and smiling at me. When he finished he asked whether there was anything I liked to hear, something I liked in particular. I didn't know what to ask for, and just said:

"Anything, everything is beautiful."

"Who is your favourite composer?" he asked. I felt myself go red in the face. I also felt very hot. I was extremely embarrassed. I didn't even know what the word 'composer' meant. The woman who had been sitting quietly in a chair near me, got up and said:

"I know, Percy, move over" and she joined him on the seat and they played together on the same piano. Their hands even reaching into each other's space. What beautiful music! Four hands! When they had finished, the woman came over and said:

"It looks to me, that this is the first time you have seen somebody play the piano?" I only nodded. I felt so dreadfully ignorant. I looked into her face. Her speech, although with an accent, was perfect and beautiful. I wanted to speak like she did, I wanted the words to come from my mouth the way they came from hers. She moved and spoke so beautifully and looked so graceful.

"Well, you will have to learn, it is not difficult" she led me to the door. "We will ask your mother, if I could teach you." My heart jumped up and down. But then I realised we wouldn't be here long enough. When we left, there wouldn't be a piano at Grandfather's. My heart sank. But for the moment, even if we were only here two weeks, I would try.

Mother came looking for me. You must go to bed now, it's late. I told her that I had been listening to real music being played on the piano, and that the lady had offered to teach me how to play. Mother didn't answer. She left it open. I asked Mother which country the lady came from because of her strange accent and she told me, that they were husband and wife, both pianists, refugees from Lithuania. Their name was Helja and Percy Waeber. They too had fled communism. I wondered if they had come through Mehlsack with all those other refugees. Was that really less than a year ago?

Almost every day new people arrived at the *Schloss*, people like us, some of them relatives of the von Schwarzenbaers, who had estates in Silesia, and had to leave because the Soviets took their land.

Four days after we arrived in Eichhofen, Mother collapsed with a biliary colic. She was in terrible pain, could keep no food down, and looked dreadfully thin and yellow. I was sure she would die.

Lisa looked after her. Apparently Lisa was a trained nurse. I admired her, she could do anything. Mother was a trained nurse too. Their combined knowledge would have to do since there was no doctor available who could advise.

We children kept out of the way. We also had to go to school. The von Schwarzenbaer and von Hallfeld children went to school every day and we were told by a Nazi official in the village, that we had to go too. Even Bine had to go to school now, the man insisted. "How had she escaped for so long?" the man wanted to know. I told him she wouldn't be seven years old until August, and one didn't start school before the age of seven. But there was no arguing with him.

So with Mother unable to do anything at all, we just went along with the Schloss children, Tissi staying with Lisa in the kitchen.

The way to school, led out through the court gate, up stream along the road past the sawmill and smithy, along the river Laaber for about three quarters of a kilometre, where it turned right and left the river in the valley below, up a very steep hill into the next village, which stood on the crown of the hill. It took us about thirty minutes to walk from the Schloss to school. I compared it with East Prussia and told the other children how I had got stuck in the snow, so much more snow than there was here. In East Prussia, it was open countryside and very flat land, here nothing was flat, everything rose and fell. The road led through

fields and meadows. A wedge of forest reached the road at the spot, where the road forked off and led up the hill to Thimsdorf. There was a small field between the road and the river. At the very edge of the river were trees, with their roots in the water, and along the road ran a draining ditch, with just a thin trickle of water running in it.

We learned from some of the children who joined us at the smithy, that the smith was Lisa's father, and the children her sisters. The smith had 18 children, all girls. I was completely speechless. Lisa wasn't even the oldest, there were sisters who lived away from home, some married, and there were little girls my age, like Hanni, who soon became a bosom-friend. Hannes said to me, that the smith wanted a son, and kept ordering new babies, but they all turned out to be girls. All the children laughed, except Hanni and her sisters. Hanni was the girl who I had seen pumping the bellows.

We were quite a lot of children by the time we left the village behind us completely. There was Hannes, Gottfried and Bärbel von Schwarzenbaer, Beate von Hallfeld, Bine and myself, the baker's son, Friedrich, Hanni, Gerda and Martha Hirsauer. Two boys joined us sometimes from Loch. Often they were too late to come with us. There was still a lot of snow, but it was too wet for sledging.

We had been in Eichhofen about a week, when I woke up in the night, frozen. It had turned bitterly cold. Tissi was awake too, and wanted to go to the loo. I put her on her potty, and waited, shivering.

Apart from the cold, I realised that the planes overhead had woken me up. Not only that, but there was bombing not too far from here, the windows rattled. I couldn't imagine what they would find around here worthy of bombing.

I put Tissi back into bed, she wanted to snuggle between Bine and myself, and we cuddled tightly. Bine moved closer too, without apparently waking up.

The temperature had plunged suddenly, this night in the last days of February, and we awoke in the morning, to a world of frozen beauty. Icicles sparkled from the eaves of every roof, the branches of the trees were covered with a clear glassy coat. There had already been signs of spring, with the buds fattening out, but now they were coated in ice. The fence posts and telegraph wires dazzled coated, spangling the village, the countryside the forest in a shimmering, translucent glaze. On our way to school we picked icicles and sucked them like lollipops, every now and then, dipping them into the new glittering snow. The air was crystal clear, the sky the colour of Mother's pearl necklace. Here and there the sun would come through the clouds in streaks of light. It was a day for awe, not war.

Why did they drop bombs during the night?

My school was a country school. It consisted of one really very large room, where all the classes sat, little ones in front and the big ones at the back. There were three large windows either side of the room. Around eleven in the morning on this beautiful winter's day, my school got bombed, without warning.

The first bomb missed the school house, but shattered all the windows. The teacher calmly led us all out into the yard.

There were huge planes overhead, with strange glass bubbles in the front, on its belly and in its tail, with people inside. Darting in and out, were smaller, faster planes. They were taking it all out on this tiny, sleepy village. There was only a church, the school and a very few houses. Larger farms were scattered across the country side. The teacher tried to lead us over to the church, but we had to shelter by a wall which divided the schoolyard from the road and the church. We didn't get any further

Screaming, the village children ran home. Some fell and lay still. The Eichhofen children huddled together, and Hannes, the oldest among us said we should try and reach the forest. It was a long way. I suggested, to lie flat on the ground with our satchels and arms over our heads, remembering what happened in Regensburg.

There was added something new, a new sound, something I hadn't experienced before. This sound made me look up involuntarily. Above me I saw an aircraft, so low, that I could see the men's faces as they sat in the glass bubble in the aircraft. On the wing of the plane shone a white star. The aircraft was still coming down at the school, but it was not throwing bombs, it was spraying something small and the sound was a continuous tatatatat. Wherever the small things hit, the snow pounced and there was a little hole. These little pounces and holes made the pattern of a giant bead necklace, hitting the wall in front of us and disappearing behind it. Hannes said:

"Mashinengewehr." (Machinegun). Yes, I knew what that was. I felt fear. If the planes came down that low, so low that I can see the men behind the gun, than they can see me. I was furious. For the first time in this war, I felt that I wanted a gun to shoot back. How dared they! Couldn't they see we were all children? It was so unfair. It was exactly what I had heard the enemy would do, only until now I didn't believe they would really do it.

Then I thought that maybe they couldn't see we were children. We would have to do something. We would have to give them a sign. But nobody could move, the bombing and shooting was continuous. Bine, Hanni, Bärbel and I squeezed together as closely as we could. Beate was crying dreadfully with Gerda and Martha Hirsauer huddled close. Hannes put his arm over them.

I lost all track of time. We all just lay there and waited. Even when all was quiet, we didn't move. My hands were very cold, and my feet hurt. Bine was shivering. The teacher called us all together and told us to go home quickly.

We turned and ran out of the school yard, and there we saw two children who were a bloody mess, and the snow around was red. We stopped just a few seconds and then we ran. Were those children dead? Hannes said that they were. He said that he had seen more children up the road and they were dead too. They didn't move. Maybe they were just badly hurt. We couldn't tell and didn't look back. We just ran.

Beate was still crying, I felt like crying. I had such a lump in my throat. But it was helpless fury I felt.

I held Bine's hand tightly in mine, as we ran down the hill. Half way down, the planes were back. We threw ourselves into the ditch for cover. Luckily, the little ditches were frozen and we didn't get wet. Gottfried said, that even though we were in the ditch, they could still see us in the snow.

"You could see a sparrow in this snow from up there." he said. They dived at us, coming straight at us and when I thought the plane would hit the ground, they screamed back up into the sky again without shooting at all. We were terrified. Again and again they came at us and when they didn't shoot, I looked up, fascinated. I could see the men in the glass bubble laughing, I could see their teeth. Finally, they flew off, and we ran like furies home, convinced, that we would never have to go back to school after this.

The adults agreed. But they would have to get permission for this from the Nazi village official, who insisted that this was not enough reason for not going to school. Defeatists talk he called it, and he would denounce anybody who did not send their children to school. He would personally see to it, that we would be on our way every morning.

Frau von Schwarzenbaer had a meeting with the schoolchildren's parents and it was agreed, that we would have to go to school, provided the school was still standing, but we would have to go the long way around and use the forest for cover.

The school was transferred into the church, desks and all. The planes continued to cross, but everybody was alert from now on. We were two weeks into March and the snow had melted almost entirely where it was exposed to the sun. Dandelions, Coltsfoots and March Violets appeared. Pussy willows shimmered in the sun, and bright yellow tails of the hazel fluttered in the wind.

Fields were ploughed, and potatoes put into the ground. Women were out sowing grain.

But for us, there was always the exposed road on which we had to walk once we had to come out of the forest. We carefully checked for planes. It would take us five minutes of hard running to get to the safety of the Schloss.

As the snow melted, the grass grew, we found shelter even by the side of the road. We could tuck ourselves into a furrow or a ditch, and as the leaves covered the bushes and trees, we found ample shelter below.

Dreadful news reached us. Refugees from East Prussia, thousands and thousands of them had drowned when the *Wilhelm Gustloff* was torpedoed in the Baltic Sea. Having their escape cut off in the west and the south by the Soviets, their only way to safety was by boat across the Baltic Sea. The lifeboats fell into the water, full of people who then tried to survive clinging on to ice floes, but they all drowned. Was Farmer Graf among them? Robert? The Kramp family, all our friends?

I was certain now, the war would not finish, until we were all dead. Was I right? I didn't dare ask Mother. She was still trying to recover from her illness. I thought about it on my own. I couldn't discuss it with Bine or Tissi. They would only be frightened.

Then I pictured in my mind, all the dead people I had seen. Their bodies looked empty, left behind. Where had they gone? I didn't believe in a heaven with angels and harps. The Catholics believed that. They also believed that one could confess one's sins and that would be like an entrance ticket into heaven. Hanni, whose family was very devout catholic, told me that. In fact

Hanni told me all about Catholicism and took me to a convent downstream from the village, and introduced me to some very kind nuns. She also told me, that if one sinned, and didn't confess, one would end up in hell and everlasting purgatory. I didn't believe that either. And how could you go on sinning, then confess it all on Saturday, go to mass on Sunday, and start sinning again on Monday. Hanni said that was ok. I felt, that if sinning was wrong then one shouldn't sin. If you sinned anyway, thinking that all one needed to do, was confess afterwards, and for punishment, you just said a few prayers on your rosary, then that was living a lie. It was wrong. It felt wrong.

What would heaven be really like?

❋❋❋

28

Mother had often told us about the time when she was little and her mother had died. A great aunt who was an artist, had painted my grandmother going into an imaginary heaven. How did people know what heaven was like? In the catholic churches I found impressive paintings on walls, ceilings and numerous altars, which showed what it was like in heaven, filled with angels and Saints. Had the artists seen heaven? If I came from heaven originally, I could not remember what heaven was like.

Why were there so many people dying now? Did God want them all back in Heaven? In most families, relatives had died because of this war. Where *did* all the souls go, once they had left the body? There were so many, as many as there were stars in the sky. Did the souls hover among the stars somewhere until there was a new baby to be born? Did the soul take on the body of the new baby and become a new person? Were there enough babies to go round? These thoughts were as enormous as trying to work out where the universe ended. Would everything go on forever, would I go on for ever even when I am dead?

Was Hell life on earth? Was this purgatory? Was it Heaven to be dead?

My thoughts went round and round with no way out. There was something that drew me to the convent I visited with Hanni. Hanni went there every day and I came as often as I could. She knew all the nuns. It was so peaceful and beautiful there. The nuns were friendly, not like the ones at my school in Regensburg, who were only friendly after Father Rappel had spoken to them.

Here in Weissenfels Convent I felt safe, secure and without fear. Nobody questioned whether I was catholic, whether I had a right to be here. Here was no war, just white, serene beauty, peace. If there was a heaven as such, would it be like this? There was a charming chapel attached to the convent. Some of the nuns were buried there too. I accompanied Hanni, watching her perform the catholic ritual, which I now accepted as being quite normal. Being catholic was part of Bavaria. I would still have to learn a lot, to know what was going on, but Hanni was a good teacher. One thing was clear; we had the same Christ, and that was the important thing.

Outside in the graveyard, were a number of Hirsauers going back into the last century. Eighteen seventy six was one Josef Hirsauer who was born in 1800. It seemed he was the first one to be buried there. This was a village burial ground were the local people would be buried. I knew that we could not go back to Silesia now, since everybody fled from there. I could not be buried at the family burial ground. Would I be allowed to be buried here, would they have me? Would it make any difference anyway? If we all had to die before the end of the war, then I would like to die in Weissenfels, or at least near it. I didn't want to be the only one left though, if the family died. I asked Hanni what she thought about dying and she said she didn't want to die, and she wouldn't die until she was old, and then it didn't matter.

I realised then, that she didn't have any idea about the war and what it could do to her and what it had already done to thousands and thousands of Germans. The war had so far passed her by completely. Even her father was still at home, never had to go away to fight. I wondered why.

It occurred to me, that until our school got bombed, the war had been somewhere else for her as it had for all the other children around here. I was aware of so much suddenly. The hysterical screaming children, running everywhere, senseless, not comprehending what was happening at the school that day. In Berlin we had been gradually initiated into the bombing until it had become a regular thing. In a way we had learned to cope with it.

I looked at Hanni and saw that I couldn't even explain it to her. I also realised, when we became friends, that she had never gone anywhere by train. She did not know what a WC was. She had never seen a telephone or travelled on a bus. She had never been to Regensburg. She had walked to the villages around, and visiting the village with the railway station to her was like travelling to a really big place. Going to the station and taking the train into Regensburg, meant, you had grown up and could go on your own, like Lisa, and some of her other sisters, who got married and lived elsewhere.

I could have come from the moon, it would make no difference to her. Berlin, East Prussia, the Moon.

They have a different dialect where I came from and people tend to call people from my part of Germany *Sau Preuss* (Sow Prussian) Hanni couldn't explain why when I asked her. Soon we learnt from the Schloss children to call the locals *Knödelfresser* ('Dumpling eaters'). It made up for being called a *Sau Preuss*. We had little gangs of Sau Preussen and Dumpling eaters, but mostly we roamed around happily together.

Hanni's innocence of war made me feel lonely. The difference between her and myself meant, I would have to keep my thoughts to myself. But nevertheless, we became very good playmates and friends.

That evening at vesper in the Schloss, the latest news item, the torpedoed "Wilhem Gustloff", was being discussed at table by the adults. They said that it happened in the last two days in January with five thousand civilians and wounded soldiers drowned among the ice floes.

"What are civilians?" I asked Percy Waeger, next to me.

"Civilians are people who do not fight in the war, people like you and me." Then he put his long and exquisitely shaped finger to his lips and said: "psst" and I was quiet and listened.

"And the town, absolutely packed with refugees from the eastern countries, Poland and Silesia. They started at nine in the evening and went on all night. They dropped phosphorous bombs which could not be put out. Somebody said those bombs were called napalm. Flames followed and attached themselves to the fleeing people and even when they jumped into the river, it would still burn on top of the water and under the water." I shuddered! How could fire survive under water?

The English bombers lit the town with fire bombs to make it easier for the Americans to find the city at night with explosives. One could see the glow one hundred and fifty kilometres away in the sky. It was a raid that lasted three days and caused such a holocaust, that the ruins were white when the fire finally died out. One hundred and seventy-five thousand inhabitants lost their lives in the first day of the raid. But the exact numbers of dead are not known because one doesn't know the precise number of refugees, which had arrived, and the remains were such, that one could not work out how many bodies there were.

A man I hadn't seen before, was telling this to the adults at the table.

I had stopped eating and just sat there listening. Mother had got up and was taking Bine and Tissi away from the table. Percy Waeger again touched my hand and looked at me.

"Go on, follow your Mother. This is not for children." I asked him:

"Where is this place they are talking about?"

"Dresden" he said, "you won't know it." I looked at him and remembered our night at the station and the horror of the fire bombs then, and how finally we had a train that took us away from the exposed platform right through the flames to safety only three or four months ago. Had there been anything left to bomb?

"Yes, I have been there" I told him, but he wasn't listening to me anymore. His long teeth bit into a roll and he was eating furiously as if there was no tomorrow. But would there be a tomorrow?

❋❋❋

Four weeks after we arrived in Eichhofen, around the 6th of March, Mother had recovered enough to be able to move from the Schloss to our own little place. With so many new people arriving at the Schloss, Mother was glad to have her own little domain.

The room above the smithy had become vacant and we were allowed to have it. Mother was also given a job. She was to be responsible for the Schloss's vegetable and fruit garden. She was very happy about that. We had not very much to move, it still fitted into Grandfather's little cart and that was how we moved. It was only about 200 metres and almost next door to Hanni's home. I was going to love it above the smithy. There was the big loft with so many hiding places! We could be as noisy as we wanted, because there was enough noise already from the wood-working shop and the smithy downstairs.

This new home had no bathroom, but the most fantastic loo anybody could ever wish for, at least that was what I thought of it. One entered it from the loft through a door in the outside wall. It led straight onto a wooden elongated structure, like a roofed in balcony, but not running along the house but away from it. At the end of the balcony, was a comfortable two seater with wooden lids, beautifully fashioned with little carvings. Lifting the lid and looking down through the seat, one found the river Laaber rushing past way below. Its clear water glistening in the sun. Little weeds bending with the flow, weaving gently back and forth.

We couldn't get Tissi close enough to sit on the seats, because she could see through the boards in the floor where the little brown knots had fallen out and she thought she would fall through as well. She would sit on the floor in front of the first little knot hole and no matter what, she would not be moved. Eventually after days, we persuaded her that it was quite safe and such a lot of fun. Bine and I would sit together and watch the river below.

There were wagtails resting on exposed rocks by the river's edge, gracefully dipping their tail. There were *Eisvögel*, (Kingfishers), which I had never seen before. Later we also saw large blue dragonflies. Large fish lived in the river too. It was a fascinating loo.

Eventually Tissi would share the seat with me and not be afraid anymore. But she had the oddest fears. One had to be really patient with her.

Across the road, immediately opposite, was a saw mill, and the whine of the huge circular saw went on almost continuously. Lorries with soldiers and POWs arrived regularly to pick up the sawn boards and load them onto the lorry and drive off again.

Herr Hirsauer, the smith, was also responsible for the saw mill. There was a regular crew of Hungarian soldiers who had been fighting side by side with the Germans. Their leader was Joseph. He and I were soon good friends. He said being here was almost like being at home, because it was so close to the Danube and that was the river that passed his own home in Hungary. Whenever he passed the river, he would spit into it and work out how long it would take to pass his home where no doubt his wife would watch out for it. I laughed, and so did he. He watched my face for a reaction. I said I didn't believe it. The spit wouldn't last that long, and anyway, even if it did, his wife wouldn't recognise it. But he said, that it was the thought he was sending which she would feel. That made sense to me. He had dark hair and very blue eyes and when he laughed he showed big, white, beautiful teeth with not a crooked one in sight.

A German soldier with a wooden hand in a leather glove often accompanied the Hungarians. He could move his thumb with a dreadful click, but it helped him to hold things with this hand. He did all the official work like signing a lot of papers. He didn't like us to hang around all the time, but I continued to follow Josef. Tissi called him Joves and soon everybody called him that, even the German officer with the wooden hand, who sometimes even managed a friendly grin.

Occasionally, the Lorries wouldn't stop, just drive past the saw mill. All the Hungarians would holler and wave and we could hear them before they came round the bend, and since the smithy was the last house in the village, we could wave from the window and watch them until they disappeared from our

view, where the road forked off to the village with our school. They camped two villages down the road past the fork. There was a camp for English prisoners of war near Josef's, which was bombed by enemy planes and almost utterly destroyed. Josef told us that and we were shocked, because we could not work out how the enemy could kill their own people. It could only have been a dreadful mistake.

The Hungarians often had their lunch on the meadow in front of the smithy. But their food was limited. They were yearning for some potatoes. They had tinned pate or cheese, but apart from some black *Pumpernickel* bread, nothing to go with it.

Mother and Joseph came to an arrangement. We would provide the potatoes and they would share their tins. We hurried home from school and quickly grabbed a bucket full, and went to the river upstream from the smithy to wash them. They were old and sprouting, the brush was big and difficult to handle and the water still very cold. Bine and I heaved them upstairs together, and boiled them on our little stove. Brown scum collected in the pot and Mother said we hadn't washed them enough. Josef, who just came in, said that was ok. All the germs would be dead by the time they were cooked, but he took a spoon and scooped up the brown foam. It was only earth that had been on them. When they were boiled the Hungarians piled into our little room. We didn't have enough plates to go round, so we doubled up. A lot of salt was put onto a plate into which we dipped the potato which we ate with our hands, throwing them from hand to hand because they were so hot, laughing a lot when one dropped. A thick slice of that strange pate with the potatoes made a delicious meal.

Josef too was worried as to how far the allies would let the Russians advance. Everybody had been talking and discussing this for so long. "Our efforts would all be for nothing" he said

"If they let the Russians in they are making a dreadful mistake." Once he told me that the Americans should know better about the trouble which was threatening Europe.

Losing personal freedom because of one's faith, not trusting in Communism, the constant disputes about borders in Europe, mad, fanatical, upstart leaders, those were all the reasons why people emigrated to the States to become Americans in the first place. America consisted of unhappy Europeans, who now lived in America next to the people who would have been their enemy in Europe. But in America they would be great friends. It was interesting listening to Josef. He said his father's brother had gone to America not very long after the First World War. He hadn't heard from his cousins for many years and wondered if they were in that army now advancing. I found it very strange and awful, that cousins would be enemies. He said, the same goes for Germans too, because they have relatives in America too.

The Hungarians came about two or three times a week, and we repeated our lunchtime social gathering every time. The Hungarians always swept the room after they had been there and washed the dishes and the big pot in the Laaber.

At other times we just waited for them to pass and waved. Once, as the lorry passed, a little parcel was thrown down and landed in front of our feet. There were some shoe soles and a little note saying: "You can now fix up your shoes, Frau Gerret." Mother was very happy. In the smithy that day she repaired her shoes. Another time a bar of chocolate landed on the road. Then one day, four Lorries arrived with POWs. They stopped, and the POWs spread themselves all over the meadow opposite the smithy, through which a tiny stream flowed whose source was only about fifty meters away in a very clear and sweet well.

These men undressed except for their underpants. They turned their clothing inside out and settled down in the warm April sun to delouse their clothes. The POWs were very thin and white but they laughed a lot. After a little while, Mother went upstairs and filled the massive potato pot with water and made 'Hitler mokka' the Érsatz' coffee which we all drank, a mixture of barley, dandelion and acorns. Mother poured the 'coffee' into the water jug, put more water into the potato pot to boil and went down stairs. She walked up to each man and asked if they wanted some coffee. The neighbours, who had been watching Mother and shaking their heads, appeared with coffee and soon everybody was drinking it.

If some of our neighbours thought we were foreigners, what must they have thought of the POWs!

Mother did not allow us to go into the meadow afterwards for at least a week, hoping the lice would have died by then. But new POWs arrived daily, and the meadow had no chance to recover.

We could not tell what nationality the POWs were, but they all came for timber, and left with loads, in exchange for lice in the meadow!

Josef told me, that the Americans were very close. He said we would all be free soon.

We had our daily ration of *Tief Flieger* (low level flying attacks), but we had learnt very quickly to dive out of sight. It was becoming just one more routine even for the local children.

✹✹✹

29

The Americans were now in Darmstadt. Josef and I were washing potatoes at the Laaber, when he told me, that soon he would not be coming any more, they were being transferred to another camp further south, closer to the Hungarian border. He looked happy. He tore off a star from his uniform and gave it to me.

"Keep this for me," he said, "I shall collect it after the war." He looked so proud and tall. I took the star and held it in my hand. My throat felt tight. Soon I would have to say good bye to another friend. I felt sad and lonely. Nothing was permanent.

Much later, I carefully put the star into my little box of treasures.

Josef and his troop left that day, feeling happy that soon they would be going home, when the war finished. They were singing a beautiful and fiery song in their own language. We stood in the road and waved until they disappeared around the bend, their song still in the air.

We were just turning to go into the house, remarking about the beautiful song when the *Tiefflieger* (Low flying aircraft) were back. This time there were German fighters in the sky too. We watched, fascinated. They kept disappearing over the top of the wooded hills, and some American planes dropped silver stuff, which we ran to collect. We felt quite safe. The enemy planes were too occupied with the German fighter planes to bother about us. The silver stuff turned out to be huge hanks of endless, beautiful, shining tinfoil tape. What ever could it have been for? Nobody could tell us and later, when we decided that it wasn't poisonous or explosive, we cut it into thin strips for next Christmas to use as angels hair on the tree.

The noise of the planes was terrifying. Huge bombers laboured across the valley, and small American and German fighters buzzed around like a swarm of angry hornets.

Suddenly, as we watched, an American plane turned nose down and started to twist like a corkscrew, down and down it came, turning and twisting with a huge trail of black smoke coming from its tail. I realised that the plane must hit the ground, and I also realised that I felt anxious for the men in the plane. Curiously, I wondered why I felt for the enemy.

I was stopping and starting and in the end found myself running towards the falling plane. But what could I do when I got there?

There were people working in the field nearby, and when they saw what was happening, they dropped their hoes and ran to the spot where the plane came down. When they got near there was hardly anything left, except a big hole and smoking debris. They told us to go home and not go near the aircraft. I wondered what had happened to the pilot.

Another plane fell and disappeared behind the hill. An awful lot of black smoke, accompanied by a deafening explosion came from behind the bend of the road to Joseph's camp. I wondered what it could be, but the people from the field yelled at us children to go home "this instant!"

We ran through the big open doors of the forge and watched the grisly battle from there.

The smith stood behind us and scratched his head. He swore constantly in broad Bavarian, and kept repeating his words over and over to give proper emphasis to his feelings, using the holy sacrament, *Heiligs Sakrament, Sakrament* changing to *Cruzyfix Sakra Türken, Sakra Türken* (Crucifix and holy turks) and ending with the *Heilige Mutter Gottes* (Holy Mother of God). It still amazed me how the Bavarians could swear. Nowhere else in Germany had I heard such swearing. And yet, I felt as one with the smith, his swearing was somehow appropriate.

The big planes disappeared out of sight and we could hear the bombs whistle down and explode. Even though they were over Regensburg, a long way away, our windows rattled, and a heavy wind came up. The planes crossed the sky until evening and it became dark outside.

When the field workers came down the road they told the smith, that the Hungarians had not made it to their camp. Their lorry had been bombed and it looked as if they were all dead.

I felt again, that sooner or later we would *all* be dead. I still held Josef's little star in my hand. I looked at it, and wondered where his soul was that moment. Had he briefly passed here before going home to his wife on his way to heaven? I went down to the spot at the Laaber where we had washed the potatoes so many times together, and where we had talked this very day, could it have been only one hour ago. Life was wiped out so quickly. I wondered why I was born, if all I had to do was wait for death. Josef was wrong. He believed he would live. Mother cried quietly.

The very next day, coming home from school, we were caught in another raid. We were walking down the *Thimsdorf* hill when we heard an unearthly roar. We flung ourselves into the ditch. There was no plane where the roar was, the roar was travelling across the valley, empty, without the object, that made the noise. Just then, I saw the fastest, strangest looking plane shoot soundlessly across the valley. It was incredible. Just as it disappeared over the treetops, its roar came up behind and followed empty across the sky. What were they? What would they do? Fascinated and scared we watched. None of us had ever seen such fast planes. It looked to me as if they were trying to catch up with their own sound.

Other planes followed, huge bombers and small fighters. The planes were so low, that although we thought we were well covered in the ditch, they still found us and strafed us. Bine and Bärbel panicked, ran from the ditch and down the middle of the road. I screamed after them. Bullets hit the road just behind them. I got up and ran after Bine, just behind the bullets. Bine came to the bend, crossed the road and ran down the meadow to the river and trees, which would give better shelter. The plane had to pull up sharply or crash into the hill on the other side of the river, and by the time it had come back the other children had followed us and we were all safely among the trees.

Bine had run so fast, she could not stop in time and fell into the river. She couldn't swim, neither could I, and she yelled and screamed and swallowed water but miraculously got hold of one of the low branches which reached into the water.

The trees did not cover us, because the leaves were only just beginning to unfold. We could still see the planes, but I was now so busy trying to pull Bine out of the water, I couldn't be bothered about the planes. There were frightful explosions nearby. I could also see our window and Tissi looking out from behind the glass. She was crying dreadfully. I wished Mother would look out. Anyone!

I asked Gottfried and Hannes to help, but Hannes was busy helping his brother, who had fallen awkwardly and was bleeding badly. Hannes helped him with something else, which looked dreadful. Bärbel saw that I looked shocked at what they were doing, and said:

"Gottfried cannot go to the lavatory the way we go. He can't-" and she pointed to her backside, he has a hole in his side, and does it into a bag. He has to wear that bag all the time."

I was stunned. I looked at Gottfried with different eyes and I was full of admiration for him. He was a real hero! Going to school and doing all the things we do, and all with this handicap and never letting on.

I was still trying to understand it all while desperately hanging on to Bine's hand. She had quietened down somewhat, because her teeth were chattering in the cold water. She was calling forlornly for Mother. I asked Bärbel to hang on to me while I pulled Bine out. But Hanni and her sisters had gone to the smithy under cover of the trees, and were returning with their father, the smith. He grabbed Bine by the arm and yanked her out and carried her to the smithy. There in front of the roaring fire, he took off her wet clothes clumsily and put a warm horse blanket around her. I dashed upstairs but Mother was not home. She was busy in the Schloss garden. So Bine was at the best place since there was no fire upstairs. Tissi came down with me and we all sat quietly in the forge with little Tissi hiccupping and sobbing and hanging on to my hand. She had been so terrified up there on her own.

Hannes had taken Gottfried home. Bärbel was still with us in the smithy. Everybody was talking and the smith made a decision.

Nobody was going back to school. He would see to that.

Nobody did go back to school. We stayed close to the village and waited now in earnest for the enemy to come.

From the Schloss we heard forbidden news. The Americans had taken Hannover, the Russians Königsberg.

April 16. Russians were heading for Berlin. Americans reached Nürnberg. Americans went into Czechoslovakia.

Hanni came home from Weissenfels, where she had attended Mass which was held every morning at six o clock. She had some great news. The village where the station was, Ondorf, had some warehouses, and the doors had been opened to the public. Nothing should be left for the enemy. We could go and fetch anything we wanted, free. Immediately, we took Grandfather's little cart and headed for Ondorf.

The warehouses were part of the railway station. Quite a number of people were there already.

As we entered this Aladdin's cave, we found some oil drums with a tap on the side and filled our two brown enamel water jugs, which Mother had, hoping it was cooking oil. We looked at many different things, wondering if any of it was any use to us. Mother said:

"Even if we can't use it, it might come in handy for barter." There were large white tablets of stearin wax, the size of a square foot. We took a dozen.

There were rolls and rolls of white paper. Good enough to use as writing and drawing paper. When had we last seen paper!

Bine found some tins. They were army colour and had nothing written on the outside except some numbers. We lifted them and shook them and listened to what might be inside. A woman who was also collecting said:

"You take first and look at it later. It's bound to be food." She was right we decided and took some from each shelf. There were friendly and happy faces everywhere. People were happily telling each other what they had found and where, giving directions. There would be food on every table that night. We found flour, oats and brown wet sugar. We took such a lot that I felt guilty. But there was so much that even the amount we took didn't make much difference to the pile.

Even some army blankets, horrid colour but thick and fluffy and always useful.

Another woman said, that this was the place where the food rations and supplies for the POWs was kept.

"They had better food than we had" somebody else said. I thought of Josef and the shoe soles and the chocolate. Chocolate! Would that chocolate have come from here? I went in search of it. There must be some. True enough I found some. Large bars, not like Josef's, but almost as big as the wax tablets and very thick and dark. I took lots and carried them back to the cart. Then on the way back for more, I discovered a sack of white powder and dipped my finger into it to find out what it could be. It tasted sweet. Bine guessed it was custard powder. We had nowhere to put it and the bag it was in was too large to lift. So I ran off to find some containers. As I came past the big entrance doors I saw burning outside. No time to stop for that. I ran on, searching, and eventually found some beautiful little white sacks. They were as fine as our pillow cases. I grabbed quite an armful and ran back to Mother. This place was quite unbelievable.

"They are bombing outside." I told them as we filled some of the bags with custard powder, some with sugar and flour and oats.

We had been hungry for so long and missed the meals at the Schloss. Since we moved to the room above the forge, we had been rationed, and often, even though we had coupons, there was no food other than milk and potatoes. But in Regensburg we would probably not even have had that.

But now we were already working out what we would cook that evening and the first thing would be pancakes and chocolate sauce. We had oil and flour. It was so difficult to wait.

Our cart could hold no more and we started for home. When we got back it was only eleven in the morning. I decided to go off for another load. We emptied the cart and carried everything upstairs. Now we had to be careful storing it because the big loft were we lived also housed a lot of mice. I left Mother to sort it out and headed back for Ondorf. Bine came too, and when we trotted past Hanni's house, she joined us pushing an ancient pram.

Having their own fields, a cow and chickens, they didn't need to look around for food as we had to, but when Hanni spotted our rich load, she decided to join us on our second trip.

As we left the warehouse in Ondorf with our second load, a train pulled into the station, desperately screeching to a halt. It had been attacked already, but as I realised this, the very planes here swooping down again. All the people in the train came rushing out, screaming and throwing themselves onto the ground. We raced back to the warehouse and waited inside until the shooting stopped.

Finally the planes had had enough and disappeared over the wooded hills. There were many wounded. Bine went over to a woman near us who sat on the ground and moaned. Her legs were bleeding. She spoke to her and the woman got up and came over to us. Bine said:

"I told her, Mother is a nurse and can fix her legs."

"It's only about three kilometres to walk" I said. She was happy to come. While we were walking she explained she came from Magdeburg where she had lost everything in the bombing. She worried, whether the Americans or the Russians would get to Magdeburg first. But she had a sister in Meran and that is where she was headed. She walked so slowly and with obvious pain, we sat her on top of our goodies in the cart and pulled her home. Bine and I worked harder that day than we ever had in our lives.

Back at home, we were greeted with a delicious smell of baking. Mother had made fresh bread! I squealed and jumped into the air. First, Mother took her Red Cross box and carefully pulled pieces of shrapnel from the woman's legs.

"I could do with some alcohol" Mother said. I had found some big cans of something, that a woman at the warehouse had called Schnapps. I fetched it and it turned out to be pure alcohol. When the woman's legs were all bandaged up, we filled a straw mattress with fresh straw and arranged a little area outside our room into a cosy place for her to recover. We all had some of the fresh bread and then Mother said she ought to go and see if there were any more people that might need her help. We took the little cart and set off for the third time to go to Ondorf that day.

The train had left for Regensburg, taking the wounded too. We filled our cart again from the warehouse and headed home.

At the other end of the big loft, above the woodworking shop, lived an old woman, *Mutter Prindl*, and we told her she could have anything she wanted from our treasure store. She gratefully accepted some flour, sugar and oats. She also took some stearin to make candles. In return, and for the first time since we lived there, she spoke to us. She had been hostile and pretended we were not there. Now she came with some eggs for us. She kept a few chickens behind the saw mill. We could have some real pancakes now. That evening we ate so many pancakes with syrup, which we found was in one of the tins, and hot chocolate sauce, that I actually heard myself say:

"No thank you, I can't eat any more." We all laughed.

What a weird and happy day that had been. And what a lot of nice people there were everywhere! Maybe we wouldn't all die. There were so many people who believed that soon all would be well. Surely, they couldn't all be wrong?

❋❋❋

April 29. Heavy Street fighting in Berlin.

I found Mother working in the garden. I told her the news which I had had from Hannes. Her eyes filled with tears. She didn't cry often, and so seeing her cry I felt my tears coming too. We were both thinking the same thing. What of Onkel Kurt and his family? Tante Ria, Omi Pless and everybody?

The Americans were in München. My heart was in Berlin. Mother said why couldn't the Americans get to Berlin first? Why, why?

"There would be no grass growing in Berlin after the Russians had been there." Mother said.

"They are uncivilized, barbaric savages. They don't send European Russians to do their dirty work, they send Asians to do that. They have a different civilization and attitude."

The road from Ondorf through Eichhofen was suddenly crowded with refugees from the East. One morning, passing through, a small group of people appeared which grew and grew as they filed past the smithy and the saw mill, slowly, tired and starving women, children and old people, their clothes only rags. Emaciated horses pulled wagons with the sick and wounded. They had lost everything too, their estates, their land, houses and farms. Tired and abandoned they knew not where to go. Their eyes were dark and hollow, their expressions of desolate hopelessness. They were hoping to find a roof somewhere, hoping to find somebody who would say: "You can stay here." Hoping to find some food, but where? There were hundreds, growing to thousands!

Another day, a beautiful lady, sitting astride an equally beautiful chestnut horse, came riding up at the head of a large trek. She stopped outside the forge. With her were several wagons and horses and a lot of people. She seemed to me like a queen among her subjects. She wanted her horses shod.

The smith came out and looked at all the beautiful horses. He would shoe them for her but he wanted no money, he wanted a horse for that.

The lady was furious and said no, she wouldn't. That was far too high a price to pay. She was still astride on her horse, which was dancing around. She calmly controlled it.

The smith was not impressed. He walked round the lovely horse and lifted the tail, picked a louse from it and flicked it at the rider. I noticed the famous Trakehner brand on the horse's side; the shovel antlers of an elk.

"This horse is thin and lousy" he said "and not worth much." When he had flicked the louse, the lady hadn't even blinked. Steadily she looked at him. The smith looked at his feet.

"Only a few days of regular feeding with hay and oats, grooming and looking after, and you are looking at a horse, such as you would never have dreamt of seeing in these parts" she said.

My heart leaped. I looked at the smith expectantly.

"Maybe" the smith said, "but that is my offer." The lady turned her horse and looked down at the smith.

"I will let you have that two year old over there, for food for all my people, hay for the horses for at least a week and shoes for them all." The smith roared with laughter, smacked his shining leather breeches, and then the horse she was riding, on the back, and said:

"Done!" Now the lady laughed too, a beautiful smile. I admired her. I wanted to know who she was, she seemed so regal, brave and unafraid. She now dismounted and went to the various wagons and spoke to the people inside. She had handed the reins to a thin little boy of her group. All the Hirsauer girls, Bine and I helped to fetch hay, sacks of potatoes, flour and milk. There was plenty for all the people of the lady's trek. Bine and I gave the lady some of our sugar. She looked at it and said it was a very precious gift.

Mother came down and invited her upstairs into our room for a meal. She had transformed the room into something from another world. She had unpacked our carefully guarded silver cutlery and the one silver bowl and laid the table. In the bowl were potatoes in their jackets, she had made some green salad from young dandelions and sorrel and cress. Some cottage cheese with wild chives in a little bowl and napkins with Mother's family crest woven into it. It was like it used to be when we were still at home in Berlin. Mother and the lady shook hands. "Gräfin Yorck" (Countess Yorck)* she said and Mother introduced herself and the three of us. It was amazing how quickly we remembered our table manners. It was wonderful to see her pick the potato with the skin and put it on her plate. Would she peel it? No, she split it, put some cottage cheese into the split she had made with her fork and gracefully put some dandelion-sorrel and cress salad on the side. We waited until everybody had helped themselves and then we started to eat together.

She had been on the move for almost three months. She had left her family estate in Silesia. Mother and the countess exchanged the history of their lives and we sat and listened. It was fascinating. The countess was in two minds as to whether she had lost her lands forever or only temporarily. It was for the first time that I saw her weaken. Her eyes glistened with tears and the end of her nose became red, but she did not cry. The same thought filled millions of hearts. Would anybody ever be allowed to go home again?

The smith was busy making new shoes for the horses. The Countess Yorck's trek was there all day, washing in the Laaber and cooking and resting. Mother offered the Countess her bed but she said she wanted to press on. She had distant cousins in Bavaria and that was where she was headed. They were now so close, and they wanted to get there before the *Zusammenbruch*, (Collapse) which we all expected very soon now.

They left in the late afternoon. The smith had his two year old, the first of many horses he would acquire in the next few days. What puzzled me was where he had those extra potatoes from and all that flour.

---

* The name Yorck has been spelled both with and without "c." The family of Yorck employed both versions. On the patent elevating the family to the dignity of Count the name is written "Yorck," but the "c" is deleted on the monument in Klein-Öls, the family's former estate in Silesia. The descendants have employed both spellings. Count Peter Yorck von Wartenburg, who was executed for complicity in the plot of 20 July 1944, generally used the "c", while his brother Paul, the present head of the family, does not. (Yorck and the Era of Prussian Reform 1807–1815 by Peter Paret)

30

The river Laaber divided Eichhofen and Loch. It looked like one village, but it was not. Coming from Ondorf, the road split, half went straight into Loch petering out into a muddy lane finally leading to the ancient castle tower and caves looming above. The other half curved and led across the Laaber where it split again into Eichhofen to the left and Weissenfels to the right. Just before crossing the bridge was an enormous tithe barn which had been almost empty since our arrival. We often played in there, jumping from great heights into a heap of straw which filled a corner.

One morning it had been taken over by a trek of Ukrainian refugees. About one hundred and twenty women, children, men and old people lived there now. They used the river for everything, cooked outside the big barn doors and looked as dirty and bedraggled as nothing I had seen before. Their clothing was very strange too. The women wore many skirts one over the other which made them stand out. Their jackets were well cut and intricately worked and embroidered and must once have been very beautiful, now they looked sad and worn.

The village children gathered by the bridge and hung about. Their children came and stood by the great barn doors and we watched each other. The girls wore just as many skirts as their mothers and grandmothers. They did not speak German. But there were lots of adults in that group who did. They called friendly words to us in their hard strange German accent.

The Ukrainian boys taunted us and threw stones. The girls stood shyly at the barn doors. One stone hit Beate and she ran off crying. There were not many boys in our group, and we had to decide to make a stand as girls. Gottfried still had not joined us since his accident by the river. So Bärbel, as the daughter of the Schloss, went up and told them in no uncertain words that if they wanted to play with us, they would first have to wash, and she pointed into the river. The boys looked a little stupid, but an old grandmother laughed and yelled something in her own language from where she was sitting in the doorway of the barn. There was more laughter and the boys looked embarrassed.

Bärbel turned and we followed her across the bridge and went back into Eichhofen. That afternoon, still tattered but clean and combed they came up to the Schloss. We all played in the forest and around the village, showing them some of our lesser hiding places.

These Ukrainian children were different from us. What annoyed me most, was that they kept picking their noses and wiping it into their clothes. Even though they were washed, there was something about them that made me not want to touch them. It wasn't the clothes. Ours were just as shabby. They had had a wash but still looked grubby somehow. They had lice and fleas as well. We hadn't picked up any lice yet and were grateful for that. They were constantly scratching themselves everywhere. But at least they were friendly and were not throwing stones now, and they wanted to learn to speak the way we did.

I suppose we were also cross, that we could not go into our barn to play anymore, but we realised, they had to live somewhere.

With all the refugees coming through, the Eichhofeners had been hoping they would all just pass by. When the Ukrainians took over the barn, some people were cross, including us, although we had no right to be.

We changed our playground into the castle, and explored the many caves that once were rooms. From this elevated position, we could look far into the Laaber valley, up and down upon the village. We were even high enough to see the large farm which belonged to the Schloss and was situated on top of a forested hill. It was called the *Rammelsteiner Hof* and had its origins from roman times, when Regensburg was Castra Regina, a roman fortress on the very spot where the river Regen joined the Danube. The Rammelsteiner Hof had even then been a large farm, producing and supplying food for the Romans.

What brought us closer to the Ukrainians, was their singing. We could hear it in the evening, and we came up to the barn and listened. They opened the doors and let us in. It was like a gypsy camp and very cosy. Their songs were deep with many different voices singing in harmony, sounding like bells and reminding me of the Russian prisoners in East Prussia. It was so beautiful, I never knew whether I wanted to cry or be happy. I remembered again and for the millionth time, Robert. Where was he now? His songs still haunted me. To me, people who could sing like that were special.

Day and night, soldiers passed through the village of Eichhofen. Endless. There were POW transports which came through the village on foot. There was an almost constant shuffling noise of tired feet from the refugees, soldiers and POWs. It was as if the whole world was on the move. Why did they all come through this remote little place? Were there that many people on the move *everywhere?*

There were Russians, fiercely watched by soldiers with guns. There was a tap at the bottom of our stairs, and often the convoys would stop here for water. Some of the men were short in stature and looked different from any human I had ever seen. Their eyes had a strange shape, very narrow and slanted, but they were wearing Russian uniforms. These convoys would pass the Ukrainian barn first since it was the first house at the other end of the village and the boys had followed this convoy all the way through the village, laughing and taunting them.

The Russians looked away and ignored them.

"*Wasser, Wasser*" (water) they were saying.

Shocked, I watched, as a Russian soldier bent down to pick up a raw potato which must have dropped accidently when I had carried a bucket full upstairs earlier.

The guard pushed him with the gun and stopped him picking up the potato. I couldn't work out why, and a little hesitant,

I picked it up and gave it to the man. Nobody said anything, but he looked at me, took a bite and handed it to his comrade, who also took a bite and handed it on. The man was still looking at me. I wanted to go and get more potatoes. We had plenty. But the guard stopped me, pointed with his thumb over his shoulder and said: "Verschwinde" (Get lost) and he also chased the Ukrainians down the road. They went back home.

I crossed the road, to the stacked sawn boards of the saw mill. We had our playhouses and hiding places there. I disappeared into one of them and found Bine and Tissi already there. Through the gaps we watched the poor prisoners. They were guarded more closely than any other prisoners we had seen coming through here. Bine said:

"They are Russians, the ones, Mother said, no grass would grow after they have been."

We watched them through the gaps. They looked as if they could not harm a fly. They were hungry, dirty, tired and had hardly any shoes. Well, neither did we. I would so much have liked to have a pair of shoes. Sometimes, it was as if there was nothing I wanted more, than a pair of shoes.

I felt so sorry for these men. If only we could feed them, but there were too many and their guards stood stiffly watching everything.

Suddenly there was movement among them. Mother appeared with a bucket, and a tin mug. She dipped the mug into the bucket and handed it to a prisoner. He drank it greedily. One of the guards came up to Mother, but she seemed to take no notice. Bine and I came over and helped. It was hot barley coffee with milk and lots of sugar, of which we still had plenty. *Mutter Prindl* also came downstairs with a bucket of coffee.

They hadn't all had a cup of coffee, when the soldiers yelled at them to get ready. They formed a long line to march on down the road. Mother and Mutter Prindl followed with the bucket, and Bine, Hanni, who had joined us, and I making sure that the rest would all have a cup of coffee too, while they slowly walked down the road away from the Village. They were grinning at us when the buckets were empty. As they disappeared we heard them hum a slow sad tune.

We turned back towards the smithy with the empty buckets, when there was yet another air raid with low flying planes shooting at anything that moved. We dashed down to the wooded riverside, and walked under the shelter of the trees.

There was a transport of French POWs. They were so different from the Russians. It was fascinating to see the many different nationalities. The French, even though their uniforms were dirty and torn, like everybody else's, still looked elegant. They moved gracefully, and when they accepted the coffee we offered them, they did so with a very polite, dignified bow. They spoke all the time excitedly, moving their hands a lot and laughing and speaking in French with Mother. The German guards where less strict as they had been with the Russians. It was all very polite and civilized. They were allowed to sit and rest for quite a while. One of the French POWs made a new key for Mother's box, which had been made for her in East Prussia. The old key had got bent and broken. He was clever and very quick. The smith watched him fashion the key from a little piece of iron in the forge with his tools. He made the key almost as beautiful as a piece of jewellery, it went smoothly into the lock and turned without difficulty. The other one always was hard to turn. That was why it bent and finally broke.

✻✻✻

It was May the second nineteen hundred and forty five.

A lorry load of POWs arrived and began to build anti-tank obstacles in front of the Ukrainian barn, on either side of the bridge, and at the entrances of the *Schloss Hof* (court yard)

My thoughts went back to last spring in East Prussia, when I had sat with August Kramp on that little foot bridge across the ditch with the amber coloured stones, when he told me about the anti-tank ditches he and his friends from the *Hitler Jugend* were digging. August had been so sure, that they would stop anything and keep Germany safe. It was such a long way away and even now it was not Germany any more. Overrun by Russians. (Four ancestors of my Mother's side had lived in Danzig since fifteen hundred and thirty-two, and lost their home of four hundred years, at Christmas of 1944, bringing with them a tiny herd of Trakehner horses.)

It did not feel as if I was the same person that I had been last year. A familiar awful tight feeling came back into my throat.

Nothing would stop the tanks! Who are they kidding? It seemed ridiculous! All was lost.

That evening we were told, that we had to pack our things and leave the room above the smithy and go with all the villagers to the *Rammelsteiner Hof* for safety, since the enemy would be here any day.

The smith locked his forge and led the horses and cows deep into the forest to a secret hiding place. Frau Hirsauer, Hanni's mother came out of her house. She came out very rarely. Hanni said she had 'open legs.' I could not imagine what that might be. Certainly her legs were for ever bandaged in a messy way. I never liked to go into Hanni's house, because the geese and ducks and chickens walked in and out, doing their business on top of the table, perching on the backs of chairs. It was disgusting, but Hanni didn't think it was all that strange.

They had small sacred containers by the front and backdoor with holy water hanging on the wall. The chickens which perched on the chairs were able to reach and drink the holy water. It was very odd that Lisa, who was so clean and tidy, came from this family?

All the other villagers took their cows and oxen and other animals and hid them in the thick of the forest. The few men, including the smith, all the boys from the top two classes at school and the very old men, had to assemble at the office of the Nazi village official, Herr Schröder, the very one who had insisted we continue to go to school. The villagers had to man the antitank obstacles and defend the village. They had no guns or ammunition, only pitchforks and sticks. I watched, as they slowly walked down the road. We made ready to go in the opposite direction. Even I could see that their efforts would be ridiculously futile. The Ukrainian men joined the men from the village with sticks. The rest of the Ukrainians went up to the caves in the castle.

We pulled a few of our things up the steep hill through the forest to the *Rammelsteiner Hof*.

There was really only one thing that worried me. I hoped that our stores would be safe. We couldn't take our treasure from the Ondorf warehouse with us. We carefully hid it among the rafters of the roof. Only children could find it, the space was so narrow, but I was still worried.

At the Rammelsteiner Hof we were told to go into the cellar, which was just as well. A dog fight in the sky was raging, but we didn't even watch anymore.

It was now the 4th of May. Anxious faces were everywhere. Was I afraid? I wondered. I realised I wasn't sure how I felt, except relief that soon it would all be over one way or the other.

A new noise took our attention. The adults explained they were canons in action. They would never be able to pull them up this steep hill to the *Rammelsteiner Hof*! The von Schwarzenbaers worried that they might destroy the Schloss, the brewery and the mills. Somebody said, that if there was no shooting from the villagers, they would not destroy anything. The villagers had no weapons, there were no soldiers here to defend anything.

Our gang was here, Bärbel, Hanni and her sisters, Gottfried and Hannes, Beate, Bine, Tissi and myself. There were the Rammelsteiner children too. We were nosy and wanted to know what the Americans looked like. We came up the cellar steps and peered out into the court. Nothing. Not a sound. No birds, no animal noises. It was so strange.

The buildings were arranged in a big square, with the farmhouse on one side. There were farm wagons parked under a huge overhanging roof, a long, neat row of them. We told the little ones in a whisper to stay there and we, the older ones tiptoed from wagon to wagon until we came to the last one and there we rushed on tiptoe to the wall which led to the open gate. There was still not a sound anywhere. Mothers were calling us back. Beate and Bine went back, and just as I wanted to follow Bine, Bärbel held me back.

"They are a long way away. There is no noise. Let's just have a quick look down the lane towards the forest." She followed her brothers.

My heart was thumping around in my chest, knowing that I defied Mother when she called, not knowing what I would find if I looked around the corner and down the lane.

Mother was calling again. I took no notice. I would face her later. The first time I had flouted her.

"Come on then, let's have a look" I said.

As we nosed around the corner, we saw some funny very round things, gliding up the hill, half hidden in the tall may grass, which was dotted with colourful, wild flowers. The meadow was so beautiful. We couldn't at first make out what the round things were, since they looked as if they moved on their own. Hannes said:

"Americans." The nearest round thing bopped up. There was a face underneath it. He came up on one knee and pointed a gun at us.

"Don't move", he said in dreadful German, but we just turned and ran towards the cellar. Gottfried and Bärbel yelled:

"They are here, they are here", and we all stumbled down the stairs and waited, out of breath. We waited a very long time, nothing happened. We could hear voices but saw nothing. All the mothers were looking at each other, wondering what was happening.

Suddenly, hesitantly the Americans appeared at the top of the stairs, some of them holding candles, others pointing their guns at us, making us all stand up against the wall. Others moved quickly through the cellar to make sure nobody was hidden anywhere, their guns constantly covering us. They found everybody's suitcases and boxes, kicked them open and spilled everything inside onto the floor. They picked up a few things here and there, looked at them and put them into their pockets.

I wondered where Mother had put the silver. If they found that, it would be gone.

One of them, with a red scarf round his neck, came over and put his hand into our box, got hold of a blanket, pulled it up and threw everything onto the floor. With his feet he kicked it around, found nothing he wanted and walked on. Another one came over to where we still stood at gunpoint and said something to Mother. She pretended not to understand English.

31

The liberators had arrived. Robert and Josef had both said that all would be well when the Americans came. There would be peace. They are a civilized, cultured people.

I looked at them with interest. They carried their helmets at an audacious tilt and were chewing all the time. What were they chewing? They popped nothing into their mouths. Their behaviour was raucous and drunken. Mother said they were drunk with victory. They did not look very civilised to me. The way they were chewing and looking at us was offensive.

They walked around the cellar, kicking doors open with their rifle butts or their feet. They bullied the women, touching them and talking to them and then when they didn't understand, they poked them rudely into the chest. They were mostly fat. Their uniform stretched over their bodies, far too tightly. Their buttocks were plump and well rounded, with not a millimetre to spare in their trousers. They were a funny sight when they walked.

They told us to go up into the farmyard. Mother hastily piled all our things back into our box and closed the lid. The sun was brilliant and warm. Most of the Americans left again by the opposite end from where they had entered, only a few guards remained.

The rest of the afternoon we played and sat around. Later, Mother gave us some milk and took out a loaf of bread, which she had baked before we came up here and we each had a round with some milk. That night we slept in the cellar on some straw.

The farmers from Thimsdorf herded their cattle back from the forest in the night. We didn't get much sleep.

Next day, Mother sat on the shaft of a hay wain and waited, the three of us standing close, watching. Two or three Americans stood at a distance, guns ready, some young village girls giggling with them.

Two jeeps screeched into the yard, spraying dust everywhere. Americans clambered out and started to mill around. The soldier that had spilled our things in the cellar came over to Mother.

"You are a very nice lady" he said in English, but Mother pretended not to understand. He stood close and touched her. Mother brushed his hand away. In German she said that she did not understand what he said. He fetched his wallet from his pocket and showed her a photograph. In German he said:

"You understand?" Mother nodded, blushing.

"I understand." The American continued in German:

"You much understand" and walked away. I didn't understand at all.

He climbed into his jeep and kept driving past, taunting us, whirling dust and making us choke. In big circles he drove about, every time he passed he yelled: "Deutschland Deutschland unter alles." After a while he stopped the jeep. He came over and held something out to us. I looked at Mother, and she gave no sign. I shook my head at the soldier and said:

"Nein danke" (no thank you). He offered it to Bine and Tissi too, but they also declined with a curtsey. He then spat at Mother and said again:

"Deutschland, Deutschland *unter* alles" and walked away, swinging his bottom, throwing himself back into the jeep with one foot on the dashboard.

What did I expect? After all, these were the men who, a few days ago had been shooting at us, the men I watched in the plane laughing while they aimed at us. They were not friendly.

I watched him, as he slowly circled in the yard, looking at the other people. There were several ladies from the Schloss. He stopped the jeep and walked over to one of them. He kicked her in the bottom and yelled: "*Essen, Fleisch, Kartoffeln, halbe Stunde, oder*" (eat, meat, potatoes, half an hour or) and he made the sign of cutting her throat. I realised with relief, that Mother got away lightly.

We slept in the straw again that night, quietly. What will the future be? I was still alive, so there would be a future. What will the Americans do now? What will happen? I was worried. This was a very new feeling. I had not consciously been concerned or frightened about the future before.

There was no food at the farm. The Americans had taken all the milk and all the eggs. The bread had gone the same way. The little we brought was finished. After three days of waiting and being hungry, the villagers trickled back one by one. When Frau Hirsauer made ready to leave, we too got ready. It would be good to get back to our little room. Maybe there was news of Grandfather too. We had sent messages to each other via the von Schwarzenbaers every now and then, when they went into Regensburg.

I even started to think, that now we could all go home. At the thought of going back to Berlin, I almost choked. It would be so good, to be going home.

As we put all our stuff back onto Grandfather's little cart, I asked Mother if we could now go back to Berlin. The war surely was over now. She shook her head.

"There is nothing to go back to, all is rubble and ash. Nothing but rubble and ash. Anyway the Russians are in Berlin. The war is not over yet, not for a long time."

I quickly put it all out of my mind. I didn't want to think about it now. Some other time. We would go back home eventually. People always go home in the end. We would too.

The way back to the village was much easier than when we had to pull the cart up the steep hill. I picked wild meadow flowers, to put onto our table in our room. A festive homecoming, a celebration. I asked Mother where she had hidden the silver, since the American had not found it in the box. She said it was in the box all along, only it was under the blanket he pulled. Had he put his hand deeper than the blanket, he would have found it, as it was, when he pulled up the blanket, he just missed the silver. Mother grinned and said.

"Somehow that clot wasn't supposed to have our silver." I laughed back and skipped a few paces. We would cook a wonderful meal. We would lay a festive table, even put on a tablecloth. A sheet or something would do as a tablecloth. Pancakes? "Yes," Mother said "we will have pancakes, and we shall open one of those tins too." Of course, it would be a surprise meal, since we could not tell what was in the tins. The pancakes would fall to pieces since we had no eggs or milk. Flour, water and salt and oil off course, were the only ingredients we had to make pancakes with. But it would still be delicious.

As we emerged from the forest, we could see in the distance a lot of Americans milling around the saw mill and the smithy. There were army lorries and little jeeps parked everywhere. We had to wait a very long time outside in the road, before we were finally allowed to enter the smithy and go upstairs.

The room was a terrible mess. There was nothing there that was of any value. But the soldiers had thrown the cooking pot and the few plates on the floor, the beds were all undone, the straw sacks emptied and the straw on the floor. Americans were still moving in and out as if it was their place, laughing as though it was all a joke. I didn't dare check in our hiding place whether our food treasure was still intact. The worry continued.

Survival meant fighting for one's life, worrying, not just for myself, but Bine and Tissi and Mother. I busied myself putting the straw back into the sacks, asking Bine to help. She said she wanted to check on the food, and get things ready for the meal. Bine was hungry. I stole a look at the Americans. They were watching us, and under pretence of being very busy with the straw, I said to Bine that we must not let them know there is any food. They must not know about our treasure. They will take it away from us. We cannot do any cooking while they are around.

Mother started a fire and put water in the large potato pot to the boil. She did not ask us to fetch any food from the hiding place. Instead she told me to go down to the Laaber and wash potatoes in the big bucket. Bine and I went off to get the potatoes.

So, after all that, we would again have potatoes and salt. Where would we get new plates? No celebration. The Americans were crazily rushing around on their jeeps. The road was not safe. They whirled their jeeps around, their feet on the windscreen or on the front mud guards chewing and chewing. Bine wanted to know what they were chewing. I suggested maybe they chewed their tongues? We tried it, but it wasn't pleasant.

We knelt on our little platform at the river and scrubbed the potatoes. The bucket was almost done, when I saw some Americans coming down to the river about twenty metres upstream from where we were washing the potatoes. They were in a very happy mood and laughing and hopping around. Then I saw one of them throw something into the river. It made 'plop' with a little splash.

The American soldiers dropped down onto the ground and put their arms around their heads. Next the river went up into the air with a most frightful explosion. Bine and I fell over, got entirely drenched and nearly swept away by a huge wave and lost the bucket with all the potatoes. My nose was bleeding, so was Bine's, and there was blood coming out of Bine's ear. She was crying hysterically and ran back to the smithy.

There were dozens and dozens of fish, belly up, floating in the river. Laughing their heads off, the Americans fished out a few large ones with a net and let the rest float away, down the river.

Mother came running to see where I was. She shot the blackest look at the Americans and one of them looked at her and tipped his helmet. It was the one that had touched her at the Rammelsteiner Hof. He was a callous monster, I decided.

I cried, unable to stop. I didn't feel embarrassed that I cried, and I sobbed:

"All the potatoes are gone!"

Mother said:

"When you finish crying, go and wash another pot of potatoes. I shall bake some bread now." I cried more than ever because now I had to wash another bucket full of potatoes. It was all too much. I didn't want to go on. I just wanted to go to bed, not hear or see anybody. I hated everybody.

"I don't want any food, I just want to go to bed." I said.

"So do we all." she said. "Where would we be, if we just did what we wanted? Even if you are not hungry, your sisters are." My nose had stopped bleeding, but Bine's hadn't. So I went down again, found another bucket in the smithy and filled it with potatoes and dragged it back to the river. I was still crying. It felt good to cry, I didn't want to stop but at the same time I didn't want the Americans to see that I was crying. Why did Josef have to die? I wished he was here now, helping me wash the potatoes. It was safe when he was around. He was good and kind. He had a soul. The Americans did not.

Worn out and tired, I dragged the bucket upstairs. Mother put the potatoes into the pot where the water was already bubbling and boiling. Some water she had taken off and poured it onto some herb tea. Now she filled some cups and put some sugar into it and handed me a cup of the hot and steaming tea. It smelled delicious. She put an arm around me and gave me a kiss and a cuddle.

"Meine Grosse" she said. (My big girl) But I still couldn't stop crying. Would I ever? I went over and finished stuffing my bed with the rest of the straw and lay down on it. I didn't wake up until the next day.

The sun was shining through the little windows and made a pattern on the floor. I could hear the big bellows down below our room. The smith was busy already. I wondered what the time was when the door opened and Mother came in. She normally got up at five in the morning and went straight into the Schloss garden, to start her day. She would be back home by about seven to make breakfast. So it must be seven, I thought.

Mother came over and asked how I felt. I said I was still tired. I also had a headache. My head felt heavy. I let myself fall back onto my straw sack. I then realised that Bine and Tissi were not in their beds.

Mother said that it was afternoon. Would I like some lunch? They had had theirs, they had had pancakes.

"Did I sleep through all that?" I asked her. Mother smiled at me.

"We were as quiet as mice, not to wake you. It was all a bit too much for you. I am to blame. I asked too much of you. Now you must have a little rest." It was wonderfully cosy. The door to the outside was shut, Mother made pancakes. She opened the little window. The birds had come back. They were singing in the trees again. I found it amazing, but they had disappeared, where, was a mystery. But now they were back and their song was glorious. I remembered in Regensburg, even after a terrible raid, the winter birds still sang. So what had made the birds go away this time? Mother had no answer either. The circular saw was singing monotonously and the traffic sounded so distant. There was such peace, and a warm feeling stole into my heart. There would be no more raids. Aloud to Mother, I said:

"Will there still be air raids now? Will they still shoot at us?" Mother shook her head and came over to sit on the side of my bed.

"That is all finished. Now they find the people who they think are responsible for the war. A lot of guilty people, hopefully all the guilty people will be prosecuted and locked up for good or even be executed, but there will also be some innocents who will forfeit their lives. And a lot of the really guilty are probably no longer in Germany. Many people, who could have stopped the war in the beginning, but let it happen either through arrogance and greed or sheer ignorance will also not be punished. They will push their guilt into the shoes of others and they also exist among our enemies, and they will always be our enemy." She smiled at me. "This is all too difficult for you to understand. Don't worry your little heart over it. In the end all will be well. There are good and just men everywhere. Unfortunately they are mostly shouted down by rowdies. The world is also full of rowdies." She tucked the cover over me and gave me a kiss and got ready to leave the room.

We were really very happy here above the smithy, except for one thing, the flies. Herr Hirsauer's cow and horse manure was piled up close to the smithy's big entrance door, not far below our window. Now that it was warm the flies appeared in millions and millions. Nothing could be left, we had to fish for flies every time we ate anything. It was a plague, such as I had never encountered before.

Lying in my bed now, the flies tried constantly to sit on my face. It was unbearable. As Mother went to the door she said that one does get used to them. For now there was nothing we could do about them and there was no use grizzling about them either.

I put a sheet over my head, and soon I was asleep again.

The smell of burnt porridge woke me up. I got out of bed and pushed the pot over to the side and closed the hole with the rings to keep the fire in. I put the porridge quickly into a bowl, so that the burnt taste would not spoil the entire porridge. I took the pot and went downstairs to put some cold water into it to soak it. Then I wondered where everybody was. In my nightdress, I went over to the door and looked out. There were American army trucks and many German soldiers, who were now prisoners of war, loading wood onto the trucks. Was it only last week, when there were German soldiers watching over Russian and French soldiers doing just what the Germans were doing now? I went back to my pot, picked up a little bit of wood from the woodworking shop and started to scratch at the burnt bits. I thought it was only fair, that the Germans were now the prisoners. That was the way any game was played. War must be a game adults play. A grim game.

Mother came rushing in and tearing up the stairs, worried about the porridge. I called after her, that I had pulled the pot off the fire. She had quickly rushed out to collect some scrap wood from the saw mill for cooking, when the American with the red scarf had held her up again. Mother was red in the face and furious. The American had followed her and was standing in the doorway, saying things in frightful German, and coming closer in a dipping walk. Mother said to me:

"Leave the pot to soak and come on upstairs. You must have your breakfast." As I rushed upstairs, she put an arm over my shoulders and led me across the loft to our room.

"I don't have to bear his dirty insinuations. I don't have to put up with his hands all over me. Does he think that German women are whores?"

There had been a lot of talk about conquering armies raping women. Exactly what raping was, I couldn't imagine, but it was something women were very afraid of.

"Do soldiers rape children?" I asked Mother.

"No, of course not, where do you get such stories from?" she asked me. I told her that I had just heard it around. People talk.

"You mustn't believe everything you hear, country people are full of old wives tales." Mother said.

"I shall protect you," I said. "I shall go out and fetch all the things you need. That American shall not see you again and when you have to go to the Schloss garden, I shall come with you." Mother put her arms around me and squeezed me, lovingly.

"That won't be necessary. I can handle him, it is just that he makes me feel so cheap." Mother smiled.

"I suppose that is part of being defeated by the enemy. As far as they are concerned, we are all guilty, and they can do with us as they please. Now get dressed and fetch your sisters, I think they are still on the loo. They have been there for a long time. Then we can have some breakfast."

I slipped on my clothes and went over to the loo. They were both sitting there, legs apart, letting wood shavings sail down into the Laaber, and watching the exquisite curls until they floated out of sight, forgetting all time.

Finally the Americans left the saw mill, and everything was very still. It was strange, how quickly this little village fell back into being a very remote spot. No one was in sight. The smith was busy, and the saw mill whined, somebody was sharpening a scythe nearby. The ding-e-ling noise it made sounded like a little bell. Mother had sent Bine and myself to fetch some young dandelions, nettle tops and sorrel to make into a vegetable. With a sweet flour sauce, it tasted very nice and made a difference to potatoes and salt. She boiled them quickly, then chopped them like spinach and left them on the side while she made the sauce. We all loved it.

Hanni came after lunch, and we decided it was safe enough to go back to playing. We hadn't played for days. We sat outside the smithy and watched the world, talked about what had happened and wondered about when school would start again.

Suddenly there was a dreadful engine noise, two jeeps came to a screeching halt. One of the Hirsauer chickens was run over by a crazy army truck. It was horrible to watch. American soldiers poured out and went over to Mutter Prindl's chicken shed. They entered the little enclosure and rattled on the door and excited clucking chickens came rushing out of their little trapdoor, trying to escape through the chicken wire fence, only to be caught by the soldiers, who twisted their necks and made them go limp. Their frightened noise was terrible. Then when they had most of Mutter Prindl's chickens, laughing so much, they could hardly stand straight, they shot at the door with their guns, splintering it and ripping off the padlock. They walked in, filled their helmet with all her eggs and left.

Crying and throwing up her arms, Mutter Prindl came rushing down the stairs, asking the smith to help. But the Americans had gone and Herr Hirsauer just shook his head and lifted his shoulders.

Hanni, Bine and I went over with Mutter Prindl to find out how many chickens there were left. There was one only. Mutter Prindl was in a dreadful state. "This poor chicken will never lay again. It would only be good for the pot." Hanni said, that there were chickens of theirs brooding in the hedge between their kitchen back door and the river, and the Americans would never find them. When they are hatched, Mutter Prindl could have some, free.

"You are a good girl." She went upstairs and wiped her tears with her apron. Hanni and I went down to where we wash the potatoes and dangled our feet into the Laaber. The water was getting warm, just right for a swim.

✳✳✳

32

Beautiful, warm and sunny days followed. Our gang had slowly gathered again, and we all played around the village, in the castle and among the stacked sawn wood from the saw mill. The trees were in bloom, the wild flowers had so many different colours. Even in East Prussia I couldn't remember so many varieties. Mother explained, that even though we thought it was warm in East Prussia, the climate was much harsher there. Here in the south of Germany, spring and summer came much earlier, the flowers had more time to grow and many more species would survive.

I had a passion for these wild flowers, and every day I picked some so that we had fresh flowers on our table all the time. I marvelled at the many colours and the beautiful and varied shapes. I put various different grasses in amongst them. For a vase I used an empty tin from our store.

Those tins were of many uses. In the smithy we converted them to cups and containers. From the lids the smith crafted crude little pots and pans for his daughters and for us, to use as crockery for our playhouses which we had amongst the stacked wood piles.

One of the Hirsauer chickens was run over by a crazy army truck. It was horrible to watch it die.

Hannes came running down the road from the castle, and told us that he had found many empty petrol cans. Nobody wanted them. The Americans had dumped them. If we tied them together, we could swim with them.

We dropped everything, and ran up the road to the Schloss. Behind the flourmill and brewery, where the weir and the lock was, the river gathered into a deep pool, and the excess water spilled over.

Often, we had waded across the slippery weir which we used as a shortcut to go to Loch from the Schloss. There had been a narrow footbridge not so long ago, but it had fallen into the river during one of the many raids. Now one could only walk on the remainder of the bridge to the far end of the lock. Climbing down over the hinge, if one didn't mind the slimy moss, one could reach the weir. Coming back was more difficult, because one had to climb up the slippery pole and wall to reach the hinge.

In the Schloss Hof we found about a dozen large petrol canisters. Copying Hannes, we clicked down the little lids and tied the handles together, two at a time, got undressed and dragged the cans over to the water.

Hannes showed us how to do it. He floated the cans in front of him in the water, and then carefully slid into the water, placing the upper part of his body in the middle of the tied cans. With his arms he pulled himself well up, so that really only his legs dangled in the water. Then he paddled himself about on the water. It looked like great fun.

Carefully, the less afraid followed him into the water. Bine and Beate wanted to come too, but were unsure of themselves. They hoped they could share with somebody. But until I knew exactly what I was doing, I couldn't take Bine.

Bärbel wasn't sure either, if she should join us or not. She pretended to be busy with her cans for all the time we were in the water. Bine and Beate begged constantly, dangling their feet in the water and splashing impatiently.

Gottfried couldn't join anyway. Because of his condition he couldn't swim. I felt sorry for him. He said, that soon, when things are better and back to normal, he would get a better device, and then he would be able to swim too.

We stayed in the water until I couldn't hold on to the cans for cold. My teeth were chattering, nobody could talk because our jaws were stiff with cold. We carefully hid the precious petrol canisters, and then went down to the saw mill, where it was very warm among the boards. I loved the smell of the saw mill. The freshly cut wood had a delicious scent of resin.

Soon we were warm again and Hannes said he wanted to go back to do some more swimming. We all got up and followed him down the road to the Schloss, but when we got there, the sun had disappeared behind the brewery and the water looked black and forbidding. Nobody wanted to go back in.

Instead, we crossed the weir and roamed around in the castle above the village. We climbed up to the very top of the hill, which was the ceiling of the castle.

There, with the heat of the day reflecting back from the hill, the ground, the grasses, everything feeling warm and soft and smelling of earth, I found a beautiful little flower, which I hadn't seen before. It was a blue-violet, very hairy bell, opening out into the sun on a very straight stem (Pasque Flower). I touched the soft fur of the flower. It resembled an anemone. Bärbel said it was a cowbell. To me it looked like the velveteen evening gown of a fairy princess.

Finally, we came down the steep hill to the river, just opposite the smithy. There was no bridge here, and to get back we would have to go along down river to the weir. Being lazy, we sat down in the afternoon sun and dangled our feet in the river.

Hannes thought it would be really clever if we could collect many petrol cans, tie them all together and make a bridge across the river.

We all thought it was a great idea when suddenly many Lorries and tanks stopped opposite, outside the smithy. Lots of American soldiers spilled out of the Lorries and unloaded some huge barrels and rolled them down to the river. We thought they were bombs and wanted to go into hiding.

The Americans waved to us and made friendly signs. Their faces were new, their uniform slightly different from the other Americans we had become accustomed to. The one with the red scarf was not among them either.

These men began to roll the enormous barrels into the water, secured them with rope to stakes which they had knocked into the soft meadow ground, then they put large sheets of metal segments down, leading from the road to the river, and backed a lorry down on top of it. The causeway and bridge they built was wider than the road itself. From the back of the lorry they got more sheets and barrels, and bit by bit they built a floating bridge. We watched with great interest.

Hannes seemed to know all about it. He said that a General had been to see his mother and now they were building this bridge. It was a pontoon bridge, he explained. They had to transport something really big, which would not pass through the gates at the Schloss Hof, without demolishing part of the brewer's living quarters.

When the bridge was finished, one of the Americans came over and said in strange German, that he wanted us to be the first to use the new bridge. Shyly and confused, we got up and followed him. He was a friendly man, and so were his comrades. These soldiers were also people!

Then I spotted a black man amongst them. Ali! My heart made a leap, but I realised my mistake and felt disappointed. He was black, but his face was quite different from Ali's. I didn't know that there were black Americans. I suddenly realised, that all the children were staring at him, and the soldiers laughed. The black man came over and took something out of his pocket. His big lips opened up, revealing many very white teeth and a very pink tongue. In his black hand he held a long, round tubular package, and when he took the lid off, some brightly coloured disks slid out. He held them out to us, and said something. I didn't know what they were, but they had a mouth-watering smell. None of us knew what to do with them. The soldier who had led us across the bridge, said encouragingly:

"Essen" (eat) and with his finger he pointed into his mouth. I took a bright red one and put it into my mouth. It tasted delicious and pepperminty. One by one Hannes, Gottfried, Bine, Beate and Bärbel, Hanni who hadn't been with us but had joined us with Tissi, took one with a *danke* and a curtsey or a bow. The black man had dropped down onto his knees and had great fun watching us chew these thin and brittle disks. From inside the doors, the smith was watching. I wasn't sure if we should have accepted these sweets, but these men were quite different from the other soldiers, who we had first met, nearly two weeks ago now.

The black man got up now and gave us a gentle shove towards the smithy, and we all left slowly and still confused and wondering what had happened to the other Americans. Where had they disappeared to? Would they come back? We all hoped they wouldn't.

Hannes, who knew everything, explained, that with conquering armies the rule was, that they send ex-convicts and ruffians to do the combatting and hard fighting, and when all the danger was over, they withdraw them and sent in the next batch, who were usually much nicer, friendlier and more civilized.

Well, if that was true, the rough and unfriendly soldiers had left and if the Americans were as nice as these men, life may be ok.

I was getting hungry. It must be nearly evening. I went upstairs but Mother hadn't come home from the Schloss garden yet. So I went down and filled the bucket with potatoes. I noticed, that the heap of potatoes was getting very low. Would we get some more? Would we have to cut down on how many potatoes we could eat a day?

I went down to the river and washed the potatoes. I watched the soldiers at the pontoon bridge. They had difficulty getting a really large vehicle across. From the meadow to the bridge was a sudden drop and they tried to overcome that with thick planks from the saw mill, but they had splintered badly.

I could see that this big thing would be far too big to pass through the village and across the road bridge at the other end of Eichhofen by the Ukrainian's barn. The bridge was only just wide enough for the milk lorry. But then this vehicle would not fit through Loch either. They would never make it, I decided, but they did. The Ukrainian children had gathered on the Loch side and were following the thing all the way through Loch and watched as it inched past their barn, and finally joined the road to Ondorf. I never found out what it was. The villagers guessed for days what it could have been, but in the end, all were convinced that the thing contained some very special and lethal bombs.

I finished washing the potatoes, took them upstairs and found that the fire had gone out. I went down again, filled our sack with bits of waste wood and shavings from the saw mill and went up again to light the fire. I asked Bine and Tissi to fill the pot with water from the tap downstairs.

They came back with Mother, who was late and I could see, had been crying. Now that the war had finished, what could have happened?

I went over and stood in front of her, waiting. I told her I had washed the potatoes and relit the fire. She still said nothing. She sat down and looked at a spot on the floor, tears were running down on top of her nose and dripping onto her lap. I took a corner of the apron she was wearing and wiped them off.

"Onkel Kurt is dead and Tante Guste and Hannele and Bärbele. They died nearly a month ago now. Exactly the day is not known. They were found by Kurt's secretary, a few days after they had died. They are buried in their garden." Mother collapsed completely. Bine stood completely still, and stared with her huge black eyes at Mother. Tissi's little face was screwed up, but she wasn't crying.

I went over and put the potatoes on. Onkel Kurt always meant home, stability, and family to me. Going back home had meant being close to Onkel Kurt and Tante Guste. Where was Hermännle? Where was his brother Kurt? Was he still in a French prison camp? Did they know? I couldn't ask Mother now. She was quietly crying, and my throat was getting painfully tight. It was all so hopeless, so utterly hopeless.

I laid the table. I had to tell Mother about the potato pile getting low. I went downstairs and picked nettles, dandelion and sorrels. I washed the greens in the river and went upstairs again. On the stairs Hanni came and said she had heard the news about my uncle. Everything in the village was known within a very short time. She offered to take me to Weissenfels after supper, there would be a *Mai Andacht* (May service) and I could pray for my uncle and his family. I said I would come.

I lifted the lid and threw the greens into the boiling water on top of the potatoes. On the remaining corner of the stove I made the sauce for the vegetables.

My mind was constantly on Onkel Kurt, Tante Guste, Hannele and Bärbel. How could they all be dead, together, no one surviving? It was terrible. I wondered how many dead people there were in Germany. I thought it was strange, that we all still lived? I had a longing feeling, that it would have been much better if we too had died. What did I want in this place? Whom did I really know and love, apart from the four of us and Grandfather? Everybody I knew and loved was either dead or lost. Thinking about them hurt so much. Where was my father? We had had no news from him since 1942. Was he alive or dead? Where was my brother? Did he live? There was envy in my heart for Onkel Kurt and his family. They *were* at peace.

I fished the green from the top of the potatoes with a fork and chopped them on a big board, which I had found in the saw mill. The flour sauce had turned lumpy, and no amount of stirring got it smooth. Tissi would grumble. She hated lumps. I put portions onto our plates and put the food in front of everybody. Mother said a prayer, and we all tried to eat, but we couldn't. I didn't feel hungry, and the food tasted awful.

Hanni knocked on the door, was I ready? Mother nodded and said I could go. She would do the dishes. She thanked me for doing the cooking and gave me a kiss.

"At least they are all safe now." she said. I knew what she meant. I left with Hanni to go to Weissenfels, feeling lost and lonely, and somehow wished I too could be safe.

✸✸✸

33

Frau von Schwarzenbaer came to the forge and spoke with Mother. The talk helped her to overcome the loss of Onkel Kurt and his family.

She invited us to come up to the Schloss for a special Sunday service. They were protestant like us and had their own private chapel there. We often joined them for services. Mother was grateful.

The following Sunday, we four walked to the Schloss, dressed as best we could. Hanni came too, even though she was a catholic and said she would have to confess the sin of going to our service. I looked at her, puzzled. I asked her how it could possibly be a sin, since it is the same God we worshipped. I was sure I didn't sin, going to her service.

She said it didn't matter anyway, because the sin would be forgiven.

It was a beautiful service, remembering Onkel Kurt, Tante Guste, Bäbele and Hannele. There were flowers for all of them. It was good, that there were people who cared, even for that brief moment. A few weeks ago, all these people were total strangers.

Percy Waeger and Helja spoke to Mother and put their arms around her. They were concerned. Since we left Berlin, there had been very few people who had done that to her and she was moved by their caring gesture.

I ran off, down to the river. I could not bear it any longer. I didn't want to cry anymore. Bärbel came running after me. She was really much nicer than I had first thought. Although she was spoilt and silly, and made a big thing about being the daughter from the Schloss, but, when everything came to a head, one could rely on her.

We walked together down the road, past the smithy and up the trail that led to the Rammelsteiner Hof. At the edge of the forest in the meadow was the little well. I loved this spot. The crystal clear water came welling out of the ground, very fine sand covered the bottom and delicious herbs, which I loved to chew, grew on the side. The water tasted sweet. Little creatures lived here. To see them one had to be very still and wait for a long time. Bärbel and I lay down on our tummies and looked into the water. Neither of us had spoken since we left the Schloss. Quietly we watched. A little newt appeared, then another. Lots of spiders rushed around on top of the water. Amazingly, their feet didn't sink into it. It seemed as if they stood in minute little bowls.

Suddenly, I felt something on the back of my hand and as my eyes slid over to see what it was, I discovered a tiny, most exquisitely shaped lizard. He was like a jewel. His colour was grey, but also golden and green. He was so beautiful. I felt so honoured, that he should have chosen to sun himself on my hand, or had he arrived there by accident? I barely breathed. Bärbel too had seen him, and slowly she moved closer. For a few more seconds he sat there, looking around with his most wonderful aureolin eyes, and then he disappeared so fast, that I didn't even feel him go. It was almost as if he hadn't been.

We could hear the bells from Weissenfels and Thimsdorf. Heavy and massive sounds mingled with light and happy, tingling ones, rolling across the forest in waves like the wind rippling a cornfield.

Mass for the Catholics was over. It must be midday. I rolled over onto my back and looked up at the sky through the grasses around my head. A buzzard was slowly circling above, wings not moving at all, just riding the air. Oh, could I fly! I would fly home. But where was home now?

Bärbel said she would have to be back for lunch at the Schloss.

I didn't want to go back to people, but I couldn't let Mother down. Who did she have apart from the three of us, and Grandfather?

Bärbel sat up and looked at me and told me about the people that had died in her family. There were quite a number, and not all had died in the war. She said, that even though she felt very sad, she didn't feel sad for long. She said that I too would not feel so sad in a little while. I told her about all the people who had died in my family, and that no one knew where my father was.

She knew what I meant. Her father wasn't home either, but she had heard from him.

I still felt, as if I would never be happy again. I looked at Bärbel. She may have been younger than I was, but she was also wise. There and then we promised each other eternal friendship for ever and ever. Strangely, I felt better after that. It was good to have such a friend.

Slowly, we went back when we saw Mother, Hanni, Bine and Tissi walking down the road towards the smithy. We all arrived at the same time. Mother was smiling and said, that in the evening there would be a concert at the Schloss, Helja and Percy would play the piano. A performance in the music room. Bärbel waved and ran home. "See you tonight" she shouted as she ran.

The people from the Schloss filled the music room that evening, and for me it was my very first live concert which I experienced.

There were two pianos in the room, and Percy and Helja played together. They announced the name of the composer, Anton Dvorak. Even the name sounded musical, I repeated it, Dvorak. And then they played. It felt as if music could talk, trying to tell me something, only I couldn't understand it. It was a language I hadn't learned to understand yet, except maybe that it spoke directly to my heart. My heart, I think, understood, because I felt strangely happy. It said to me that there is far more in this life than everyday misery and sadness. There is something which is above the awful thing that people do to people.

With a happy little smile Helja introduced something else by another composer. His name was Frederic Chopin. It was a happy, dancing piece. Helja played it in such a way, that I could almost see her dance to it. When I closed my eyes I saw elves on flowers floating and dancing; only in my imagination. In reality, I had never seen elves because I am so big and they are shy and small.

A Piano Concerto by Ludwig van Beethoven was next. This was music which would always be with me, would be a part of my life. His music especially.

I closed my eyes. I could understand and hear better with my eyes closed. The music had colour. It was a miracle, when I closed my eyes the music I heard was colour.

Percy and Helja read their music from a book with very mysterious signs. These signs made no sense to me.

Afterwards, Mother promised, that she would see to it that I would learn an instrument and had music lessons, when school began again. Probably not the piano, because that would be too expensive to buy, but something small.

"We will see." she said.

❋❋❋

Things became really quiet now. Hardly any refugees, apart from a few stragglers. Soldiers on their way home, pushing little carts with very few possessions. Mostly they were ordinary soldiers released from prison camp, or from field hospitals, limping, bandaged and on crutches. It seemed that there was always one amongst them with only one leg or one arm. Incredible how they could walk such distances with only one leg, but they were going home!

And there were some stealing home in disguise during darkness of the night.

Most of them came in for a drink from the tap by the smithy door. Often we would share a meal with some of them. They would stop and ask where the road led to, and we would ask if they had eaten and the answer was always: "No."

Happy for the company we invited them up. We never had anything other than potatoes to eat. Either as a potato salad, or with homemade cottage cheese and wild chives, or just in their jackets, or as a stew. There were endless different ways of having potatoes. Our flour had come to an end.

I had begged some chicken wheat from Hanni, who let me have a bag every now and then, although nobody was allowed to know that she had given it to me. Bine and I put the wheat through the coffee mill, and Mother baked bread with it. It was very hard work to grind the wheat with the coffee mill. I held the mill between my knees with all my strength, and Bine had to hold it down with her hands as well as I turned the handle.

Mother always asked where the *Landser* (vagrants) as we called them, were headed and where they came from. What company they used to belong to.

They told us about their time in the army, where they fought, their anguish with the Nazi Regime and Hitler. How they hoped that such a man, in whatever disguise, would never be able to come to power over the German people again, or for that matter any people or nation. Most of them could not understand how he ever became leader in the first place. There were many arguments as to how he achieved it. One even said, that if the art critics in Vienna, some of whom were of the Jewish elite, had given him a chance, he might have become a famous artist. The world would then have been a better place.

I thought that was strange. How can anyone be either an artist, or an oppressor and warmonger?

Desperately some wanted to know what they themselves should have done to stop this madness! But what can an ordinary, simple soldier do, except take orders and do the best for his fatherland? One would be shot for insubordination if one didn't.

These discussions went on and on. To me they went round in circles. It always started at the same spot and finished at the same spot. The keywords were 'Nazis, Gestapo and Hitler'.

Listening to them, I came to realise, that grown up men were strange. When the soldiers talked, I felt distinctly, that they had also enjoyed parts of the war. They talked excitedly as if it had been a great adventure, a game, which they enjoyed.

"Some of it I wouldn't have missed for anything," some of them said.

It was no adventure for me. Just a nightmare. And war was a game that adults played.

The news of Germany, which they brought to us in this quiet little village, was terrible. These lost wanderers had been coming in from the east, from the west, using little unknown roads through sleepy valleys, just like ours had become again. We could hardly believe what they had seen, what they were telling us. How utterly destroyed the land was. They also found that their families where not where they had left them. Having got home, they could not even make out the street were they had lived, there were no officials, no offices, no papers, no neighbours, nothing. There was a new word which was used all the time now, *Der Zusammenbruch* (Collapse)

Dates of events were now counted as before the collapse and after the collapse.

Under the circumstances, we still enjoyed these cosy peaceful times, when we had guests from the road. Mother had produced something else, which she got from the Ondorf warehouse. A huge roll of leaf tobacco. She always produced a few leaves when the table was cleared, and the faces of the visitors would light up and laughingly, they would ask: "Where did you get that precious stuff from?"

On a board from the saw mill, now named the tobacco board, they cut the leaves into fine shreds, and then rolled them into a carefully trimmed piece of paper from the roll which also came from the warehouse. Some had a pipe. But all were quiet, when they began to puff. It was like a ritual.

They always did something in return for us, like mending the ancient iron, or the little immersion heater, which hadn't worked since East Prussia. One of the men even built a radio for Mother in an old cigar box. It only received a weak signal from the local station but it was better than nothing at all. On Sunday mornings we could now listen to beautiful music. We could also hear the news, and they read long lists of names of lost people, people looking for one another. We always sat around the radio and listened intently to the crackling voice, hoping to hear familiar names.

There was no end to the things these clever men would do. They made *Klapper Sandalen* for the three of us. These were sandals made with wooden soles which they cut and shaped in the woodworking shop downstairs from scrap wood. The soles were then cut into three pieces and held together with canvas or leather, and when one walked, they rattled. That is why they were called rattle sandals. They were the envy in the village.

Our stores were dangerously low, but we always stretched what there was and enjoyed great company. They were grateful for anything which passed as food in our room, and also for the little rest and shelter.

We were coming home from the Whitsun service at the Schloss, when Mother thought we could go for a walk through the forest to remember our last Whitsun walk in East Prussia.

Four German soldiers were walking just behind us, pushing a cart, 'country-road-friendly-adaptable-cart' they called it. It was a rickety thing with four different size wheels for a start. I thought it a miracle that it didn't fall to pieces, even on the short stretch to the smithy.

We invited them home instead of having our walk and went back to prepare a Whitsun feast. They had 'acquired' eggs, which they would have cooked that evening somewhere. We even had a little cake. Mother made a big bowl of potato salad from potatoes we had cooked previously.

At the 'Collapse', the four of them were stationed at the Hungarian border in a field hospital, where they had worked. They had walked all the way since then. One of them looked very strange to me, but it was impolite to stare. In the end I had to know. I whispered to Mother and she laughed. "Yes one of them is a girl" she said. They all laughed at that and explained to us, that to save her from the 'Amis', they had put her into men's uniform and give her a man's haircut. She was a field hospital nurse, two of the men were doctors and one was a chemist. They were headed for Hanover and home. Such a long way. From Hungary to Hanover.

Before they left late that day, they made their cart a bit more roadworthy in the smithy. One of them left an address. Would Mother write to his wife in six weeks' time, telling her he and his friends had been through here, and were on their way home, provided of course the mail worked by then.

Mother wrote as promised, and he himself answered, saying he would never forget the Whitsun he spent with us and telling us how they managed to get back. Luckily he said, his place was not bombed, which must have been a miracle. The other three found themselves homeless and stayed with him in Hanover. He was the chemist, the others found work in a Hanover Hospital.

It was soon after Whitsun, that we went back to school. But there were no books of any sort, which we were allowed to use. Everything had to be censured, in case they contained Nazi propaganda.

There was no paper for us to write on, no one had a slate which wasn't broken. They got broken during the many times we dived into the ditches during the air attacks and there was nowhere, where we could buy new ones.

Most of the time we should have spent at school, learning, we were sent out to the potato fields with tins containing some paraffin. We had to move up and down the rows of potatoes, checking each plant for Colorado Beetles, which we had to put into the paraffin, where they died. The beetles were yellow with black stripes down their backs. We did not have this pest in Germany until the Americans dropped them in some of their special bombs. That is what our teacher told us. I hated this task. It was dreadfully boring and endless. But if we didn't do it, there would be no food in the autumn.

Another thing we had to do, instead of going to school, was planting new forests. They had cut so many trees to build barrack camps for POWs, refugees and wounded soldiers, that in large areas which used to be thick forest, only a few trees remained. In the remaining space, we planted baby firs. I liked this task much more than beetle collecting.

On a hot and sunny day in June, Bine was playing by the river, when a solitary soldier asked her, if she had any matches. She took him upstairs to Mother, who had just had her thirty-eighth birthday the day before.

Bine asked Mother for some matches for this man, and Mother turned round. They looked at each other, and she often said afterwards, it was as if she recognised somebody very dear from a long long time ago. They both felt this way. He was tall and blond and from Reichenbach in the Vogtland which was a hilly stretch of Germany in Saxony. They produced musical instruments where he lived, he said, but he was an aircraft builder by trade. His name was Wolfgang Tuschek. As he looked at Mother, he slowly slid his huge Rucksack off his back and put it down. Mother said:

"Have you eaten?" He shook his head. There was still potato salad in a bowl which we kept for the evening meal. She now put a plate in front of Wolfgang and a fork and he said:

"There is something that would go nicely with this potato salad" and he produced some *Spec.* (smoked bacon). I wondered what else there was in the Rucksack.

He stayed that day, and happily Bine and I fixed him the straw sack which we still had from the time when the woman from Magdeburg recovered on it in the loft outside our little room. She had left long ago for Meran, just before the Americans came. But her cosy corner was still there. Now we hoped Wolfgang would stay. When he saw the cosy corner he laughed:

"I couldn't refuse such a comfortable spot," and he dropped his Rucksack in the space between the wall of our room and the slanting roof. I liked him and secretly hoped that he was meant for us.

Apart from the *Speck* he had something else which we had never seen, smelt or tasted before: Nescafe. He also had chocolate. He stayed the next day and the next. To us it was as if a dear member of the family had come home. We were so happy to have him, and he loved us all.

Nobody asked how long he would stay. We all knew, that it could not be forever, yet. He had been home to Reichenbach when he was released from the army and found his mother weak and starving. There was even less food than we had here. Mother asked him if he couldn't get her out of Vogtland and bring her here, but he said she was far too ill. He had come back to Bavaria to find food. He said most of what he had in his rucksack, he earned from the 'Amies'. He was working for them. They needed good aircraft engineers. He spoke Polish, English and German. Very useful at this time too. He still had the job with the Amies. They gave him leave to return to his mother and if possible to bring her back.

Wolfgang got up at the same time as Mother and went with her, to the garden at five in the morning, every day. We had breakfast together at seven, Bine and I would then go with the rest of the children to school. Times were almost normal.

After two happy, secure and wonderful weeks with us, Wolfgang was ready to go. We had become so used to having him. Mother and he had such long and deep conversations in the evenings when we were already in bed. Often he would sit with us and tell fairy tales from Russia, which we hadn't heard before. We wished he could stay. But it could not be. Not yet.

His last evening, we spent together quietly and anxiously. When he first came to us, the borders which he had to cross were closed. He hoped that things would sort themselves out, and they would open again. But they hadn't. Now the Russians controlled the borders, he must cross, and they would shoot if they caught him. His home was now in the eastern zone. But he was confident he would make it and return to us. He had papers and an official pass from the American authorities. A rare thing in those days.

With love, he hugged us all individually. Then he picked up his Rucksack, into which we had put some of our very precious tins and some sugar, and walked away. We watched as he crossed the pontoon bridge, stopped, turned and waved once more.

"I'll be back" he shouted, his blond hair shining in the sun.

34

My birthday was here again. A year ago I had gone with Robert to fetch the horses in the morning, and he had given me a doll which he had carved himself. I could remember almost every minute of my birthday last year. I could feel and smell the corn. When I closed my eyes, I could feel the fresh East Prussian wind which danced unhindered across the wide, open land, racing with the clouds and laughing sunshine.

This first of July 1945 was a hot, cobalt blue, burning day. Giant, ugly horseflies were biting. I could never feel them landing on me, and by the time they announced themselves with their dreadful bite, it was too late.

Thunderstorms usually gathered purple black by three in the afternoon, making the air stand still, and the atmosphere sticky. By four o clock it would be all over, the blackness vanished, the air fresh and spicy, the sun shining once more and the earth steaming in the heat, the refreshing rain settling the dust.

I felt excited about my birthday but I also missed Wolfgang. It seemed, Mother expected him around every corner, even though we knew he wouldn't be back for six weeks, if ever. But the "if ever" we kept to ourselves, we did not speak about it. I also felt a little guilty for missing Wolfgang more than my father. Did Mother miss our father? She never mentioned him to us, since she had been to Berlin to be with Grandfather at his trial. I sensed, that whatever happened, or whatever was said, she did not want to talk about it. I only knew, that she had talked to neighbours and they had seen him in our lockup cellar during the time we were in East Prussia.

Mother wanted to surprise me with a present. She had a beautiful white dress with Hungarian embroidery and a matching red embroidered waistcoat, which she had taken to a woman in the next village, to be altered to fit me. It once was her best dress, but now it was very worn and Mother couldn't wear it herself any more. But there was enough good material in the skirt alone to make a dress for me. The embroidery was so beautiful. The waistcoat needed only a little alteration.

When Mother went to fetch it a day before my birthday, the woman said it had been stolen. She could find it nowhere. Mother was very cross and suspicious but there was nothing she could do.

I had ground some of Hanni's chicken wheat and exchanged an egg for some buttons she wanted. With the rough flour, Mother had baked a cake. She had worked out that if she soaked the flour overnight in a little water, it turned into a fluffier cake. We had also been to the forest to pick forest strawberries. They were big and juicy and sweet. They shone bright red and grew in such abundance on sunny banks in the thick dark forest. We had enough for the cake and some over.

Mother had collected sour milk for days and drained it in a sack to get soft cottage cheese. This we made into *Quarkspeise*. We always had some dripping in a stool turned upside down with a fine cotton cloth tied to each leg. A bowl underneath caught the greenish water which had separated from the curd. This Quark we could make into anything at all, sweet and savoury, and when we had it with potatoes, we mixed it with salt and precious paprika, wild onions and chives. It was a meal we always enjoyed.

But for the birthday treat the cottage cheese was stirred until it was soft and creamy, then we added a little sugar and the fruit. Any fruit of the year would do. It was important not to wash the forest fruit to make sure it would not lose its unique flavour. Now we added the strawberries with the odd pine needle still attached to it and watched the white creamy substance turn into a delicious pink. Beate, Bärbel and Hanni came in the afternoon. Bärbel brought a semolina pudding as a gift, Hanni a small piece of *Speck* and three eggs.

We started my birthday with the usual swim in the Laaber which we had done daily since we had the petrol canisters. Then we roamed in the forest, where we went most days, to see what we could find for lunch. Breakfast and supper were the two meals at home. The rest came from the land. It was a challenge, and we worked as a team, with the motto one for all and all for one, which was only valid for members of our gang. We guarded our food sources very carefully.

When we got back, Mother had made some barley coffee and cut the cake. I put my finger through the *Quarkspeise* and licked it. It tasted heavenly. Just as we were ready to tuck in, Gottfried and Hannes knocked on the door.

They had also been invited, but a few days ago, they had said to Bärbel, that a girl's birthday party was not for boys. But here they were, with the excuse that they had to ask us a very important question! Mother cut two more slices and put a dollop of *Quarkspeise* on top of it and offered it to them. Hannes said:

"Well Frau Gerret, now that you have already used a plate, we had better have it." Mother laughed and said:

"You had better." We all laughed. We never found out what the important question was.

Later, after the semolina pudding, we idled down and sat on the pontoon bridge, dangling our feet. There were less flies, but the mosquitos were biting. We wiped them off with water. It was a warm and peaceful evening. The air was filled with a hundred different scents. Butterflies, beetles and colourful flies were lazily buzzing about.

I had had a lovely birthday. Mother was leaning out of the window above the smithy and looking into the country. The Moon was slowly rising brightly just above the treetops of the Rammelsteiner forest. Where were Mother's thoughts, I wondered.

Daily, the German prisoners of War came and used the saw mill. Sometimes they brought dried potatoes and vegetables, or egg powder and Mother cooked a soup for them. Frau von Schwarzenbaer contributed a few things for the pot, the best was a giant bacon rind, which could be boiled in the soup over and over for flavour. She also provided some bread whenever possible. Even when the German prisoners had nothing to give, they still expected a meal when they came.

Their American guards did not mind. In fact they were civil and polite, one of them spoke with Mother often. Mother remembered now that she had learned English at school. The American asked where we were from and bit by bit he learned our history. He often had a cup of our Ersatz coffee and one day he left us a small tin of Nescafe. He was from Pittsburgh, Pennsylvania.

One day, we had run so short of food, we could not provide the soup for the Germans POWs. When they didn't get their food, they wondered what was amiss, and sent a spokesman. Mother had to explain, that there was nothing, no food. They hadn't brought anything lately and Mother had run out of provisions.

The POWs had been under the impression, that we were local farmers and had plenty of food. Their spokesman apologised that he and his comrades had eaten everything we had, and hoped to do something about it. Mother said, that she was always happy for the company and they shouldn't worry, something would turn up, it usually did.

They left a big sack of dried potatoes mixed with vegetables outside our door, with a note, asking Mother not to question where it came from or how it got there. Mother asked no questions. She continued to cook soup for all of us again.

Once they brought us a tin of peanut butter. It was something extremely rare and wonderful. My first ever taste of peanuts and I thought there could not be anything better. Except I remembered some nougat, Father had brought home one day, when he returned briefly from Italy.

The weeks passed and the main occupation of the day always was where to find the next meal, even the way to school was a food finding expedition. Everything was tested for its eatability.

One very early morning, we heard a jeep blow his horn outside the smithy. We went to the window and looked out. In the jeep was the American guard from Pittsburgh who had accompanied the German prisoners all these weeks. When he saw us at the window, he stood up in his jeep and saluted, waved and drove off. Mother was puzzled.

A day later the Germans were back with a different guard. They told us the other guard had gone home to America. He would not be back.

"So," Mother said, "That was his way of saying goodbye then." Another valuable and good person gone from our lives. She said he had become a friend.

Mother and I began mending flour sacks for the miller and for that he gave us flour or crushed grain. Every evening we sat until the light faded. Every morning Mother took the smelly sacks back on her way to the garden, and fetched another pile on her way home. The miller had very busy mice, and we had a little food. We had to wash and sort the grain carefully, because of the many mouse droppings in it.

It was the time of the year when the wheat and barley was cut and stacked in the fields. We helped and got our legs scratched, since we did everything barefoot, even walk in the stubble fields. We learned how to walk on the stubbles by sliding our feet along and bending the stubble first before we trod on them.

Our wooden sandals were only for best. We didn't even wear them to school. Everybody walked barefoot, even the children from the Schloss.

When the grain was loaded and driven home to the barn, we would gather, with other refugees and poor people by the side of the field and wait for the farmer to finish raking the empty field with the large horse rake. He would then give us a signal and we would start picking up all the ears he had missed. We kept a sharp lookout on the wheat cutters to be on the spot, when the farmers gave the signal for us to glean.

With our sacks, arms and aprons loaded, we would go home and eagerly rub the ears between our hands, blow away the chaff and feel the heavy grain. I would put some into my mouth and slowly chew it. The taste was at first strange, but soon it tasted nutty and bready and was very satisfying. First we left the grain to dry in our loft, where Wolfgang's cosy corner was, and then we put it through the coffee mill. It wouldn't go through the coffee mill when it was fresh, but turn into a paste.

After dark, I would slip out and quietly go to the barn and through the boards, I pulled more ears. I knew it was stealing, but we were hungry and there was little food to be had. Anyway, in the barn was plenty. I did that every night.

Wolfgang's six weeks were over and every day we waited for him to return. The weeks passed into seven and eight.

I had started to steal potatoes from the field. I lied to Mother, as to where I had got them from. She didn't really press me too hard. She probably guessed where they came from but said nothing. I felt I had some right, since I had been up and down the field, picking Colorado beetle. I had a method by which the farmer didn't know somebody had been to his field. I went out in the darkness and carefully dug them from underneath the plant, leaving the plant intact, and only taking potatoes from every tenth plant. We had to be careful not to show that we had potatoes, washing and eating them in secret. I swore Bine and Tissi to secrecy.

And so October arrived. We helped with the potato harvest and earned some honest potatoes which we stored for the winter. Nobody worked for money, payment was a tiny percentage of the harvest.

Grandfather wrote and said that the house was now more or less rebuilt and safe enough for us to return. The Americans or the housing office would have taken the spare rooms and put American officers or refugees into them. So Grandfather was eager to have us back, rather than have to take in strangers.

We had been in Eichhofen nearly ten months. It seemed such a long time, but when I looked back to East Prussia or even Berlin, it was no time at all. Now we were packing again with a heavy heart. We all had started in a very small way to feel at home here, to grow very thin tender roots. As we collected our few things, we counted the many times we had moved since we left Berlin. In two years we had moved seven times, not counting the stay with Grandmother in Silesia before going to East Prussia. Moving back to Regensburg would be our eighth move. Often the move had been a wrench. I did not look forward to going back to Regensburg. I would miss the river, the saw mill, the smithy, my friends, the well and the forest, the castle. But, by then I had learned, that it was no good to be sentimental. It only hurt. Look ahead. We continued to pack. But that lump in my throat was back and hurt.

We still fitted everything into Grandfather's little cart. There was more in it than when we came here because we had the paper roll, the wax tablets and a small amount of tobacco left. We also had the extra blankets and a sack of very precious potatoes. Carefully, we rolled up our feather beds which were still with us from Berlin, which gave me a sense of permanence, continuity. It felt strange to think that I had slept in these same feather beds in Berlin and East Prussia. It seemed to be from another life, another world.

We tied it all down very securely and took our leave. We promised to visit. It was difficult to leave our peaceful room. We had been happy here.

Hanni and I had been to Weissenfels the evening before. I did not want to leave without saying goodbye to the nuns. I would never forget those friendly women. They taught me to trust in people regardless, whether or not one was a catholic.

Frau von Schwarzenbaer came to the door, thanked Mother for having been her gardener for all these months and said her door was always open to us. What a good and generous woman she was. Hanni and Bärbel came with us to Ondorf. There we put the cart into the goods wagon where it travelled with animals and other luggage and large bales. We had to travel on the foot-board of the train, because there was no room inside the train at all. Mother put the three of us on the top step, with our feet dangling between hers. She was standing on the bottom step, holding on to the two handles, either side of the door.

At breakneck speed, with soot and grit getting into our eyes we raced along. My eyes were watering and hurting, but I kept blinking and after a while the tears washed the grit out. Bine and I, had Tissi in our middle holding her tight and with our other arm we held on to the same handrail, Mother clung to, so I had no free hand to rub my eyes anyway. Bine had the same trouble. Tissi sat with her eyes tightly shut. She was utterly terrified, the little thing. Actually I thought it was a great adventure and fun. The wind was in my hair, I felt the speed in my face, it was great. Mother's arms started to ache but she made a joke about it. I couldn't hear all she said, even though she was yelling. But she was laughing. She also seemed to enjoy to hang there in such a precarious way.

Half an hour after we left Ondorf, the train slowed down and crawled along at snail's pace. Soon we knew the reason why. We had to cross the *Mariaorter Brücke*

Suddenly, all land had disappeared around us. We seemed to float in the air. There was just yawning emptiness around us. There were screams above us. Mother looked up:

"My God, there are people travelling on the roof." she said. I turned to Tissi and said that whatever she did, not to open her eyes now. Bine and I put both our arms around her and held onto the step behind her. There was just the width of the footboard between us and space. We we're quite secure, as long as the train didn't fall. I said to Bine, that they wouldn't send the train across, if it wasn't safe, more to reassure myself. I could see the way she looked at me with those huge black and serious eyes, that she too was terrified. It took ages to cross because the train travelled so slowly and my hands were sweating and my heart was beating. But after that I would never be scared of heights.

At the Regensburg station, we collected our little cart and pulled it through the park down the Gabelsberger Strasse past the Bayerischer Lloyd, round the corner to our house. The house was roughly repaired, but all around us the heaps of rubble were still there. The crater in the garden was still there, but a new one in the road was in the process of being filled in.

Grandfather was happy to have us back. The housing office was leaning heavily on him, to release the rooms. We four would have one room. A young German refugee girl, who was engaged to an American soldier, would have, what used to be our bedroom. The American, who visited the girl, also stayed the night, but we were not supposed to know that. Our room was so cramped, there was nowhere to spill over into anything else, like the great loft in Eichhofen, and outside the house.

After the peace, space and freedom of Eichhofen I felt terribly trapped and depressed and could not pull myself out of it. Even when the sun was shining, the days were grey and ugly.

35

We moved back into the *Bauernzimmer*. The housing office was constantly at the door to check who occupied what. There were not many private houses which were habitable. Grandfather had manoeuvred carefully to fill the rooms in his apartment with people he wanted, and Mother was angry. He hadn't told her all the facts. The *Bauernzimmer* was only half the size of the room we had above the smithy. There we also had the use of that large open loft outside our room, the loo which might have been cold in the winter, but at least we had it more or less to ourselves. We would have had more than enough wood for heating and cooking and many more possibilities to lay our hands on some food. Here, in the city, was nothing, just ruins and desolation and thousands of homeless, sick and hungry refugees. The streets were noisy with military traffic. Army lorries, tanks, jeeps. It was an endless, restless, seething movement.

Our room was so small, stuffy and airless, and with winter coming and fuel scarce, to preserve the heat, we would open the windows only briefly for fresh air. Before we went to Eichhofen, we had the bedroom too which was double the size of the *Bauernzimmer*, and was now occupied by only one woman. The four of us had to squeeze into this small room.

Mother thought it was very unfair, but went to work on the room. We had to have some furniture and Grandfather let us have two wardrobes which Mother arranged in such a way that it partitioned the little room into two cubicles. The wardrobes also hid everything which made the room look untidy. One cubicle was a sleeping area for the three of us, the other a living area with a table, where we could also do our homework, and adjoining the kitchen, wash up and bath area, which consisted of a little canon stove with a cooking area for one pot, a stool with a large basin on top, and a box, which contained our foodstuffs. To move around in the room, was a frightful squeeze.

To be able to survive, I established my domain on top of the cupboards. From the table via another piece of furniture and a short arm stretch I managed to get up there. I had all my treasures there, even did my homework there. Seldom did I come down and mix into the family scrummage.

Grandfather had no beds for us. Mother had a sofa in the sun lounge, and we three had to sleep on a mattress, on the floor.

We seldom saw Grandfather these days in our room. Mother was bitter. His door was locked. I saw him occasionally in the corridor, and then our eyes met. Did I detect a tiny friendly smile in his eyes? I couldn't tell. Bine and Tissi were scared of him. Mother avoided him. I searched his eyes whenever I had a chance. There was a bond between him and me, but for now, the door seemed locked. He too had a difficult time and he was old.

Mother went to the Protestant Relief Work Office, to find out whether there were any beds. She met a giant of a man from Bulgaria there, but of German origin, who was himself a refugee now, and the boss of the relief work in Regensburg. There was nothing he wouldn't do for all the suffering people around. He was also a doctor of medicine and a vicar. He managed to get us a tiny stove.

Mother didn't get any beds, but she found an unpaid job with this man, who, in the world of refugees and displaced persons was called 'Papa Kröning'.

The school of St. Clara was under repair. My new school was a long way away and undamaged. It was also a catholic school. Our local catchment school was still a field hospital on the ground-and first floor, and the two upper stories were filled with refugees.

The official new start of school was announced and there was only one school available for our area in Regensburg, when normally there would have been four. In Eichhofen the schools had started earlier after the collapse than in the city. Here the schools, if they hadn't been bombed, had been taken over to house refugees, who seemed more numerous than local people-, wounded soldiers and prisoners. Slowly, they had been released back to be used as schools.

Bine and I went off to the *Pestalozzi Schule*. At the main entrance we had to part. Bine was troubled and a little scared since she had never been to a school where I had not been sitting somewhere close. In Thimsdorf all the classes were in one room. Now I was two flights of stairs above her. Two years separated us. I gave her a kiss and said I would wait after school and we would meet in the interval. My heart ached when I saw her little creased face, biting back tears and trying to be brave, and so I quickly made sure she found the right classroom, and then I went off to find mine. I was a little late but I wasn't the only one.

Our classroom spilled over with children. In my class were about sixty children and the room was no bigger than the one in Thimsdorf which held eight classes and housed no more than twenty seven children in all.

The children here were aggressive and kept picking on me and some others. One could tell the natives by their clothes. Their clothes were not tattered and worn. They also had shoes. I had to wear Grandfather's ski boots again. My feet hadn't grown much more since last winter and the boots were still huge on my feet. I felt embarrassed. I looked around to see whether there was somebody I knew from the time I was at St. Clara, but I could find no one. I held on to my satchel and melted into the background.

A man and a woman came in and told us to be quiet. There were not enough places to sit, and some had to sit on the floor. There was fighting and shuffling for seats and desks among the pupils, who were all girls.

When all was reasonably quiet, we were asked one by one to come forward, give our names, place of birth and religion. We were put into three groups. Catholic locals, catholic refugees and protestant refugees.

We ended up with two groups of about thirty in each, and one group with two, myself and a girl from Bartenstein in East Prussia. We were told to stand over to one side. We whispered our names to each other and stood close, feeling, that whatever happened we two had to stand against the other sixty. We felt uneasy and out of place; was there something wrong in being a protestant? The other children looked at us tauntingly. Instinctively, Marie Luise and I held hands. She whispered to me that she was called Ise, at home. I whispered back that they called me Ange. We smiled at each other. I was worried about Bine. Would she have to endure the same ordeal?

The man tapped on the desk and waited until all was so quiet one could hear a pin drop. The woman, who was short, round, and ancient, glared at us. He said that there were too many children in this class and they would have to be split into morning class starting at seven and finishing at twelve thirty, and afternoon class starting at one through to six thirty. Every week there would be a changeover so that the parallel class had a chance to sleep in. They all laughed a little at that. Ise and I still had no class.

He now looked at us. He sighed and wrinkled his forehead "And what am I going to do with you?" Well I didn't know nor did Ise. I was embarrassed. Ise shrugged her shoulders and grinned. All eyes were looking at us. The two teachers had a private little conference. Then the man turned around and said:

"I certainly thought there would be more children of the other faith. But we have to see what can be done. Now, I would like to mix the two groups, I want an equal amount of *Einheimische- und Flüchtlings Kinder*(native-and refugee children) in each class. It is very important that we integrate and make friends. We are all Germans." He then lined them up two by two, always taking one native and one refugee child thus dividing the two groups into equal parts.

He led his snake of thirty odd outside into the corridor. He then came back into the classroom and turned to the woman. Aloud he said looking at Ise and me:

"I think we keep those two together and they should stay in your class." Then he turned to the rest of the children and said:

"There is a severe shortage of teachers. We have to cope as best we can. This is *Fräulein Ampfer* (Miss Ampfer) and she will be your teacher for the time being. She needs your cooperation. These are hard times for all of us." He shook hands with Fräulein Ampfer and left. Now there was almost room for all of us to sit. Fräulein Ampfer said that in the basement there were some benches and we would now go and get some. She made everybody line up two by two, and marched us down the stairs. We picked up eight benches and brought them back to our class room. We were then asked to line up again and slowly snaked down stairs into the yard for the interval.

Ise and I looked around for Bine. She was standing by the wall, and I could tell she had been crying. She was the only protestant in her class. I put my arms around her. Poor thing, at least I had had Ise. The three of us were hungry, but we hadn't brought any food. Only the native children had bread and an apple. We looked away, pretending we didn't see.

Luckily Bine too was in the morning class so we would always be able to go to school together. It turned out that Ise only lived about a hundred metres from our house. We were practically neighbours.

When we were back in the classroom, the teacher said that she wanted to explain about the two faiths. She said the problem was that there was at present, no protestant school which there had been, before the collapse. We were now in a catholic school, and teaching would be a problem. But they would sort things out.

We were then given a timetable and some ancient books. There were pages missing in the German reading book. The same pages in every book. Fräulein Ampfer explained that soon she hoped we would get new, approved books. Most books were banned now. Many teachers would have to wait for denazification before they would be allowed to teach. Until such time we would have to do the best we could.

We did a little arithmetic and read aloud from the reading book, about three lines each. It was a very slow and difficult process and very boring. There were children who couldn't read at all. There were even children among the refugee children who couldn't speak German properly. The native children laughed maliciously, as they struggled.

Our teacher had to give a long explanation, but the native children did not really grasp the situation. I had to think of Hanni. She didn't know either, couldn't comprehend. These children only knew their own town. Very likely they had not been outside this city, except maybe to visit a relative on a farm nearby. The teacher put all the children, who had difficulty with the language, together into one group. She then made them stand up and tell the rest of the class were they were from. They were from Bulgaria, Yugoslavia, Hungary, Romania and Lithuania, Latvia and Estonia which was close to Finland and whose language was similar to the Finnish language. We even had a girl from as far away as Kiev in the Ukraine.

The teacher explained to the rest of us how far away that was and which countries they had to cross to get to Germany. She told us, that it was up to us to teach them German and to make them feel at home, until such a time, when they were allowed to return home into their own land. The teacher said that when the peace treaty was signed, and things were sorted out, everybody would be allowed to go home.

We were given some homework, reading, some writing and some arithmetic. I was very happy when we were released to go home.

Bine was already waiting in the yard, and the three of us walked home. We were all dreadfully hungry. We promised to meet in the afternoon when we had done our homework. I was very glad to have Ise for a friend.

Tissi was all alone at home, sitting on the mattress and crying. Where was Mother? She couldn't tell. She didn't know. Mother had gone to work and hadn't come back.

I boiled some potatoes and we had those with some salt.

Mother came home. She explained, that there was so much work, sorting out all these poor homeless people, trying to find mattresses, filling in forms, going to the various camps and finding more room to house them. It normally meant shoving the mattresses closer. In the end, the shelter per refugee adult with one or more children, was no more than the space the mattress occupied. People had to walk over other people's mattresses to get to theirs. There was no food, no washing facilities and winter so close. The nights were bitter.

Mother said it was just terrible and how lucky we were to have the room. She would not grumble again. She looked at the three of us:

"You have to help. I will not be able to be at home much, until things have eased a little." She gave me the food ration coupons and some money.

"Now you have to do the shopping and see to it, that there is food on the table. Bine, you help your sister. Tissi, you can play in the garden or be in our room until your sisters come back from school. You must not wander off on your own outside. Promise?" Tissi nodded. Mother got up and went out onto the veranda, which she had arranged to be her private bedroom. It was almost like sleeping out in the open. She lay down on the sofa and was almost instantly asleep.

I did my homework. Bine had no homework at all and played with Tissi.

Ise came at four in the afternoon, and the two of us went off together to explore the neighbourhood. I learned that day, that I must never go anywhere, without the ration cards and money. I also learned that day, that when there is a queue, one queued first and asked questions later.

We saw a queue and asked what there was. A woman said that they had had a salt herring delivery.

I dashed home to get the coupons and the money. Ise did too. We both got into the queue but by the time it was our turn, the fish had gone. From now on I had to be alert to find food wherever.

Ise's mother was a strange woman. She was much older than my mother, very tall and wore long black dresses which came down to her ankles. She did not work, and therefore was at home all the time and free to do the shopping. There was only Ise and her mother. Ise had a father and a sister, but they were both in a sanatorium in the hills just outside Regensburg because they had tuberculosis. Ise's sister was already twenty four years old, her father was sixty nine.

Ise did not have to do any shopping, but she came rushing over after school and told me, her mother had found oats, or fish, or potatoes in that and that shop. I would drop everything and we would run to see if there was any left. Often I was too late. Because of school, I missed out. I was more successful, when I had the morning off, and school did not start until the afternoon.

We could tell from afar, whether we were going to be lucky or not. Because there was nothing else in the shop to sell, it just closed when the supply ran out.

The small cinema cum theatre opposite our house was turned into a refugee camp. It housed about two hundred people from Silesia. In the evenings we could hear familiar songs, and Mother, when she was home, was drawn across to sing along. They were happy-sad gatherings.

November came and with that heavy snow. We sat in our classroom in the coats which Mother had made for us in East Prussia, the arms getting a little short and tight, our hands in our muffs, feet hurting with cold, noses cold and getting colder. Every hour, we went downstairs, into the school yard to do warming up exercises. By the time we made it upstairs, we were cold again.

Then something incredible happened. We were told to bring anything which would contain food and a spoon.

Every day, at eleven, or three in the afternoon, two American soldiers appeared in our classroom with a big milk churn full of food. They ladled out the food. It was a sticky porridge with bloated raisins, very sweet and a little slimy. But I loved it and licked the old army canteen afterwards. There was no more. Very soon though, I realised that the native children didn't eat theirs, and I asked them to pour it into my canteen, rather than waste it. I could take as much as five portions in my canteen. Bine did exactly the same and so did all the refugee children. The native children were happy to give their food away and boasted a little, that they helped feed the poor and starving.

The food was monotonous, but Tissi and Mother loved it and Bine and I ate it again, as we sat around our table, in the evening. Occasionally, we had green pea soup with ham flavour, which was always our favourite, or potatoes boiled in milk and flavoured with vanilla ice cream powder, which was sickly, especially when the potatoes were still a little raw.

By the beginning of December, we were sent home until further notice, because it simply became too cold in the classroom and no way of heating it. There were no coals at home either. There were power cuts too. In fact, during the day, when we didn't need it, the electricity was on, but as soon as it got dark, it went off. So our stearin wax from Ondorf came in very handy. We learned to make candles.

We missed the food from school, which we had started to rely upon.

Life had become unbearably cold and very, very dark.

✳✳✳

36

Many farmers with loaded wagons of sugar beet, were passing our house on their way to the sugar factory, which had been put into working order again.

The roads were cobbled with big, rounded granite stones, and many beets fell off and landed on the road. It was fortunate that the road was rounded, high in the middle and receding to the sides. This way, the beets rolled of their own accord to safety, away from the endless American army traffic.

We had collected a number of these beets and kept adding daily. They were stored on the veranda. We cooked one to eat, but it tasted sickly. That didn't stop us from collecting more. We hoped to make sugar, only we didn't know how.

The Winkelmanns were lucky in their bad luck. Because members of their family had tuberculosis, they were given a room to themselves above an old disused fire station. The beautiful, ancient fire engine was still parked downstairs, shining red, gold and black, even in the gloomy darkness, it occupied.

Having this space, allowed Ise's father and sister to come and visit them at times, without the fear of infecting other people.

The fire station was part of the clinic complex to which the sanatorium also belonged. It stood by itself in the park grounds of the clinic. One entered into Ise's living space through the big garage doors, squeezed past the old engine and up via a beautifully wrought iron spiral staircase. A tap and a loo were downstairs. The space was very small and dark, but it was all theirs. The beauty was, they didn't have to share with anyone.

Frau Winkelmann found a source of wood and said she would share it, if we helped out with our cart. So we took Grandfather's cart, and made many trips to a saw mill a few kilometres outside the city.

Tall, dressed in black, slim and white haired, Frau Winkelmann strode beside us. It seemed, nothing could shake her dignity.

We covered the wood carefully, so that nobody could see what we had in the cart, guarded it all the way home and divided the wood between Ise and us. These trips became part of a daily routine, until that supply ran out.

Frau Winkelmann taught me how to make syrup with the beets we had. She too had collected some and I asked her what she did with them, and she showed me the deliciously brown, treacly substance bubbling on her stove.

From that time there was a pot on our stove too. Shredded beets were constantly on the boil. Carefully I had to judge the right moment to strain the juice, and then I would squeeze and press the pulp with Bine's help until it was quite dry. The juice would continue to boil for days, until it turned into syrup. We filled several containers with that delicious syrup. It became an important ingredient to our daily food. Mother said she was proud of her girls.

One Sunday, Mother had come home tired. She had been helping Papa Kröning with the church services in various refugee camps and hospitals. It was afternoon and she collapsed onto her sofa. After she had rested and got up, she couldn't find her glasses anywhere, and for several hours, everybody was anxiously looking for them. Mother was in a state. Where could she get new glasses? Not for money or for barter, could she get a set of spectacles in times like these. She tried to remember where she last had them, but to no avail. We continued to search high and low.

I found them in the evening when I was stirring the syrup, although I did not know at first what I had hanging there from the wooden spoon, dripping in long thin threads into the syrup. It took a while to sink in, that they were Mother's spectacles. They had been happily boiling away in in the syrup pot, but how they got in there, was a mystery. Miraculously, they had come to no harm. They were a good as new, after Mother carefully washed them.

Bine had made friends with twins, who had a third floor apartment just around the corner. They joined the school, a week after we had, and were also protestants and natives of Regensburg. I wouldn't have believed that there were native Protestants in this town.

We hardly saw Bine these days. She was forever with her new friends, the Bussigel twins. They had not been bombed and never had to leave their home and had everything one could dream of. Bine came home and told us about dolls and dolls houses and dolls prams, toy stoves and pots and pans, tiny crockery and mini cutlery. The list went on and on. The three were inseparable.

The twins also had children's books, but hated to lend them out. When they came to our house they brought one or two books which I could read, but when they left they took them home again before I had a chance to finish. It was pure torture for me.

The twin's father was still in a prison camp outside the city. On Sundays, we could see their mother, the twins and their older sister, dressed immaculately, in beautiful coats with fur trim and shoes walk past our house on their way to visit their father. We always waved at each other from our window.

It was also due to Frau Winkelmann, that we found two wooden beds. They came from a prison camp and were collapsible and needed some repair. She had seen them and hidden them and we would have to hurry with our cart. Ise, Bine and I ran off, found the beds, loaded them and took them home. Just in case, we made sure nobody saw us, as we loaded them up. Mother had got one bed from Papa Kröning. Now we had three!

After Father Rappel mended them for us, we stacked them on top of one another. Bine claimed the top bunk and I had the cosy bottom one. Tissi's stood opposite mine. There was just enough room between the two beds to dangle one's feet. We had a real bed each. Things were looking up again.

By now, we all had caught lice from somewhere and were riddled. Once a week, Mother made paraffin packs for our heads and we sat for two hours, trying to fumigate these vermin. But I think they only got drunk, because they seemed to recover very quickly, once the pack was off. The consolation was, that everybody had lice. A lot of discreet scratching went on, even among very respectable people. The only one, who didn't suffer, was Grandfather; he was totally bald. We never had scabies but many children we knew had it and most people in the refugee camps had it. It became quite common to say: "don't shake hands with her, she's got Krätze." The other thing we never had were wanzen (bed bugs), but it seemed, it was a regular thing to have them. I always wanted to know what they looked like, but even Mother could not tell me.

Mother's date for denazification came closer. Every German citizen whether or not they were a member of the party had to go through this procedure to obtain an identity card, even Grandfather who certainly had never been a member of the Nazi party.

Mother had not been associated either. She tried to join in 1935, but then they admitted no more new members. By the time they reopened the doors for new membership, Mother had changed her mind and decided this was not the party she thought it was, and never joined. But our father was a member.

The day also arrived when we were told we did not qualify for a refugee pass. Therefore there would not be any compensation or help for us at this stage. We were not in the trek from Silesia because we had travelled to Regensburg to be with Grandfather in his fight for life. The fugitives left Silesia six weeks after we left. We were very grateful that we did not have to be in that frightful escape, but we had also lost everything, but in the bombing and that was different from having lost it to the Russians. The authorities decided, that Grandfather would have to support us, which was difficult since he only had a pension and just as little or no food. He already provided a free roof over our heads. Things did not work out very well and Mother and Grandfather avoided each other, even more. It was very sad.

But one day, when I met him in the corridor, he had a shadow of a smile for me, which I had missed when we first arrived back. One day, he invited me into his study and asked how we were and if we have enough food. I guessed, that he too, was hungry.

He had employed a woman from Czechoslovakia, Frau Grudczinsky, to cook for him, but he must have been very lonely. Frau Vasner, who Mother had called the blond poison, had vanished very soon after the Americans arrived. Grandfather had become withdrawn. I asked him if he had food, and he said that his cook and he had enough. Father Rappel, his faithful servant and friend, brought him what he could. He had connections in the country. If Grandfather also had connections, he kept them to himself. Anyway, I could see that we would have been too many mouths for him to feed. It was everyone to himself. I gave him some of our syrup, and he was very grateful. He spooned it straight from the glass. He said, he would ration himself to a spoon a day.

The young woman who occupied our former bedroom, a refugee girl from Upper Silesia, was working for an American family as cook and nanny, and was engaged to a GI. She was able to bring home the odd bit of coffee or tea, white bread which the Americans considered stale, and the water in which they had boiled their ham. This was the most prized food supplement because it had large bits of white fat swimming in it and it tasted of ham.

She paid the rent with food. Grandfather didn't want money. The American soldier shopped in the American store, which was called PX, to pay the rent. We never saw what he brought Grandfather.

The food Inge brought home was extra, and we got most of it. Inge used to go shopping in the PX with her American family. Absolutely everything one could think of was available there and also things one couldn't even dream of. But it was only for Americans and the currency was dollars. Very occasionally she brought a little Hershel's chocolate home.

The Americans had a habit of only half smoking their cigarettes, and throwing the rest away. I began to collect the butts and put them aside. I picked them off the street, around park benches, in fact, wherever I saw one, I bent down for it. They became important currency, better than money, even better than silver spoons. With money one could buy nothing, but tobacco, bought anything that was available.

We did, however, qualify for a pass to use the soup kitchen at the Palace of the Prince of Thurn und Taxis. Mother thought it ironic, to be a guest at her godmother's soup kitchen, for the poor and homeless.

I asked her why it was, that the princess was Mother's godmother. Was she other children's godmother too? Mother said, she probably had other godchildren. I asked her to tell us what it was like then, remembering the little story about the apples.

"Your grandfather and the prince and princess were good friends once. My mother was the princess' companion and confidante. Grandfather's second wife had been lady in waiting to her. The racecourse at Regensburg, the Tattersall, riding hall and the collection of coaches and the noble stable of horses the prince possessed, were all due to Father's initiative and drive while he was captain of cavalry at court. And of course he took the hunt." Mother said. I sighed:

"That must have been great. I wish I could do Grandfather's job. Could I learn? I think I would like to spend my life working with horses and music."

"Perhaps," Mother said.

"How did Grandfather ever come here in the first place?" I asked.

"He was with the Kaiser in Berlin before that, and the Prince von Thurn und Taxis asked His Imperial Majesty, if my father could be released, and permit him to come into his service. The Kaiser granted it, and on parting said to your grandfather:

"Will he remember, that the Prince is of the catholic faith? He may find life difficult in Bavaria, away from our court. He is always welcome to return into our service. Our door is always open."

"Grandfather must have been proud, that the Kaiser had such high regard for him?" I replied.

"Your Grandfather was always loyal to his Kaiser, even after he abdicated, after the First World War. That is another reason why he never accepted Hitler." Mother responded.

Now, we gathered every lunchtime with hundreds of poor people and queued for lunch at the palace, paying with a few points from our ration cards. Mother recalled incidents of long ago and pointed out various buildings where she had been, when times were so completely different. The clothes she wore, the people she saw. The black and gold coach she rode in. The many beautiful dolls the princess had given her. The events were of a different time, a different life, even.

I asked her why she couldn't just go and visit the princess and tell her how things are and Mother said:

"There is a wise old saying 'Gehe nie zu Deinem Fürst, wenn Du nicht gerufen wirst' (Never go to your prince unless he asks for you)." I tried to argue, that she didn't know we were here, unless Mother told her, but Mother was adamant and said we were no beggars. "Anyway, everybody is in the same boat, and we have to work together to get out of it. We all have to start rolling up your sleeves."

The food in the soup kitchen was good and the only food we had apart from one slice of bread a day and the flour soup in the morning and maybe the odd bits Inge brought home in the evening.

We met many friendly and interesting people and made lots of friends. It was like a friendly social gathering every day.

I met a young man of eighteen who had just been released from the army, and had no clothes other than his grey army uniform. I looked out for him and when he was late, I kept a place for him next to mine. Every day we met and talked. He could play the accordion, and so one Sunday, he came to our place, to play on Mother's little squeeze box. He was delighted. A Hohner Accordion!

There was still a curfew every night, and one day, he missed it and couldn't go home. We made a bed under the table for him, which we rolled up the next day and stashed it under my bed for the day. From then on, he stayed with us. He had no possessions at all, but he had a job with the city surveyor's office, as a land survey technician. It was great to have him. His name was Günter.

Having a man around the place, who also worked for the city, brought in a few perks. He was allocated a sack of coal from time to time, which he said he received as part of his wages. Coal burnt so much longer and gave more steady heat.

I knocked on Grandfather's door. When he said: "Come in," I entered and invited him to join us in our warm room. But he wouldn't. He smiled and thanked me. He had a little wood burner stove, and it was quite warm in his room, where he sat in front of a beautiful huge upright desk with many little drawers and secret compartments, surrounded by books. Candle light was the only source of light. It shone onto a lightless brass lamp with a green shade. It all made reading a little difficult.

Father Rappel had provided the wood for his burner. He asked me if I had any books to read. I shook my head and told him that I only had the one from school. He got up and from a shelf, picked two books. He had hundreds of wonderful books. He said:

"Read these, look after them and then when you finished them, bring them back and fetch another one." I thanked him and gave him a kiss. I am sure he was embarrassed by that, but I didn't care. I loved my grandfather.

The books were girl's adventure stories. When the girls in the book were children, times were different. They didn't have to spend their time hunting for food, they could wear beautiful clothes and eat wonderful food. They all had fathers who provided them with everything one could think of, even trips to Italy, where most of their adventures took place. But I loved reading about it and dreaming and forgetting reality. The trouble, was that candles were rare and during the day there was little time to read. But in the darkness, waiting for Mother to get home, I told Bine and Tissi what I had read so far. They loved it and couldn't wait for the next bit.

Mother still went to work with Papa Kröning every day. Ise and I spent most mornings roaming the town, to see what we could get for our coupons. There was no school, but we assembled, even we two Protestants, at the church of St. Anton for Christmas Carol singing.

I slipped into a strange Christmas mood. In a way, I was optimistic for the future. The reason for this, was the many visits to the hospitals, singing carols to the wounded soldiers.

I saw such terrible wounds there! I couldn't imagine that anyone would want to start another war if this was the result.

I thought it was amazing, that one could live with such wounds. There were soldiers whose arms were attached to various parts of their faces by the skin with half their faces missing. Eyes staring at us that had no lids and could not blink. They had to spray the eyes with something every now and then. Mouths with no lips, teeth, what was left of them, bare. Faces with no noses, faces with the teeth wired together because the bones in their faces were shattered. They had to drink all their food. Faces with the skin so taut and out of proportion, it seemed to be only an enormous yellow scar.

There was a terrible foul smell in the room too, like tinned meat, when the tin had exploded after it had gone bad. It was grotesque and shocking.

Some of the children would not go into the wards because they were frightened. They were almost all the native children. The refugee children had seen things in the war and on the long flight to the West, they had not been sheltered like the children here. I had seen people die and people being shot at. What I saw here was the result of the games adults play.

I looked at these men. Did they still like being soldiers? Was this still exciting? I suppose some of them wished they were dead. Where was my father? Did he lie in a bed in some hospital somewhere? Was he still alive? What did he think of his Führer now? The argument was that one didn't have a choice then. Had adult men learnt their lesson? It was clear to me that men made war. I also wondered whether it was a man or a woman who had completed the slogan we saw at the many stations we travelled through:

"Räder müssen rollen für den Sieg und Kinderwagen für den nächsten Krieg" (Wheels must roll for victory, and prams for the next war).

I felt very sorry for these men, and we sang beautiful Christmas songs for them. They were listening with open hearts and some were crying. Did they know where their families were? I sang better than I had ever sung. I wanted to make them happy.

Ise and I were always together, and I knew she had the same thoughts. There was a bond between her and myself. We felt alike and knew what the other was thinking. Only two days ago, she had revealed to me that she also had had a brother, but he had fallen in 1943 in Russia, almost at the same time as my uncle. We confided in each other, told each other secrets, we told no one else.

We went from ward to ward. There were other wounded soldiers. The limbless and the ones with wounds in vital organs. Belly shot and lung shots. They had been ill for so many months. There were not enough medicines for them, and many, especially the ones with wounds in their stomachs, were on morphine. Mother had explained that to me, because she had been with Papa Kröning to the same hospitals, registering the names of all those wounded, who were looking for their families. All those who were from the east and had now lost their home to the Poles or Russians. Everybody had to be registered, and Papa Kröning would distribute their names throughout Germany. He in return, received lists from other parts of Germany, and tried to match up families who lived here. It was a mammoth job for both Mother and Papa Kröning and his team. He also looked out for his own wife.

There was one ward we didn't enter. There the patients had dreadful head wounds. They were more dead than alive, often with bullets still lodged there. The nurse who led us from ward to ward, explained the difficulty to us, and why we couldn't sing to them. An operation would probably kill the soldier, and so, hoping to find a surgeon who was skilled and could successfully do these operations, the soldiers just lay there and waited, some in a coma like sleep. The nurse said they didn't feel much pain and she was hopeful. "As soon as everybody is denazified and allowed to work and as soon as the German soldiers are released from prison camp, we will also have doctors and surgeons." The nurse said. And teachers I thought. And my father maybe?

I had saved provisions for Christmas. There was a little flour and oats. Outside Ise's house was a beech tree and we had collected the nuts and halved them between Ise's family and ours. We had syrup, sugar, which I had hidden long ago and a dollop of precious margarine. We still had some of that oil from Ondorf.

Mother began to bake for Christmas at weekends and evenings. The smells were heavenly and expectations were running high.

I found Grandfather sniffing in the corridor. I promised him some cookies. Everybody was busy again, making presents for Christmas. The ideas were endless, the hiding places many. I was sitting on top of my wardrobe and pottered, drew and painted.

We went to the hospital again and again. The soldiers were expecting it, and sang along with us, tears running down their distorted faces. We got to know some by name. Some also died before Christmas.

✷✷✷

37

During the nights beautiful ice flowers formed on our windows which slowly melted as soon as our little stove warmed up the room.

On the 23.rd of December 1945 we were to sing in the Cathedral of St. Peter in Regensburg. There was something special which attracted me to this splendid, ancient church. It had been God's House for endless generations, and would be here for many more. It was a place of reassurance and permanence in this time of utter chaos. We were now to sing all the songs and carols we had been singing throughout the Advent time to the wounded and the refugees, in this special gathering place. The Cathedral Choir, the *Regensburger Domspatzen* took the lead in singing with us. We had two rehearsals in the *Dom* beforehand because there were a number of children from other schools in the city of Regensburg also taking part. Even though we were so many children, we were dwarfed by the size of the *Regensburger Dom*.

On the evening of the Christmas carol service we walked down the Ostengasse and turned into the *Alte Korn Markt* (Old Grain Market). The ringing of the bells filled the cold crisp air. The evening was clear and wind still. The stars shone brilliantly. Everything was dark because there was no electricity in the evenings, and yet visibility was good. Candle light shone from some windows, making the snow glisten pale vermillion in the darkness. Indigo shadows were crunching in the snow, moving in the same direction as we did, getting lost in the blue darkness every now and then. Some people carried wind torches, lighting their faces as in a Rembrandt painting.

The bells of the Dom were swinging powerfully deep and slow, the bells of *Niedermünster* church, *Karmeliten Kirche and Alte Kapelle* were almost above us pouring the slow sound down upon us and further to the left the *Kassians Kirche was answering back.*

*Obermünster*church was gaping roofless and silent, exposing the high altar to the merciless winter.

Deep and moving, the sound of all the bells enveloped us like an ocean. The ancient *Emmerams Kirche* and the *Schotten Kirche, Dominikaner – und Dreieinigkeits Kirche* made the undulating flood of sound complete. Was there ever a city which offered more houses to God? He had held out a protecting hand over his houses, saving most. The bombers had destroyed many houses around them.

The bells surged through the city, and the mass of people arrived at the gigantic double doors of the cathedral on the crest of such a wave.

People, who moved rubble and cleaned bricks and hunted for food and fought for survival clad in rags, suddenly had shining eyes, happy faces and seemed to walk on air. The Bavarian greeting of *Grüss Gott, Fröhliche Weihnachten* (Gods greeting, happy Christmas) was heard everywhere. Men took off their hats as they climbed the many stairs to the double doors, their hard and troubled faces, now unusually soft and expectant. People coming towards each other, taking each other's hands and holding them. "Are these your children?" And Mother put her hands on our shoulders and looked proud and happy.

The doors to the cathedral were wide open and the light of a thousand candles flooded out towards us. The frost on the intricately carved stone of the portal shimmered and glistened. The cathedral was transformed into a sea of light.

I left Mother and the sisters and went over to where my group was gathering. Slowly, row upon row, the children threaded their way in, until the southern aisle had almost filled to capacity. In front of us all, were the *Regensburger Domspatzen* boys' choir.

There was a service first, and the bishop and priests looked splendid in their white, red and gold vestments. I was filled with awe. Then, for almost two hours we sang together, the entire choir on their own, or with the congregation. It surged on wings and echoed back from the immensely high and lofty ceiling of the cathedral and nobody wanted it to end. When it seemed that it had come to the last song, somewhere in the crowd somebody would start yet another hymn and everybody would join. In the end, the candles were dying out, and the Bishop of Regensburg gave the blessing. Everybody left as the Dom slowly fell back into darkness and cold. Tomorrow would be Christmas Eve. Protestants would not come to this church then.

This Christmas Eve was very quiet and subdued. Grandfather made an effort to be nice to Mother, and Mother was friendly to him. But the gap could not really be bridged. I am sure neither of them gave the other enough thought and understanding.

Because of the coal merchant down stairs, we were now not allowed to play in the garden, even though it was Grandfather's. I think that Grandfather was shattered and disillusioned, when the coal merchant did not get punished for what he had done to Grandfather, which to me, was no better than an indirect attempt of murder. I thought, that it would all emerge in the denazification, but as yet, nothing had happened. Grandfather had said something to me like 'Money is stronger than justice' and I puzzled over that. In my world it should have been so easy. Honesty, truth and honour should always win. It seemed to me, that in the real grown up world, this was not so.

There were quite a few visitors for Grandfather around Christmas time. A number of them had known him from his Poznan and Silesian years. Now, living a long way from their home and knowing no one, they looked up anybody they knew. Some Grandfather knew very well, others only vaguely. Then there were the local people. It amazed me, how many people Grandfather did know. I wondered where they were, when Grandfather was in trouble with the Nazis.

There were also some friends, whom he knew from way back, when he was at court in Berlin, and later when worked for the prince, the times he called the good times.

Whenever I was at home, I was on door duty. Every time the bell rang, I had to open the door, lead them into the corridor and ask: "Who may I announce?" and they would tell me their name. Then, I knocked on Grandfather's door, waited for his: "come in" and announced the name, giving Grandfather sufficient time to sort himself out and take on the part of happy host, and then lead the person into him. It was all very formal. Grandfather would then introduce me to his guests, and if they were titled, I had to curtsey to the men and kiss the hand of the lady. If they were not titled, a simple curtsey would do. I didn't like it much, but I did it to humour Grandfather and I was curious to see the people who visited him.

Bine teased me about it and I said: "Just wait until you are old enough, you will have to do door duty." She insisted that Grandfather would have to catch her first. She knew how to keep well out of his way. In fact she knew how to keep out of anything, mostly domestic chores, including the washing up and cutting up paper for the loo.

Papa Kröning often visited us in our tiny room. He was still hoping his wife Else would be found soon. He was worried about her, not knowing what had become of her.

Also, Onkel Jo von Geöczy came to see us. He was looking for his family. He had married Mother's cousin, Tante Fee von Gerebrecht of Mönchgut and taken her to his estate of Dornitz as his bride. His family had owned the estate for generations, which was bordering the estates of Mönchgut.

He had been in the war, and now, coming back, his home was in Poland. He thought maybe we had heard where they were, but we hadn't. When we last saw them, her mother, Tante Mieze had even offered us to stay and live in the hunters lodge. Six weeks after that they too had to leave everything and flee into nowhere, always assuming that they had managed to get away. Tante Fee had two small children by then.

Onkel Jo didn't stay long. He continued with the search for his family on foot, only carrying an army rucksack which contained all he owned now. He promised to let us know and left a forwarding address, should we hear from them or even see them. The war had blown everybody into all directions. How was anybody to know which way to point their feet? Was our father on the road somewhere, looking for us?

A poem appeared just about that time in the local paper, and I thought it was very appropriate, cut it out and kept it:

In den letzen dreißig Wochen
zog ich sehr durch Wald und Feld.
Und mein Hemd ist so durbrochen,
daß man's kaum für möglich hält.
Ich trag Schuhe ohne Sohlen,
und der Rucksack ist mein Schrank
Meine Möbel hab'n die Polen
Und mein Geld die Dresdner Bank.
Ohne Heimat und Verwandte,
und die Stiefel ohne Glanz.
ja, das wär nun der bekannte
Untergang des Abendlands.
(Erich Kästner)

(In the past thirty weeks
I wandered much through our land
And my shirt is worn so thinly
That it's unbelievable.
I wear shoes that have no soles
And the Rucksack is my wardrobe.
My furniture is with the Poles,
My money was in the Dresdner Bank.
Without home and without family
And my boots have got no shine.
Well, that would be that familiar
Downfall of the Occident.)
(My own translation)

We watched Onkel Jo go. He was a little shorter than Tante Fee, but somehow seemed to stand tall. He was utterly correct, a total gentleman, a knight in his own right with values that could not be shaken, totally honest and loyal. Mother hugged him and wished him God's speed. Fee was her favourite cousin and like a sister.

We also heard from Munich, that Onkel Kurt's youngest son, Hermann von Stückerodt, had left his aunt's place and had disappeared. Tante Guste's sister, enquired if Grandfather had seen or heard from him. Hermann was only two years older than myself. And now he was gone and nobody knew where or had seen him. We were all terribly worried. Papa Kröning sent lists off in all directions with descriptions, should he show up. It was a bitterly cold winter.

Grandfather had a sad duty to perform. Onkel Kurt's other son, Kurt, had written to Grandfather from Depot de Prisonniers de Guerre, 182 Marmande, lot et Garonne, France. He was asking after his family, since there was no answer from Berlin.

Grandfather had to tell Kurt the awful news of the death of his family, a year earlier. The carte postale, correspondance des prisonniers de guerre, only permitted a few words on dotted lines. He could not use enough words to break it gently to Kurt, and sat, agonising for a long time as to how to word it. He also had to mention Hermann's disappearance.

I hoped Hermännle would come to us. He could be my other brother. I would love that.

Günter, who had slept under the table for some weeks, was now given the broom cupboard as a bedroom. It had no window and had only floor room for one mattress, but at least he had his own four walls. He was still searching for his sister Lieselotte, who he said was just a day older than myself, his brother Werner who would have been fifteen years old and his parents. Günter's family was from Oppeln in Upper Silesia. He had no idea where they were. Papa Kröning was hopeful. He was also looking for my brother Dieter, who had been in Obernigk in Silesia last with our grandmother.

Slowly this black year of nineteen forty five crawled to an end.

There was no electricity, no coal or wood. We were constantly on the move to provide both wood and food. The woods were crawling with people, also collecting wood and cones, scraping fuel from under the snow. Soon there was not a stick to be had in any of the forests far and wide. The farmers, who owned the forests, had a hard time, protecting their trees from wood poachers, who would just go and cut them down.

Luckily the miller from Eichhofen had contacted Mother. He still had sacks which needed mending. So Mother and I sat and darned and patched no end of flour sacks in the evening by candle light, for which we continued to receive a little flour and crushed grain. Mother also asked for waste wood from the sawmill and the miller would bring a sack full each time he collected the mended sacks in exchange for new ones. He told us that waste wood was getting scarce. So was the flour and crushed grain. What would we do when there were no more sacks to mend, because there was no corn to grind? We were worried.

Günter had a sack of coal once every three weeks. We had to ration ourselves and wear our coats and mittens most of the time.

New Year's Eve, Mother was invited to Grandfather's room. He had a few guests and from his larder they had some of his pre-war homemade elderberry wine. They were toasting to a fresh start. We were allowed to join for a toast before we went to bed, already wearing our nighties underneath the overcoats and muffs.

In Berlin I had a dreadful recurring nightmare. It stopped while we were in East Prussia, but had now returned. In this nightmare, our apartment was on fire. Ebony chairs, which stood in our living room, covered with rose coloured velvet upholstery, were burning. Crimson flames leaping about. Beautiful Meißen china figurines shattering in the heat. Every time, just before the flames reached me, I woke up, feeling relieved that it was only a dream.

This night of New Year's Eve, into nineteen forty six, the same dream woke me up. It felt as if I had screamed. Vividly I recalled the dream of so long ago, and wondered how I hadn't even remembered it in the meantime. It had completely left me, only to come back so vividly. I sat up in bed shaking and scared. I knew it was only a dream, but I could not help it. It was not yet morning but I did not want to stay in bed. It was freezing cold. It was too early to light the fire. I got dressed, but was still cold. I ended up wearing all my clothes including the coat, scarf, woolly hat, mittens and muff and Grandfather's ski boots. Quietly, I went outside. The dream would not leave me even though I was now awake. It was like a fever. I had to take deep breaths and still had not enough air in my lungs. It felt as if the dream was real and I had only just escaped the fire.

It had been snowing for two days continuously, and I still expected it to snow. But it had stopped when I got out and the moon was shining, between racing clouds. It was bitterly cold. I went to the henhouse and looked at Grandfather's thermometer; twenty two degrees celsius below zero. I walked through the forbidden garden and marvelled at the new snow. I came round to the bomb crater, carefully walked around it and onto the street. I couldn't go too far, since there was still a curfew. There was absolutely no noise, just overwhelming peace. The bombed houses were dressed with thick fluffy white coats, their ugliness covered and the world not only looked cleansed but as if created new. No engine noise broke the silence, no dog barked. Not even the bright moon light showed the blemishes of the war.

But Hermann was still missing. Where was he in this terrible cold? Where, with all the refugees in this city alone, was my brother? I stood so small and helpless in my enormous boots, which weighed me down even further.

Again, I wanted to fly. I wanted wings. I wanted to be away from here. I never wanted to touch the ground again.

I dipped my mittens into the snow and licked them. The clock on the Ostentor struck four. I was dreadfully cold and went back upstairs. I took some things off and quietly crawled into bed with Mother who just moved over a little to make room and put her hands onto my ice cold feet. Soon, I felt so warm and safe and looking out from the veranda windows watching the stars, I was soon asleep again.

38

The '*Kohlen Ferien* (coal holidays) and power cuts continued well into the New Year. There was no school. Mother was worried. What was to become of us? Untaught and uneducated?

I didn't mind. I hated school and the children who chanted after us:

"Go home you Prussian pigs." *Bombengesindel, Bombenpack* (Bomb trash). They followed us around with sticks and hit us on the head. When we ran away they came after us. Adults took no notice. When I carried the shopping home, I could not run fast enough, because I was afraid to spill the milk, which I had to carry in a little jug and often I was hurt. The native children were constantly on the lookout for refugee children. They could easily tell, by the way we were dressed, that we were refugees, and they ridiculed, taunted and tormented us, and tried to steal our precious rations.

At home we were asked to speak High German, and although we had learned to speak the Bavarian dialect in Eichhofen, many children in my neighbourhood, including Ise, had not had that chance to mix with native children, the way we had in the village, and they spoke in their own native dialect. In Eichhofen the children were sweet, friendly and helpful and took simple pleasure in teaching us the Bavarian dialect. Here in the city they were prejudiced, spiteful and callous, afraid we would take something away from them.

I was scared of these children. They were unpredictable. When I told Mother about it, she advised me not to show fear, to stand my ground and look straight and unblinking, into their eyes. I supposed it was worth a try, especially since there was no alternative. After all, Mother had no time to sort things out for us. Ise's Mother, also thought we would win by not showing fear.

Bine, Ise, Tissi and I had gone down to the Danube, past the Royal Villa, which was a beautiful palace set in its own little park right on the banks of the Danube. It was literally across the street from us and Grandfather had told me that it was built less than a hundred years ago for King Maximilian II of Bavaria. It was a mysteriously beautiful fairy tale palace. There were intriguing little gates in the wall, leading into the park, and there was also a large piece of the wall missing because a bomb had hit it. We often sneaked into the park to play hide and seek.

We rounded the outer wall and came down to the Danube embankment to watch the ice break up. Huge ice-floes were rushing down river, threatening a wooden makeshift bridge which connected the large island and the other side of the river with this side. The four lane *Nibelungen Brücke* was still lying in the Danube.

It was fascinating to see the huge blocks racing wildly down the river, chasing large pieces of wood and trees. The water between the floes seemed milky-viridian with brown patches. Our breath hung white and heavy in the air. The crashing sound of the colliding floes was tremendous. Right out in the middle of the river, a dog rode on one of the ice-floes, barking wildly. Would somebody rescue him before he got to Hungary? He looked doomed!

As we watched, a horde of children came down the little lane, past the Villa and started to taunt us, wielding large sticks. Tissi started to cry and my throat went dry. Ise wanted to run, but then thought better of it. There were too many of them. Bravely, she took Tissi's hand and stood behind Bine and myself, protecting Tissi. Bine's black eyes shot daggers. She took my hand. In a deep voice, which somehow wasn't mine, I said:

"Don't you dare touch any of us" and then I made myself stare at them in silence. I did not budge. Bine and I stood firm, holding each other's hand tightly, giving each other strength.

With amazement, I saw the children, mostly boys, get embarrassed and slowly back away. It was difficult to keep staring at the children. The boys looked ridiculous with their haircuts. All of them had their heads shaven, except for one patch on their forehead. The one patch looked so out of place and why should they all have the same cut? Their ears sticking out from the bare heads, red and luminous against the pale, ice cold sun. I had to stop myself from saying something. It would have spoilt the effect I was trying to achieve. They looked absurd.

And it worked! Bine and I stood until they had all gone. Then I found my knees going weak. I began to giggle and stopped myself, in case they came back. Bine wanted to sit down, but slowly, silently and shaking we went home. They did not bother us again. They taunted us from afar, they called us names, so what.

From then on, they ignored us completely, and pretended we didn't exist. I didn't mind that. Having the Bussigel twins as friends helped as well, since they were true Bavarians.

The city of Regensburg had managed to clean up the park and proclaim it safe and free from all explosives. The playground had swings again and two wonderful see-saws and an enormous sandpit. Here the children gathered to play, and as winter entered into early spring, we had more or less established our right to live side by side with the local children.

There were no adult people in the park during the day, in the evening the benches were taken over by American soldiers and young women. The only sound, healthy, strong men of all ages, were Americans. Mother insisted that we were not to go into the park after five in the afternoon.

Very early in the morning, before breakfast, I would dash out and collect all the cigarette butts around the benches. I found I had to be really early, because other people had the same idea. I had to be careful that I wasn't spotted, because sometimes rough looking men would take the collected butts from me.

A gang of German POWs came to fill in our crater. I always wondered where all the earth had gone, that had been there before the bomb fell. It had vanished. Now they brought several loads of rubble, to fill the hole. But before that, they had to check the foundation of the house, do any structural repairs.

We all stood around and watched, when suddenly, they discovered an unexploded bomb. It had been buried in the ground all these months. What a miracle that it had not gone off. If it had, the house would have been totally destroyed. It was lodged in the foundation wall into the cellar. Grandfather stood, legs spread and looking at the monster, scratching and shaking his head. He went without a word, collected his stick and hat and slowly and majestically he strode into the city to his local for a beer.

Our house and the ruins around us and the refugee camp opposite in the cinema, were cordoned off, the refugees and everybody were herded into the park which was declared a safety zone.

We sat on park benches, below the Bussigel house, just around the corner from our house and waited, listening anxiously.

By six o' clock in the evening, we were told we could go home. The bomb had been defused and been made safe. It was still lying on the pavement. It looked enormous. I had never seen a bomb that was still intact, so close. To think, that one of those could destroy a house, or even several houses. It was much taller than I was. In fact, I could easily have fitted inside. I shuddered at the thought of it exploding. We had cheated death again.

School had finally started, in earnest in the last week in February. We still had Fräulein Ampfer as teacher. School meals had resumed and hadn't changed. Still sweet porridge with bloated raisins, ham flavoured pea soup without the ham, sliced potatoes flavoured with vanilla ice cream powder.

It was a very warm and sunny March day, the chestnut buds were thick, brown and sticky, and the green shimmer in the trees had become a firm promise. There was a fragrance in the air which made my heart soar.

We arrived at the *Pestalozzi Schule* along with an army truck filled with American soldiers, wearing white helmets with the letters M P written on them. They also wore an armband with the same initials.

That day we had a strange lesson.

Our world, which had collapsed around us, had not managed to drag me down with it. I was still looking confidently and trustingly into the future, keeping my head up. I was consciously taking part to rebuild my world by helping to clean bricks, by not complaining about being constantly hungry, by making do with the little we had, not grieving about the possessions we had lost or where we were and how we were forced to live. I was totally prepared to start fresh, give everybody and everything a chance. I had faith in people around me and hoped for my father's return.

When our teacher came into the classroom that morning, she looked pale and worried. She busied herself at her desk. Then the door opened and two MPs entered. They planted themselves either side of the door.

Quietly and nervously, our teacher started to tell us that we would never use the greeting of "Heil Hitler" again, which we hadn't for a long time anyway. We had used no greeting at all, which made us feel strange. Before the collapse, we always stood up when the teacher entered the room, and a crisp "Heil Hitler" greeted him.

Fräulein Ampfer made us stand up and practise the new standard greeting of "Grüss Gott" and then started to explain that Hitler had died almost a year ago, nobody knew exactly what had happened to him. No trace of him could be found. But it was clear he did not exist anymore. She went on to explain, that he was the greatest war criminal of all times and that his crimes were such that ordinary human beings could not really grasp the extent of it.

Hitler's portrait had hung in all official buildings, in every classroom, in many households. His presence everywhere was so common, that one noticed his absence. The greeting of *Heil Hitler*, among people in the street, had also quietly disappeared, as if it had never existed. I had noticed that his portrait had disappeared off the walls too. I had given him no more thought, than that he had lost the war. Everybody said so. We were all far too busy with our own struggle, than to think of him.

Fräulein Ampfer was shaking, she was visibly upset and very ashen. She looked nervously at the two MPs, who were still standing by the door, stony faced. She went on to explain how Germany, as we knew it, would not ever exist again. It was divided up amongst the four powers. The Russians would have the east and northeast of Germany, the English the north and northwest, the French the west and the Americans the south and south east. Berlin, my home, would be divided too. Half was occupied by the Soviets and the other half was carved up between the three western powers.

The MPs had not shifted until now. One of them came over and put something onto the desk in front of our teacher. She sighed. She began to tell us how Hitler had made it a law, that non Germans had to be interned. That was the same in any country. I knew that too. There had been such a camp near where we lived in Silesia. We could see the women walk around, hang up their washing and children playing. It seemed a normal life, except that they lived behind barbed wire, in long wooden houses. They had gardens in front of their huts and grew vegetables. Mother had explained that they lived there until the war was over and then they would be reunited with their husbands and go home. They had committed no crime and they were in those camps also for their own protection.

Now Fräulein Ampfer went on to say that not all people were kept alive in those camps. On Hitler's orders, Jews were separated and put into special camps where they were then killed. She mentioned a number, but it was so high it didn't mean a thing to me, only that I just could not believe it, could not grasp it.

The MPs came over and stood silently either side of Fräulein Ampfer. She straightened her shoulders and looked at us.

"They were gassed. They were put into large rooms, and then gas would be put into the room until they were all dead. Then their bodies would be incinerated and the ash scattered." Fräulein Ampfer looked at the MPs either side of her. They stood there like statues.

Inge Schäuble, a girl behind me, vomited. I could hear some children cry and pleading to be allowed to go home.

One of the MPs barred the way to the door, as some children wanted to leave, the other lifted something he had put on the desk earlier. It was a large photograph of a mountain of shoes. Why show us all those shoes? All I could think of was, that there were so many shoes of all sizes and we had none. He picked up two more photographs, all of shoes, mountains of them. Nobody spoke a word.

Slowly and sickeningly, it dawned on me. These were the shoes of the dead people. My head began to swim, I felt very dizzy and very hot and then I vomited. It shot out of me like an explosion. We had been standing all this time. I felt wretched. Who could do such a thing and why? Who were Jews? Had I ever known any Jews? They had never been mentioned in our family.

The American MPs picked up their wretched photos and walked to the door. One of them stopped and turned to the class: "Deutschland, Deutschland *unter* alles" he said and left.

Why "unter" alles? It went round and round in my dizzy, spinning, aching head, puzzling me. I told myself, the MP didn't know what the words really meant. He translated the words wrongly. In my heart, Deutschland would be "über alles", I loved my homeland above all. Nothing anybody said could shake that. But what of the people around me?

Something evil was now happening. To me, honesty and honour had gone. Trust in people? Somebody was telling the biggest untruth of all time, surely.

Suddenly, everything around me was swimming. Was I drowning? What sort of people could do such killings? Had they happened? Were they committed by the German people? And if they had not, why tell such preposterous lies? Our teacher was still speaking, but I didn't hear what she said. I felt so ashamed, betrayed, cheated.

When the children left the classroom with their satchels, I followed. We came downstairs and everybody went home. I felt Ise next to me. She was crying quietly. We went to her house, because there would be no one at home, except Grandfather. Did he know? Who had known? Had anybody known? Did I know anybody who knew?

Ise told her mother what had happened at school. Then I suddenly remembered Bine. My God, had they told her class too? She was still in her first year. I excused myself to Frau Winkelmann and ran home. Bine was not there. I ran back to school taking the normal route. When I got to the school, I found they were still in class. I waited opposite the building until school had finished.

When I finally spotted Bine, a twin on either side, happily laughing, I knew they had been spared this horrendous lesson.

When we came home, I climbed onto my cupboard and lay down flat. I found that I could not talk about it to anyone. I could not ask Mother if she had known. I could not talk to Grandfather. I felt guilty. In the end I went to Ise's house.

Even sitting down, Ise's Mother was tall. Her white hair piled into a loose bun on top of her head. She looked very severe, in the black clothes she always wore. Unsmiling but very kindly, she looked at me:

"You must not always believe what you hear," she said. "Always remember, we are now in enemy hands. An enemy which has finally won. Germany is a coveted prize, and now it is theirs to do with as they wish." I was grateful for those words, although I did not really understand. She continued:

"Don't ever lose your pride, your hope, and the joy of knowing you are German. Our spirit cannot be crushed. We are a noble folk and an army of criminals cannot change that. My son never died for that."

"But did we really kill all those Jews?" I asked.

"If they were killed, there must have been a reason, they must have been an enemy of Germany", she said, "and traitors die in war."

"But women and children?" I asked back, but she did not answer. She just looked at me silently. After a while she said:

"You must ask your Mother. Let us go together. It is a long time since I last saw your mother."

Slowly we went to our house. Bine had gone to the Bussigel twins, Tissi was playing with pebbles on the floor in the sunny veranda, and Mother was polishing the parquet floor where it was exposed.

She was pleased to see Frau Winkelmann. Mother made some coffee and cut two slices of bread, spread them with *Vierfrucht Marmelade* (four fruit jam) and then cut them into little strips and arranged them on a plate. Daintily we picked up a small strip and slowly nibbled, and then washed it down with *Ersatz Kaffee*. Nobody spoke except Tissi who told Mother a story about her pebbles.

There was a mother pebble and a father pebble and all the children pebbles. There were six of them. Then there were all the children's children pebbles. They had four children each.

"Heavens" Mother sighed, thinking of other things, "Where do all these children come from?"

"From their mother's tummies of course." Tissi said without looking up. Mother was going to say something but then checked herself and just smiled. I was so relieved to be able to laugh a little. Ise too gave an embarrassed little giggle, but Frau Winkelmann never laughed. It suddenly occurred to me, that I had never seen her laugh.

Then Mother asked what exactly had happened at school. Frau Winkelmann explained and after listening carefully, Mother shook her head.

"All lies." she said. "The German people are not capable to do such a thing."

No, of course they were not. It was all a lie. But there was a shadow, a doubt, which would not go away. Ise and I left our mothers to discuss the matter. I had shoved the dreadful feeling of guilt, which had weighed me down, onto my mother's shoulders.

✸✸✸

39

It was difficult for us to understand what had happened to the Jews and why, and asking the adults did not help. They had no answers. I wondered whether they were as puzzled as Ise and I was. Mother said we were too young to trouble ourselves with such things, so did Ise's mother. I had to put it out of my mind in order to cope with everyday life.

The upper school classes had been taken by a convoy of army lorries to Dachau, but when we asked them about it afterwards, they could not tell what they had seen, except that they had been led through a number of empty rooms and had listened to a lecture given by an American who spoke perfect German. They did not believe what they had heard. It was all a lie, some of them said.

Was Hanni right about hell and the devil taking over man, possessing him, to enable him to do his awful work? The devil was always out to tempt souls, promise them a good life and as a reward he would get their souls at the end. Were there still such people who sold their souls? They did in fairy tales, but those stories happened so long ago. Goethe had written a story about a man called Faust. He sold his soul to get the woman he wanted, and for worldly riches, and when the time came for him to pay, he regretted it bitterly.

I found myself looking at people and wondering whether they had had anything to do with the killing of Jews. I was sorting them into 'yes they could' and 'no they wouldn't' categories. Mother told me to stop it. She got very cross with me. My mind went round and round, always finishing at one point. Who could, who would do such a thing and why. Mother said:

"They are criminals, the people who did this, and they will be caught and punished." She sat down on a chair and stood me in front of her, our eyes level and she looked at me:

"Believe that the soul is eternal and uses this body as a vessel while journeying on earth. Believe also that the soul does not die. When the time on earth is over, it sheds the body like an old and worn garment, which is of no use any more. The soul will come back, which is called reincarnation, and for the next journey on this earth it will have new apparel." Mother looked at me very seriously. "Believe that things are designed outside this world and while we are here, we do not understand. But there is someone who does, believe in Him and believe that He is good whatever He is called, and he has many names, He is our life force. He is the God for all mankind."

I could believe in my soul, I could feel that the 'I' was more than flesh and blood. It was strange, I seemed to understand it all, as if through patches of fog. Clearly one moment and hidden in haze the next. Mother gave me a kiss and a shove towards the door.

"That's enough, off you go and play. Be happy my little sunshine. We are not forsaken." Outside, the sun was shining brightly, but it was a cold and shivery day.

Papa Kröning came to our room with a new job for Mother. Mountains of Caritas parcels from the Lutheran communities of America had arrived at the Protestant Relief Work Office with clothing for the refugees. Papa Kröning needed reliable staff to sort them out into various piles and sizes, and cope with the resulting paper work. The city had made a little church available for that purpose, and would she do it? Mother was glad for the job.

There were two elderly sisters, the *Fräulein von Unruh*, whose brother was Grandfather's friend. They first met when they were both young cadets at the Academy in Wahlstatt near Liegnitz. General von Unruh was in the war, but no friend of Hitler's. He said he was in the war for Germany not Hitler. I often saw him at Grandfather's, where he came to play cards. His twin sisters did everything together. Sometimes they even said the same thing at the same time. I was fascinated by them.

Herr Sailer, a very shy school teacher was running the office, Herr Fischer was processing all the application forms.

It was a job, where Mother could take our tiny Tissi. She had spent her mornings or afternoons, according to what our school rota was, entirely alone at home, hugging Mother's apron. Now Tissi helped sort out the clothes. Blouses into that pew, skirts over into that one, dresses, pullover, men's jackets and trousers etc. Tissi loved it and changed into a happy completely different child. She hoarded impossible dress jewellery, shining and sparkling in all colours into a large casket and lived a life of pure fantasy. She was full of funny stories when we were all gathered around the evening table. She laughed about the clothes the Americans wear. She had been trying them on, and teetering around in shoes that had heels as high as her entire foot was long. She imagined that everybody in America walked around in long evening dresses and silk slips and high heels. Some skirts were so tight, that one could hardly make a children's skirt out of it. Her sweet little face looked so funny imitating what she imagined they looked like, wearing high heels and tight skirts. We laughed a lot and kept asking her for more stories.

Mother was more serious. So many garments were totally unsuitable. There were slinky thin long evening dresses in crazy colours. For every garment that was useable, there would be two that were not.

"Don't worry, they will be glad and happy for anything they can get, and you will be surprised what they can turn those dresses into." Papa Kröning said, laughing happily. "The colours alone will brighten up their lives. Every little scrap of material is needed and can be used. They are gathering possessions again, and these things are the beginning of a new life. They are thrilled with everything."

Hundreds of people, of both faiths came every day, filling in forms, answering the questions of where they had come from, their names and how many members in the family, what ages, what clothing they needed most of all. Usually they needed everything. Then they were taken into the vestry where the two elderly sisters von Unruh fitted them with the requested and suitable clothing.

Mother said that it was wonderful to see the happy faces, as they found things which fitted, and the plans they had for the things that Mother thought were totally useless. Mother marvelled at the ingenuity of the people, their will to survive and turn anything around and into something useful. Usually there was something for everyone including shoes. Mother would listen quietly to the heart breaking stories they had to tell. She could see they needed to talk. It was as necessary as the clothes for the family, Mother said.

Once two women came to Mother asking for nightshirts among other things. Mother could find only one, and nothing else that might have been a suitable alternative to double for a nightie. At a loss, she looked at the two women. Who should have the only nightie? Then she asked:

"Are you married?"

"I am." one of the ladies said. Without hesitation, Mother gave the nightie to the other woman and turning to the married one she said:

"You have a husband to keep you warm, you don't need it." Happily laughing, the women left.

The crowd in the *Bruderhaus Kirche* was a friendly and happy team. The schoolteacher, Herr Sailer, wrote funny poems about the people who worked there. It was a sunshine place and I loved going there.

Among the bundles of clothing they found letters from the people who had donated the clothes, asking the recipient to write and make friends. Many people could not read English, and the letters were handed to Mother and Herr Sailer. Mother got in touch with many of the generous Americans. In one letter, an American lady had written back to Mother, saying, that people among people will always be human and not fight or make wars. It is the politicians who mess things up.

Mother translated the entire letter to us, and I felt glad, that there were Americans who thought like that. There were so many letters, that Herr Sailer and Mother sat for many hours in the evenings, answering the letters, and telling the American families and clergymen, who headed the organisations over there, of the happiness they had created with their gifts, and of the families who had received their clothes, and of their various fates.

One American lady in particular had formed a close friendship with Mother, and they promised to visit when times were better. This lady also had three children our age. Her husband was a soldier in the Pacific. I would really like to go to America one day.

But what I would not forget, ever, were the men in the planes, laughing, as they shot at us. They were Americans too and they enjoyed killing people.

I had hoped, that we too, could have some clothes. But Mother said that we were not special cases, and we would have to fill in a form like everybody else, and so we did. Then, one day we were fitted out as well. I felt so excited, I could hardly wait. Would I be able to get some shoes?

The three of us came into the vestry, which had beautifully carved wooden panelling. The Fräulein von Unruh were already waiting and started to fuss with a tape measure and then they bustled off. They came back with the most wonderful garments I had seen. They had such pleasure in finding clothes which fitted and to see us happy.

For Bine, they had found a lovely warm dress in a deep blue and black fluffy, almost velvety material with wide sleeves and a lace collar. For me, they had secured a bright red skirt, and a sky blue pullover, which they said they had put aside especially, because they knew, I would come sooner or later. They were such dears. They looked so alike even though they were at least seventy years old.

Tissi had a blouse, a wide velvet skirt in bright green and a brown and yellow striped cardigan, all of which she had put aside for herself with the permission of the two ladies. The clothes were all too big for us, but Mother said, that by the time winter comes again they would fit. Bine and Tissi were lucky to find some shoes, but as hard as the two Fräulein von Unruh tried, they could find nothing which fitted me. I was deeply disappointed and hung my head. I was so jealous of the other two. I tried to squeeze my feet into some shoes, but I could not walk and Mother said I would ruin my feet. There was a pair which fitted, but the heels were so high, I could not straighten out my knees, and Mother would never have allowed those.

It was going to be another barefoot summer for me, but the Fräulein von Unruh promised to put the next suitable pair aside for me. After all, my form granted me a pair, so I was entitled. I felt a little happier then.

In the Easter holidays, which were cut very short, to make up the time we had had off for the coal holidays, we helped Mother with sorting the clothes. I did not find a lot of pleasure in sorting clothes. Bine and I preferred to be out in the open, but Tissi was in her element.

The *Bruderhaus Kirche* was separated from the soup kitchen by the *Emmerams Platz*, a beautiful large square, dominated by an outstanding ancient church, the St. Emmerams Kirche. When we crossed the square to have lunch in the palace grounds, I could see a man standing by the gate. For days I had watched him. As soon as we came through the gate, he would follow us, get into the queue behind us and then sit very close to where we were sitting. He looked frightfully ugly, had very deep lines in his face, so deep that I thought they were scars. Whenever he saw me looking at him, he smiled and his face was not quite so ugly then.

One day as we approached the gates, I pointed him out to Mother and asked her if she had noticed him too. She hadn't. When we were all sitting at the table, Mother started a conversation with him.

He was so happy to talk, spoke very nervously and fast in Silesian dialect.

He had finally been released from the hospital where he had been for nearly a year. They had given him his ration card and pointed the way to the nearest refugee camp. He remembered me from Christmas carol singing, and Mother had registered him, because he was searching for his family. When he saw us, he recognised familiar faces. He knew no one here and had a mattress in the refugee camp on the other side of the Danube. He had been very ill with a head wound and now he suffered agonizing headaches and had to take painkillers all the time. He had also come off the morphine and missed that very much. The surgeon told him the headaches would stop in time, he would have to be patient. His name was Benno Katczmarek.

Benno only went back to his mattress in the evenings, the rest of the time he spent with us. He was waiting at the school gates when school finished, then he walked the long hot way with us to the soup kitchen, he supervised our homework and carried my shopping. He went on walks with us. But, in a way, we looked after him. He desperately needed people who cared for him. He would suddenly have frightful fits of headaches, where he could not walk anymore and had to sit down. Sometimes he would lie down on the pavement or wherever we were, and moan and roll around. Bine and I would then just quietly sit down by his side and wait until the fit stopped, reassuring the people who stopped, that everything was alright. After a while he would sit up, complaining about a terrible headache. Bine and I would then take him into our middle and walk him home. He never left our side, except twenty minutes before curfew.

Because he was always there, the other children thought he was our father and mentally handicapped.

I asked him one day about his wound, because I could not see a scar anywhere. He took by hand, looking into my eyes and guided my hand to the top of his head. His eyes were locked into mine, as he gently immersed my four fingers into a hole up to my thumb. I recoiled in horror. The hole was entirely hidden by his thick, blond and curly hair. Poor Benno. He took my hand again and marked an area on top of his head and said that under the skin was a silver plate, because his own scull bone was shattered. I was amazed that he lived at all. Bine and I took great care of him, but made it look as if he looked after us.

After Christmas, a lot of strange people had arrived in the city. The curious thing about them was the way they dressed. It caught our attention. All of them wore black riding boots, men and women alike, the women wore elegant fur coats of a variety of exotic animals, and the men camel hair coats and tall, Russian typed fur hats. They filled the trams and the streets. They lived on the outskirts of Regensburg in confiscated flats, apartments and housing estates. Nobody spoke about them. There were just some other strange looking people crowding the ruined city. Travelling next to them in the tram I could smell garlic salami, something I hadn't tasted for a long time. When I asked Mother and other adults who they were and where they so suddenly came from, seven months after the collapse, they said they didn't know.

Their arrival was sudden and mysterious. They spoke among themselves in a strange German dialect. If they were refugees, like all the others, then they were lucky to have saved all those elegant clothes. They attracted attention by having things, other people had not. They didn't look hungry either. As the year went into late spring and early summer, they wore elegant summer dress, but kept their boots on. Among all the strange people who were now in Germany, they were the strangest.

I had filled my two large tins to the brim with *Zigaretten Stummel*, (cigarette butts) a treasured prize, worth more than all the money and ration points. Tabaco was top currency for the black market.

Proudly I showed Günter my treasure and watched his face light up. I asked him if he could go to the black market in the city and find some extra food. It was time we celebrated something. We hadn't had any festivities for many months. Mother also thought it was time for a feast.

Papa Kröning used to say when he came to work in the morning:" What are we celebrating today?" and then look around at his staff, and wait for any good news that might have come in overnight.

If there was no reason to have a party, we would find one. Having food on the table would be reason enough we agreed.

Günter and I went off to the *Gesandten Strasse*, (Street of Ambassadors) where the black market was. There I saw the people with the black boots busily trading. This street seemed to be their street.

As Günter and I, walked down from the Neupfarr Platz to the Gesandten Strasse we were approached by some of these people. "Do you want to do a little business?" they asked. Günter asked back: "What have you got?" But they had nothing edible for us. Finally he was offered some *Speck* but there was no meat on it, only white fat and he would not have it. They came after us, pulling Günter by the sleeve: "Any silver? Any jewels, diamonds? Gold?" Günter shook his head, holding on to my hand. I was intrigued. I had never met people like these, and it was the first time we had spoken to each other. They seemed friendly but difficult to shake off. I whispered to Günter: "Who are they, where do they come from?" He answered:

"I don't know where they all come from, but in the office we think they are Jews."

As the Gesandten Strasse mouthed onto the Bismarck Platz, Günter found what he was looking for. A few farmers, looking healthy and presumably with real food for sale and eager for cigarette butts, looked at us as we approached. We picked the one who seemed to have the largest bag and I held up my tin with the butts to him. The farmer looked at it, weighed it in his hand, stirred them around with one finger, grinned, and then put his fist into a dirty potato sack. We opened our shopping bag, and like lightning I saw a chicken come out of the sack and into our bag, a large bag of potatoes, a small bag of flour, some carrots, onions and four eggs and a little ball wrapped in greaseproof paper which turned out to be butter! Butter! He also had a quarter of a six pounder loaf of farm bread and a little cottage cheese, also wrapped in greaseproof paper. For that, he was happy with one of my large tins of cigarette butts. I was very honest and had removed the filters, if they had any. The tobacco weighed about a pound. He beamed and so did we. It surely was a bargain.

We did not go back via the Gesandten Strasse but turned towards the Ludwigs Strasse and followed the tram lines onto the Haidplatz. This was a very ancient old square, lined on all four sides with proud patrician town castles, each one flanked with a tall square tower. On one of the castle fronts was a huge mural of two jousting knights, one of them was Parcival.

We came past the *Alte Rathaus* (ancient town hall) and I told Günter how Mother and I had run here to try to help Grandfather, only to find, we had stumbled into a nest of the Gestapo. He squeezed my hand: "You have to forget these things now. They are past."

We entered the very narrow Kramgasse and in the tight gap between the roofs of the houses I saw just one of the twin spires of the cathedral reaching for the sky. We crossed the *Dom Platz* onto *the Alter Kornmarkt* and entered an area which was totally in ruins. I hated to walk along here and always avoided the place, when I was on my own. Buildings which had survived hundreds of years and proudly bore witness to the building skills of people long dead, were destroyed in a few seconds.

Eventually, we came to the Ostengasse, past the Inn with the bear on the chain. The roof was badly damaged and many houses in the Ostengasse were destroyed. We walked through the Osten Tor and home. I put the food on the table:

"Look what we got for my butts." I said proudly. Mother smiled happily and sent Bine and myself off to invite Papa Kröning for the next day. Mother said: "Just tell him we want to celebrate." We invited Grandfather and Frau Gruczinsky too. But Grandfather did not come. He said to me:

"It is good of you to ask me, but how many people do you want to feed on one chicken?" He gave me a friendly grin. "Next time."

I was very sad. Bine whispered as we walked back along the corridor to our room: "Never mind, so much more for us." I gave her a push into her ribs.

✻✻✻

40

My second birthday, after the collapse was near, also the most beautiful time in the year. It was hot and the trees that had survived the bombing, were thick with leaves, hiding part of the hideous ruins.

I was limping badly, because a day before Mother's birthday in June I had ripped open the sole of my foot from end to end on a steel pin which was sticking out of the pavement. It was one of several, which once had held a lamp post. I was skipping along barefoot, just outside the *Bayerische Lloyd* when it happened. It was very painful. The only time it eased a little, was when I put my foot up. I had an enormous bandage and could only use the outside edge of my foot to walk on.

I still had to go to school, but I was allowed to put my foot on a stool which was brought especially from the headmaster's office. I enjoyed the fuss they made over me in class.

Limping to the soup kitchen was painful, but I had Benno to lean on. He said that one old soldier deserves the help of another.

The other children finally believed that Benno was not our father. He was still missing. We did not know whether he was dead or alive. However, we were able to trace one of our neighbours in Berlin and left our new address, should Father come back to Berlin first. The mail was not yet working properly, mostly because the addresses were missing. Any mail within Germany took weeks to arrive, and then there was the problem of delivery.

We had heard nothing of our brother, although Mother moved heaven and earth to find him, and we read through endless lists of names daily. But every day, lost people turned up. Ours would too.

Going to school, we had to cross the Landshuter Strasse which was a main route to Munich. The military traffic, which was almost the only traffic on the road, was so heavy and endless, that we were often delayed for school, trying to cross over. There were no traffic lights, nobody to stop the vehicles for us to cross and they would not stop on their own accord to let us cross. We had to wait for up to an hour, watching military trucks full of Americans, tanks, jeeps, red cross vehicles canon trucks and other strange looking vehicles go by. It was an endless to-ing and fro-ing. The road surface was ripped open by this constant traffic and huge bits of black tar flew through the air as the great tank chains churned up the road even more. We stood patiently on the pavement, looking on and counting how many trucks with soldiers, black and white, how many jeeps, tanks and canon trucks, how many red cross, and so on. The only reward for this long wait, might be a few packets of chewing gum, which we had learned to chew by now. These gums were a prized sweet.

Our teacher made us write a hundred times:

"I must not be late for school."

We also encountered American soldiers on foot. A hospital which was on the corner of Weissenburger Strasse and Landshuter Strasse was an American Army Base, and we had to pass it every day going to school.

Often black Americans approached us and asked us, in very strange German, to teach them to yodel. Bine, Ise and I thought that was very funny, because we could not yodel either. Only Bavarians in the mountains or mountain people could.

The black Americans did not understand, that we couldn't teach them, because we didn't know how, they thought we didn't want to. They offered chocolate and sweets and begged if we would only consider it. So Ise started to squeal as best she could, getting red in the face with embarrassment. Bine and I joined her, feeling equally embarrassed. The black soldiers looked suspiciously at us. Eventually, they realised we really couldn't do it.

Presumably, they thought all Germans in Bavaria could yodel. They gave us a bar of chocolate to divide among the three of us. This game continued for quite a while. We tried to learn to yodel for the black Americans, but it was just too difficult. Father Rappel said he could yodel when he was young, but that was long before I was even born. Father Rappel said that not even all Bavarians in the mountains could yodel. One had to have a special talent for that.

After school, two days before my birthday, Benno took us to Papa Kröning's office in the *Silberne Fischgasse* (silver fish lane) instead of the soup kitchen. There would be a surprise.

Mother and Tissi were already there. A rather large, middle aged woman was sitting near Mother, looking very happy, continuously smiling watching Papa Kröning, who was sorting through a mountain of papers on his desk, speaking to two people at once. I saw him looking up every now and then, searching for the eyes of the woman. When their eyes met, there was such joy, it was infectious. I guessed it was Papa Kröning's wife. I could feel their joy in my heart. Would it be like that when my father came back?

On a canon stove in the corner, Mother was cooking something in a large pot. It was unbearably hot in the room. Even though the Silberne Fisch Gasse was entirely in the shade from the scorching sun, the heat was heavily pressing down on us. The canon stove, with the long black stovepipe reaching through the entire room along the ceiling, made things even more oppressive. Beads of perspiration were running down people's faces, and large wet patches showed under their arms.

Benno, Bine and I had stopped near the door and waited. There was no way of getting any further. Mother had spotted us, smiled and signed us to wait. A strand of hair had escaped from her thick plaits which she curled around her head, and clung wet to her face.

Papa Kröning suddenly put his papers down, lifted his enormous frame off the chair and looked around.

"For those who have just come," he said, and pointed to the large woman "this is my Else, we have just found each other again.

She needs looking after, she lost a lot of weight." He smiled all round and then sat down again and carried on with his papers.

A lot of milling and squeezing went on in the two rooms of this ancient building which could easily be a thousand years old. Everybody wanted to shake hands and welcome Frau Kröning. Papa Kröning, whom they all loved, and upon whom they looked as their anchor stone in foreign seas, had missed his wife so much and worried about her. He had often said to Mother that she was his support. He was only half a man without her. Now she was here and safe.

Papa Kröning asked a man next to him, Anton Novak, who had worked closely with, with him for some months now, and who we all knew wasn't using his real name for some reason or another, to close the door for lunch. Nobody asked questions because if Papa Kröning thought the man was honest and had honest reasons not to use his real name, then there were no more questions to be asked.

Anybody who was in the room now could expect some food, it would be divided in such a way, that it would stretch all around. Amazingly, a meal at Papa Krönings always fed anybody who happened to be there.

Thick, delicious lentil soup was bubbling in the pot. Mother started to hand plates around. The three of us had to share one, but Papa Kröning promised us a second helping.

After the meal, Else Kröning started to tell her story. Nobody had heard it yet, since she had literally only arrived this morning.

She had been shunted around in a cattle wagon, with hundreds of other refugees from the Balkan states. She had travelled as far as Hanover, and then all the way south again, she'd even come through Regensburg, in March, without knowing that her husband was here. Sometimes, they were stationary somewhere outside the towns on the shunting lines for days, waiting. They had to cook in these wagons, there were no windows, only the big sliding doors in the sidewalls of the wagons. Several families with children in one wagon, no lavatories only a bucket. She hadn't been allowed to leave the train anywhere, there were guards who would not permit it. They had been allowed to use the facilities, such as they were in some stations and had been looked at by the locals as if they were prisoners. Many stations had been totally destroyed with no facilities except for a cold water tap. They ended up in a camp in Austria, and then they were told, that they had to go back to their homes in the Balkans, in Frau Kröning's case Rumania. The refugees in the train were in uproar. They had fled because they could not live under Communism, because they were not wanted there, even though their nationality was Rumanian or Hungarian, Ukrainian and Bulgarian. If they went back it would be certain imprisonment, labour camps in Siberia or even death.

She stopped and wiped some tears and perspiration beads off her face. Papa Kröning put an arm around her and she smiled at him.

The allies insisted that we should all be handed back to the Russians. No amount of explaining could change their mind. It seems the English had some sort of agreement with the Russians and had to stick to it, they insisted. We pleaded, explained that for many, it would be certain death, but they would not budge.

She started to cry bitterly, and with tears streaming down her face she said:

"I could finally contact my sister Magda, who had married to Duisburg, and she persuaded the authorities that I could live with her so I was spared the return trip. But Oh! Those many thousands who had no choice but to be sent back into the jaws of the Bolsheviks. Not knowing whether they had you, dear Papsel (her name for her husband, which we all adopted) already, and if I went back, would I end up with you? Not knowing I nearly went crazy." She looked up at him with such affection.

"We were told we had the British Authorities' assurances and promise that we would be safe." She dried her tears again and blew her nose noisily. "The English are either very naive or worse, very arrogant if they believe that." She looked around at us. "How much more do we have to endure? I am thinking of the women and children, deliberately separated from their men. They will either be executed or be prisoners for life. It is unbearable."

Nobody said anything.

Robert had told me about Communism and that it was bad for people who wanted to live and work as a free people. He had also told me that if one did not agree with the rules of Communism, one would simply be removed, and that would mean Siberia and death. I believed, I knew that I was glad to be with the Americans and not the Russians.

The homeless were queueing outside in the Silberne Fischgasse, and Papa Kröning had to go back to work. Mother offered to take Frau Kröning to the room where her husband lived, she could make herself at home in the meantime. We took *Muttel* (little mother in dialect), as everybody called her, home and left her there to rest. She was so grateful, that her Odyssey of many months was over.

"I will never forget the many people on that train. We had become friends you know. Their faces when we said good bye, they will haunt me for ever." she cried again.

"Maybe it will not be so bad after all." Mother said.

"Now you sound like the English." Muttel said. "I would not have been able to bear to go back, even though it was my beloved homeland."

Papa Kröning's room was on the fifth floor in a house in the Landshuter Strasse. It took us a long time to get up there, because Muttel had to stop for breath all the time.

When Muttel entered Papa Kröning's room, she walked in, as if she had always lived there. She was home.

On my birthday we went out of the town very early, before six in the morning, because then the heat would not be so strong, and we had a long way to go. The sun was already above the horizon lighting up a cloudless, cerulean sky.

Mother had made a pot of potato salad, we had saved some extra bread rations and margarine. She had also baked a cake. We put it all carefully into our Rucksack, also packed a blanket and set off.

Günter said, he had found this spot we were heading to while out surveying something.

We took the tram as far as it went in Prüfening, and then walked along fields and finally came to the Danube just below the Mariaorter Bridge. I looked up in amazement. There were two arches missing altogether and the rails stretched across the abyss only supported on what looked a very rickety iron structure. Twice we had crossed this bridge, once on foot, once by train, and each time it was a hair raising experience. This time we took a ferry, which was a very sturdy wooden boat with square ends and benches running along either side. The ferry man stood on one side and held a long pole under his arm with which he steered the ferry.

There was a big iron cable which stretched across the river. A rope attached to the ferry at one end and a wheel runner on the cable held the ferry in place while the strong current of the river pushed the boat across. All the ferry man had to do was to steer a little. The Danube was very wide and fast flowing. It was quite an exciting trip. The ferry man took ten *Reichspfennige* per adult for the trip, children free.

As we were in the middle of the river, a train crossed very slowly overhead. I looked up. By now the regular travellers had become used to this spectacle, and were not worried any more. But they would remember the first time forever.

By the time we reached the other side, it was already eight o' clock. The sun started to become really hot. The horseflies were biting. The day was glorious. No ruins, no houses, no people except us five. Over to the left, nestling against the hill was the Mariaorter church.

Slowly we wandered along the meadow paths between the fields, only wide enough for one person.

Günter turned right, along a tall rye field. Blood red poppies and blue cornflowers were in full bloom. Mother said not to pick them until we are on our way home, otherwise they would wilt. There were many more wild flowers. Mother was, as always, on the lookout for herbs which she collected for her universal tea.

At the end of the rye field was a strip of meadow and the River Naab. We looked at the river's edge to find a suitable spot for the day. Wherever we looked, was big step down to the water, a tiny sandy ledge and then the river. The water was crystal clear, one could see the bottom but not how deep it was. The river was fairly wide, about the width of a double road. If it was too deep to stand in, we couldn't go in since we had no swimming aids, but Bine and I did not admit to that. We took our clothes off, and looked a funny sight, because nobody had any swimming clothes and we had to use underwear. Günter had closed his front with a safety pin and Bine and I giggled discreetly, openly we took no notice.

Günter tried the water and found it safe for us to go in. It was a firm and sandy bottom. In no time we were all in except Tissi. No way could she be persuaded to get into the water even when I promised her I would hold her up. Bine and I wished we had the petrol canisters from Eichhofen.

Mother didn't take her sleeveless blouse off and kept her skirt on but had rolled it up to expose her legs. We had lots of fun pretending to swim with one foot on the ground. We stayed in until we were so cold that we couldn't speak. We crawled out and lay on the blanket in the sun, curled up and shivering until we were completely warmed up. It was so peaceful and quiet, listening to the larks as they climbed ever upwards singing their little hearts out. Far away, on the Munich to Nuremberg road we heard the distant roar of army traffic.

Bine and I were in and out of the river exploring further afield. We found a sandbank in the middle of the river, where the water only came to our ankles.

Suddenly, as we were "swimming" back, with one foot still firmly on the ground, the ground had disappeared. Bine and I started to sink at the same time, swallowing water and splashing about wildly. Seeing Bine in such dreadful trouble, eyes wide open with terror, I collected myself and splashed towards her, and found I could keep my head above water. I walked wildly in the river with my feet and pulled Bine to where I thought the sandbank was. Bine was gurgling a yell. I gurgled back, trying to tell her to keep her mouth shut.

My legs were going like mad and I realised that I moved. I turned my head to where I still hoped the sandbank was and kicked and kicked and willed myself to walk in the water towards that spot, pulling Bine. I suddenly realised she wasn't so heavy any more, and when I turned round to see what was happening, she grinned at me. She too had found her feet. Just then my toes felt the sand below. A few more kicks and we were firmly back on safe ground.

We sat on the sandbank, having a rest, shivering. We didn't say much, and we didn't tell Mother afterwards either. She believed we could swim anyway. We had never told her we could or couldn't swim, she believed we could and we left it at that. She probably got the impression in Eichhofen that we could swim and now it was the truth. We both realised we had been in danger. When Bine stopped coughing, we went back to where we knew we could reach the bottom and tested our new found skill. That afternoon, we became good swimmers, real swimmers, with both feet up. It was a great thrill for both of us, and we felt quite proud. It was a pity, we couldn't share this with the rest of our family. It was just between Bine and myself.

We started back for home about four in the afternoon, and as we came back to the ferry, another ferry man was there. He asked where we came from and we told him that we spent the day swimming at the Naab. He shook his head and he said that only good swimmers can go there. It was dangerous to swim there because some bombs had been dropped in that area, when the Mariaorter Bridge was bombed and huge craters were still there and one didn't know exactly where they were and so the entire stretch at the river mouth was off limits for non-swimmers. Also, he said they weren't sure about unexploded bombs. Hadn't we seen the sign?

Bine and I looked at each other, thinking the same thing. At least we could tell them where one crater was for sure.

When we finally got off the tram at the Ostentor stop, tired sunburnt and happy with a big bunch of wild flowers, we found Benno in a state of deep depression sitting on the wall by the tram stop. His elbows were resting on his knees and his head was buried in his hands.

When I called him he stood up immediately and came over to us, asking where we had been, throwing his hands about wildly. He had come over, only to find we were not in, not a note, nothing. He spent the day outside our house in utter misery. By the time he reached us and seen the flowers and the rucksack, he had also remembered that we had planned to go into the country, and he had had to make other plans, because he could not walk so far and therefore couldn't come with us. Poor Benno! We took him home with us and prepared a nice evening meal, putting more on the table than we should. It would mean, that we would have to have a few lean days afterwards, but it put Benno into a much better mood, and rounded off my birthday beautifully.

I was now ten years old. I could hardly believe it.

✳✳✳

41

In August we heard that Hermann had arrived in Berlin two months earlier. I felt a great relief to know he was safe.

He had travelled secretly on goods trains, slept rough, stayed with farmers and stole away when they questioned him too closely. When he came to the east zone border, he carefully watched controls, listened to what people said and how they were handled by the armed Russians and decided to slip away quietly into the forest and scrape through the wilderness, feeling safer that way. All he had to find his way, was his school atlas which he guarded with his life. He slept in barns and ate raw eggs and raw potatoes or whatever he could find. When he thought he was well and truly across the zone border he headed back to the railway stations, careful to avoid passenger trains and only travelling on goods trains since he had no money for tickets.

Only once, did he confide to a woman who found him in her barn, that he was on his way back home to join his family in Berlin. He even gave her his name and she persuaded him to stay a while because it was so bitterly cold and he was ill with bronchitis.

In fact, he was very ill with a high temperature and he stayed several weeks. The woman got very attached to him. She had a son and a daughter and her husband had not yet returned from the war.

When Hermann felt he was fit enough to carry on with his quest, he took his atlas, left a note and promised to write and departed secretly.

He arrived in Berlin in the last days of May 1946 and found that it wasn't so easy to get to Wilmersdorf as he thought. Guards and soldiers of various nationalities everywhere. He wasn't sure of the sector zones. He couldn't work out what had happened to his home city. He didn't recognise entire city sections. Landmarks had totally disappeared or altered. He was bewildered and in complete and utter despair, having come so far and through so much.

Confused and tired, he saw a street sign, hanging on one screw, on the wall of a ruin and he recognised the street where his father's secretary lived. He went down looking carefully at the houses, of which some were only badly shot at from street fighting but otherwise lived in. He found the house and, with his last strength, he dragged himself up the stairs. He had no need to go any further. She took him in as her own, indeed she was waiting for him, since she heard he had left Munich. She guessed he was headed for Berlin. She was the closest link in Berlin that was left of his family now. It was she who wrote to us. Hermann's quest was a true modern miracle, at least that's what I thought. Mother was so relieved that he was safe, and happy he was in Berlin, if that was where he needed to be.

All summer we had practised our new found skill of swimming in the military swimming pool, which was an area in the river Regen, cordoned off with huge oil drums. There were also diving boards of various heights. Bine and I even dared to swim through the drums into the open river. Our confidence was endless.

We also had walked out into the open country side to glean the fields. Our search for food continued just the same. Nothing had altered.

When school started again in September, something strange happened. A man and a nurse appeared one day in our class room and we had to line up one by one. The man pinched the skin on our necks and then he would either send the children back to their seats or ask their names and the nurse would write them down before they were sent to sit down. Ise and I were worried. Whatever did it all mean?

We soon found out. When everybody had been tested, the man read out the names. Mine was there but Ise's wasn't. All the names on the list had to be sent to an *Erholungs Heim*, convalescent home, a camp where we were to be fattened up. We had to pack a Suitcase and be at the Regensburg station a week later.

When I came out of school, Bine, flanked by the Bussigel twins, came running and said:

"I have to go to a home for thin children."

"So do we" I said. Ise felt left out because she wasn't chosen.

"What makes me thinner than you are?" I asked. I wasn't aware of what I looked like and never realised one had to have a certain thickness. Bine said:

"They pinch your skin, and if it stays pinched than you are too thin, if it springs back, you are just right." We pinched each other's necks, and with amazement I saw Bine's skin stay like a little bit of folded paper, and Ise's didn't. We looked at each other carefully and consciously for the first time. Bine's legs had a funny shape. Big feet, straight up to the knees and then very big and knobbly knees, and then straight again and shapeless up to the hips, and no bottom. Ise and I laughed. Bine pointed at my knees.

"You can laugh" she said and all of them, including the twins, laughed at my knees, which looked as weird as Bine's.

Ise said:

"It's probably because we get some extra rations, since my sister and father are in the sanatorium. Mother and I are under special observation from the clinic."

"Lucky you." I said turning to the twins. "Do you have to go?" But even as I said it, I knew they didn't have to go. I suddenly was very conscious about my ugly legs and felt embarrassed. To me, Ise's and the twin's legs looked elegant, they had an attractive shape. I would never look elegant, I thought, looking down my thin legs and enormous feet. Why were we so thin and ugly, when others were not? I felt depressed.

A large transport of children left a week later for *Hohenfels* (Highcliff) in the Bavarian Upper Palatinate. Nearby was an American camp where they had army manoeuvres. We could hear the cannon fire and bullets hitting targets, and I hated it. It sounded too much like war.

The home was dreadful. Hard, cold beds. The straw sacks were almost empty and no new straw available. The wooden boards which held up the straw sacks were loose and if one didn't check them before going to bed, it could happen that one crashed through them in the night. There were no sheets. The pillows had no covers and the stalks of the feathers poked through the case, scratching our faces. Scratchy, dark grey blankets. Dirty tables, horrible chipped plates, scratched rough, incredibly light aluminium spoons which cut the lips if one wasn't careful. They felt unwashed. There was always sand in the food, and millions of tiny black insects in the green vegetables, too many to pick out. It tasted good, and I didn't notice the black insects until I had eaten quite a lot. I felt ghastly and didn't want to eat any more, but the attendant said we have to eat it and the insects were dead and wouldn't harm us. I closed my eyes so that I didn't have to see what I was eating, but I retched. No matter what I have eaten since I left Berlin, strange as a lot of it was, I always knew what I was eating. The stuff we had in Hohenfels was unidentifiable. And worst of all, after eating it I had a deep pain in my stomach and some very painful stuff came up in my throat which made my throat very sore.

We got up early, had breakfast, which was always white bread, jam and coffee. Then school, then lunch. Two hours sleep after lunch, afternoon cocoa and a piece of raisin bread, homework, supper and bed. Sundays we went for a walk into the forest, picking mushrooms and late berries.

Bine cried a lot, and we clung together for comfort. Some of the children had parcels sent to them. We always crowded round to see what was in them. Bine and I hoped maybe Mother would send us a parcel too, but she didn't. Anyway, what could she have sent?

One girl had a tube of tooth paste in her parcel, and we ate the lot. She squeezed a little strip onto our fingers and we licked it slowly, savouring the pepperminty taste.

The weeks crawled past very slowly. After six weeks I gained 3 pounds. A kilo and a half! At the very end of October we were home again.

Polio had broken out at school, and three of my classmates had caught it. We were all vaccinated against polio, tuberculosis and small pox.

One girl in our class died. One lived on in an iron lung. We visited her from school. Only her head showed and she could not move. I felt I could not breathe while I visited her.

To think, that she had been running around, playing cops and robbers in the ruins with us, laughing and jumping, and now she couldn't even breathe on her own. She needed this horrendous machine. There was a mirror above her head, to enable her to see what was going on behind her. In front of her was only this machine.

Opposite our house in the Royal Villa Park was an empty firefighting lake, with slightly slanting deep concrete walls. A boy pushed me into this lake and I slid down on my side, rubbing all my clothes off and then my skin to the bone. Mother tried to cope with the wound herself, but it became very septic and inflamed and I had to go to hospital for four horrible weeks.

My bed was near the window and I watched Mother go to work in the morning and come home in the afternoon. She waved and tried to mouth words which I had difficulty to understand. She was not allowed to come in, because in the week, she was never free during visiting hours and they made no exceptions. Saturdays and Sundays she always came and stayed hours. I loved my mother.

Benno came and talked and talked about things I did not understand. For the first time I wished he didn't come, but I understood that it was somewhere to spend his time. When we were at school and everybody was working, there was nowhere for him to go, no one he knew. Poor Benno.

There was one good thing about hospital. The food was not bad at all. I even had a banana. I remembered the day when I sat on my father's shoulders and watched the parade go by at the Brandenburg Gate. That was my last banana then. The memory seemed to come to me from another life.

Soon after I came out of hospital, we had a visitor. One evening there was a knock on the door and Mother said: "Come in" and the door opened and a very tall man shyly looked in. Everything on him was long. His face, his nose, his neck, his arms. He was strangely, vaguely ugly. His eyes though were beautiful and very kind.

"Mrs. Gerret?" he asked almost timidly. Mother got up and asked him to come in. He squeezed into our tiny room and we all moved up a little on the bench to make room for him to sit down.

In strange German he said: "Herr von Stückerodt sent me to speak with you. He said you can speak English? My German not good." Mother smiled and said her English was not very good, but she would try. He said her English must be better than his German.

It turned out that Grandfather had put a collection of Shakespeare into the window of a shop on the *Domplatz* (Cathedral Square), and this man was interested to buy them. But Grandfather's English had become too rusty now to negotiate a price.

Mother went to Grandfather to find out how much he wanted for them. Grandfather wanted a lot of food, chocolate and coffee.

Two days later the transaction was completed. Grandfather had the food he asked for and the American had the German edition of Shakespeare's complete works, translated by Tiek. It was of double value because one page was in English and the opposite page with the same text in German. Happy and contented the man left with his many books. His name was Arnold Ewan.

Two days later he was back. He had a small tin of Nescafe and a roll of biscuits under his arm. Awkwardly he placed them on the table. It was evening and we were all gathered around the table. He asked if he was intruding. Mother said no, and we all budged up on the bench to make room. He showed us how to make the Nescafe properly. He did it in a very complicated way and was very pleased with himself afterwards. Then he unpacked the biscuits and handed them around. Mother had started early to bake for Christmas and fetched a tin with cookies.

The conversation was general, where were we all from? Mother told our story, he told his. He spoke in German. He was very eager to learn. He thought it was a beautiful language with 'backfire words'.

In the war he was a marine engineer in Japanese waters. He told many hair raising stories of how Japanese sky fighters would fly their planes into their ships, making the planes, with the pilots still inside, into bombs which could not fail to hit the target.

He came back three or four times a week in the evenings around seven thirty or eight. We began to wait for him and plan him into our activities. He was Mother's age. One evening he said something which indicated that all Germans were Nazis, criminals and untrustworthy. Mother said:

"You are sharing their table." Arnold and Mother looked at each other. We were all quiet. Our eyes were on him. He in turn looked at us. I felt hot and strange and very, very sad. A long time passed.

"No, not all" he said, "I am sorry. It is a mistake we have made, and it must be changed." He got up and shook our hands one after the other, a custom he had learned from us in the short time we knew him. He left. We said nothing. I thought; would he ever come back, or did he really think we were bad Nazis?

The next day he was back, a little earlier than usual, saying he hadn't eaten, but he had been to the PX and bought a few things, enough for all of us and would Mother prepare it? Would she! We all helped.

It was difficult to prepare anything, because there was so little room. There was only room for us all sitting down around the table. Mother's chair was by the stove, so she could cook, sitting down.

Arnold had brought thick slices of ham, eggs, a big loaf of sliced white bread, which we couldn't toast, a tin of pineapples and some cheese. He had his own ideas as to how this should all be eaten. Mother could really only fry the eggs, everything else was totally un-German. So Mother got up and pointed to her chair.

"Here, you do it" and Arnold and Mother changed places, laughing a lot.

He put the ham into the big pan, fried it on both sides. He made a big deal out of every clumsy move he made. Secretly we grinned at each other. While the ham was frying, he took slices of bread and lined them up on the black stove pipe which extended from the back of the stove for about a meter along the wall before it climbed up and along the ceiling, giving extra warmth. Then he piled up the ham on one side of the pan and threw in the eggs, breaking each one, grumbling, looking apologetically at us over his shoulder with a funny grin. We had lined up the plates behind him and he now put a slice of warm bread on each one, a slice of ham, then the egg, a slice of cheese on top of that and a pineapple ring finished it off like a crown. We looked on in disbelief. One ate all that? He sat down and pushed a plate in front of all of us.

"American breakfast" he said. Breakfast?!

"What do you have for lunch?" Lunch in Germany was always the main meal.

"Mostly Steak" he said. But no matter how he described steak, we did not know exactly what it was, except that it was beef and if the size of it was not exaggerated, it would feed an entire family!

What a feast we had that evening, and Arnold had great pleasure to see us eat. Arnold soon became part of our life. He came often, even when Mother was not at home. He singled me out to teach him German, saying, that I showed more patience than anybody he knew. For hours we sat and spoke and I had to make sure he pronounced the words properly. Often we laughed at his pronunciation. Difficult words he would read using the English alphabet, giving the word a completely different unrecognizable sound.

Arnold had a camera and often we went on photographic expeditions around Regensburg. We found many beautiful corners which despite the destruction were still beautiful. Goethe, coming through Regensburg in 1786, during his Italian journey said:

'Regensburg is situated delightfully. The area had to attract a city. In the town stands church by church, chapter by chapter. The Danube reminds me of the old Main'.

Ernst Moritz Arndt, Historian and Poet on his travels in 1798 said of Regensburg:

'Heavenly and delightful was the view, which I enjoyed as I came over the hills above Regensburg with all its towers, pinnacles and battlements, spreading itself in the beautiful valley far below along the banks of the Danube. In spite of the glowing heat of the midday sun, I wandered happily down the hill past fields, vineyards and meadows and along the Danube. I crossed the beautiful bridge at *Stadt am Hof* (the little town at the other side of the bridge, now part of Regensburg itself) and took lodgings at the Inn of the White Lamb'.

We learned this from Arnold's German book from which he had to read. I wondered what Goethe would think of Regensburg now? What would Napoleon say, who had given precise orders not to destroy the old city? His cannons breached the walls from the *Winzerer Höhen* (ancient vineyards), but the city was spared. I wondered what made Napoleon spare the city, when the leaders in this war had not.

I enjoyed roaming around with Arnold, finding motives for his photographs, watching him get all excited and then awkwardly get his tripod set up and his camera fastened and get it all just so. His photos were excellent. Günter caught the bug and later bought a second hand Leica very cheaply and learned to develop his own pictures.

Arnold lived in the Parkhotel Maximilian, which was a beautiful Rococo stile building, all in white and totally elegant and hardly damaged in the war. It was one of the first buildings to be renovated after the war. Probably because the Americans wanted to live in luxury. He had invited me sometimes to eat with him there. I was overwhelmed by the beauty, elegance and richness of everything. The carpets were so thick! No noise as I walked.

There was something very strange about Arnold. He did not like babies, and both Tissi and even Bine he still considered as babies. I said to him:

"But you were a baby once."

"No, never" he said. "I was not a baby." If he could ever be called cross or short tempered, it was when he denied the fact that he started life as a baby.

He had the use of a staff car, and sometimes he took us for a drive. It was a wonderful experience. Günter sat in the front with Arnold who was driving. Mother, Bine, Tissi and I sat in the back. In this Ford Taunus, a German built car he said, we explored the surrounding areas of Regensburg.

❋❋❋

42

We discovered the Walhalla, a copy of a Greek temple, squatting high up on a hill above the Danube, dominating the view all the way back up river to Regensburg. Mother had a book called 'Gods, Tombs and Scholars' and there was a picture of the Acropolis in Athens, which looked exactly the same.

A man with only one arm was our guide and explained that it was built under Ludwig I, King of Bavaria. It was to commemorate the 1813 war of liberty when Germany fought Napoleon and won freedom from French domination.

In the old Germanic faith, Walhalla is where the fallen heroes are carried after death by the Valkyries. King Ludwig filled the Valhalla with famous kings, princes, field marshals and generals. Our one armed guide said there was a rumour that King Ludwig fought at first on the side of Napoleon, and almost noticed too late that he was on the wrong side before he changed sides and fought with Blücher and the freedom fighters. To compensate for this mad error, Ludwig built the Walhalla and a similar temple up river on the crown of a hill above the town of Kelheim. He also installed famous poets, philosophers and composers in Walhalla and the *Befreiungs Halle*. (Hall of Freedom)

Arnold was fascinated by it all.

"In America we copied Roman and Grecian architecture on public buildings but we have nothing like this. One cannot compare the temples in Mexico with the ancient buildings and temples of Greece and Rome. Then there is the continuance of medieval and gothic architecture in Europe. We have no historic background in America as such. There is nothing older than at most two hundred years. The cradle of civilization as we know it comes from Europe." Arnold looked at me so intensely and with such enthusiasm, it was catching.

"The North American Indian culture, although great, was not as sophisticated and civilized, and has not left any written records of their history or laws as it existed." I found it fascinating listening to Arnold. He had himself only learned some of these things recently from his German teacher. His sentences usually started with: "My teacher says" which added a certain authority to what he said.

His teacher had also told him, that a significant vote took place two hundred years ago in America. When they decided to become a nation, with their own identity, they also had to decide what tongue should be spoken as their national language. The two languages in question were English and German, and English won by one vote. I found that quite incredible. Arnold thought, it would have been much easier for him to learn English now, instead of breaking his tongue over these German "backfire words".

Arnold asked me about our father. How long was it since we had seen him? I answered that it was about four years or so. He asked me if I missed him.

I wanted to be honest, but somehow I felt disloyal if I were truly honest. Then I thought of the time I last saw him, the way he ignored us. He was not concerned about the bombing and all the things we lost, and that we might have died in Berlin as so many of our neighbours had, and that we had to be evacuated. It all didn't appear to matter to him.

Our last meeting coincided with his brother's death, but, at a time like this, did he have to side with his mother against our mother, trying to separate Bine from us, causing Bine and us great distress? It should have been a time for keeping together, for loyalty to one another.

I now wondered why Mother had to marry my father. His mother hated her so much. Her father was against it. She must have been very headstrong. I would never marry a man whose mother did not love me also. Both families are involved when people get married. That includes each other's parents and brothers and sisters. Anyway, that was what I believed.

Over the years, I had missed my father, now I wondered why and suddenly realised that I missed a father, but I didn't miss my father. This realisation jabbed me like a dagger into the heart. It was strange, but the truth. Could I tell Arnold that? I looked at him, his big droopy eyes, full of kindness, looking at me.

"No, I don't miss him" I heard myself say and felt a red heat in my face. "I don't think my father loved us," I added hesitantly. I felt tears running down my face.

This conversation took place in the Parkhotel Maximilian, in a side lobby with enormous easy chairs with beautiful blue and pink covers, low tables and enormous chandeliers hanging low from the ceiling. Arnold flicked his fingers and a young man came over, and in English Arnold asked him something and handing me a fine, beautifully pressed white handkerchief at the same time.

A little while later this young man came back with two very tall glasses full of white-orange-pink-yellow ice cream spiked with mysterious bits and nuts, with whipped cream on top and a brown sauce running down it and a very long spoon sticking out of it all. I forgot what we had been talking about and concentrated on this extraordinary and delicious ice cream. Arnold was very proud of himself. He had managed again to impress me profoundly.

This man was totally different from the friends I had made before. I would never forget Emil, Robert, Josef, Wolfgang. They had all shared the war and its horror with us, and helped me to understand it all. Their friendship had affected me deeply and they were all buried in my heart. Arnold shared peace and hope with me. I was slowly coming out of my darkness when Arnold was around.

He and Robert were poles apart, and yet in a way they were linked through me. Maybe one day I would tell Arnold about Robert.

Although Arnold never took Bine and Tissi to the Parkhotel Maximilian, he always gave me something to take back to them. He never forgot.

Later I asked Bine, if she missed Father and without hesitation she said: "Yes, but I want a father like the Bussigel's father. He is a real father."

Bine thought of our father only in terms of being separated from her mother and sisters, having to make a choice and being threatened into making only one decision, namely, staying with Father's mother.

Tissi could not remember her father at all since she was an infant, the last time he had been with us. I did not ask mother whether she missed him. There was no trace of him, no money from him, nothing. Mother could not even find out for certain where he was last stationed in the war. He had not written to Mother since Silesia.

I was trying to face facts. Either he was dead and we would probably never find out where he was buried, or he was in a Russian Prison of War Camp, and there was never any postal exchange between the Russian camps and Germany, not like France, England and America. The last possibility was, that he didn't want to be found.

I told myself that it didn't matter, that it was his loss if he didn't love his family, or at least only my brother and Bine. I wondered a little why he didn't love me. At school, I pretended he was missing, presumed dead. So many fathers were missing, presumed dead, so why not mine? But deep down, I remembered my father from the time before he went to war, when we were all at home in Berlin, he was a wonderful father. I loved him very much then, and that Father, I still loved now, but I knew, from the time I last saw him, that things would never be the same again.

The winter was cold, dark, miserable and without food. Arnold visited us as regularly as always. He picked his time outside mealtimes in the evenings when the stove was still on. He never found out, that we were cold during the day and had very little food. It had nothing to do with him.

Mother continued her work with Papa Kröning and his wife, and would come home utterly exhausted. He never rested, which meant Mother never rested. She was very worried about Papa Kröning's health. His work as minister and clergyman never stopped. As a doctor of medicine he visited the sick without transport. Apart from that there was all the administrative work for the refugees. His wife cooked and typed endlessly.

We never lit the stove until everybody was home in the evening. When we children were home from shopping, sledging or just wandering around after lunch in the soup kitchen, we made a nest on my bunkbed, where we were warm and cosy, and played or read Grandfather's books. There was still no school because of coal shortage. We called it the coal holidays.

Bine spent a lot of time with the Bussigel twins, but I stayed home because it was just as cold in Ise's room as in ours and it was easier to look after Tissi at home. Ise and her mother huddled up in their bed for warmth, only coming out to get some food or to go to the loo. Ise and I missed each other, but it was too cold to play.

Tissi was very content and happy to have somebody at home. Grandfather lent us a horse racing game. One had to throw the dice, and then one could race one's horse, which was a beautiful lead model on a little spring with a stand, over as many fields as one threw points. We played that game a lot.

Without much notice, Arnold left for the States a week before Christmas.

Christmas came dark, cold and miserable. There was no carol singing, it was far too cold in the church. There were power cuts and no candles. Even the locals felt the lack of clothes and food and resources.

1946 crawled miserably into 1947. The Danube was frozen solid, the temperatures were 20 centigrade below zero most days. Often it was colder than that. Grandfather, always wore his thick fur coat and hat, his thick socks and gloves, even to bed. He had stopped looking at the thermometer.

The chickens had been eaten when they stopped laying eggs. The air was cracking. The washing froze to hard boards in the loft, and had to be carefully taken down from the line in case it broke and tore the cloth.

All our usual sources for gathering food and wood were stripped bare. In the forests there was not a stick to be found. The rangers guarded the forests carefully because people had started to cut down real trees. There was hardly any black market. Collecting cigarette butts was difficult in the snow. Americans did not sit on park benches in the winter.

Mother and I still mended flour sacks from Eichhofen for a little food. Our clothes were worn and getting too small. We were always cold, even when we huddled in bed together, which was where we spent most of our time. There was no source of warmth anywhere. When the stove was on we crowded around it, but we did not feel the warmth. My toes usually hurt. Bine pinched my neck, and with big, serious eyes, looking at me, said:

"We have to go to Hohenfels again, what is the bet?" That was something new with Bine. She emphasised everything with: 'Want to bet?' Or 'what's the bet?'

Slowly, the days became longer and by the end of February the snow started to melt. It was still bitterly cold. The Danube was expected to flood, which meant the cellar would be under water, which in turn meant that the miserable supply of coal would be flooded. There was nowhere else to store the coal.

Arnold was back. One evening in the beginning of March he was outside our door. We had had two postcards since he had left. One from England and the White Cliffs of Dover, and one from Boston. Nowhere had he indicated how long he would be away or when he would be back.

He had a loaf of white soft bread under his arm, a piece of ham, cheese and a tin of pineapples. He handed it to me, and although we had already eaten, we cooked it just the same and all sat around the table with Arnold in our midst. He told us of his trip and what a wonderful time he had had.

After the meal he rummaged ceremoniously in his jacket pocket and eventually produced a giant bar of chocolate. Very pleased with himself he put it on the table. We all looked at it and nobody touched it. I looked at Arnold, he looked at Mother and then he pushed it towards Mother who carefully unwrapped it and broke off a little square each. Günter counted the remaining squares and announced that the chocolate would last three more days if everybody had a little square each. I made mine last and last, licking slowly, savouring each lick. This was not Hershel's chocolate, this was real thick wonderful stuff with a softer centre which tasted so good but I could not tell what it tasted of.

Dear Arnold! He was so very pleased with himself. It was lovely to have him back. Life wasn't so black any more. He had a message for me. Another American from the Parkhotel, who sometimes waved to me, when he saw Arnold with me there, had also returned from the States and he had a little present. He invited me for the next Saturday. Arnold seldom wore uniform, but this American always did. I asked him what the various badges meant on his uniform, and Arnold said, that he was a Lieutenant, and some of those things were medals of distinction.

The Lieutenant presented me with a tiny parcel and told me, it was from Florida. What a beautiful name I thought and asked what it was like in Florida?

"Warm sea and sunshine. It just beautiful" he said. How I wished I could be in Florida and be warm. I sat down in one of the enormous square club chairs in the lobby and undid the little parcel. Arnold and the Lieutenant watched, as I carefully unpacked the fine silky paper. Such luxury! I found three tiny exquisitely made animals, crafted cleverly from sea shells, so expertly put together. I had never seen anything like it. There were two little birds and a turtle. The turtle stood on a little coral rock. I didn't know what to say. I beamed at the Lieutenant and Arnold, who was obviously pleased with my pleasure.

The waiter came and brought three ice cream dreams and put them down on the low table in front of us. Arnold must have ordered that without me even noticing. The three of us tucked in with my three animals placed beautifully in front of me at the table. I would like to be in Florida. It sounded like music in my ears. I would have to ask Arnold more about it later. The Lieutenant took his leave because he had to be on duty. I got up and thanked him and curtseyed. He said awkwardly: "Aufuiedersayn." Arnold and I grinned at his pronunciation.

❋❋❋

43

Just as the sun rose over the horizon, one bright spring morning, there was a knock on our door. A little boy about my age, stood there with a note for Mother saying:

"Please come immediately. Papsel is dead." It was signed, Muttel Kröning.

Mother dropped everything and rushed over to Papa Kröning's tiny room. There he lay, as if peacefully asleep on his bed. One of his desks piled high with papers, a half-finished form, still in the typewriter, which he was going to finish just after he'd had 'this little rest'. Muttel Kröning sat at the other desk, which doubled up as a table and kitchen top. There was nowhere to stand in that little room. One entered and sat down on one of the two beds. Muttel said nothing, she didn't even cry. Mother sat down next to her and put an arm around Muttel's shoulder. What was there to say?

His day did not stop when he came home in the evening. The stream of people seeking help and advice was never ending. The day before his death, they had been to the refugee camp at the Messerschmitt works in Prüfening and held a service there. As usual, Günter accompanying the hymns with the 'squeezebox', the altar cloth was an old sheet. Mother was in charge of the crucifix and the candles. He was a wonderful preacher. Many people of various beliefs came to his services.

He was also the one and only minister and doctor who cared for the 'fallen girls'.

He would sit behind his desk either at work or at home and listen to all the people's grief, sorrow, distress and trouble with never ending patience. Then he would give advice and offer help. And he helped so many people. It was incredible how one man managed all this. Now he was dead. It was as if the world had stopped.

He pinned a saying on his wall which he tore off a calendar, and it said: 'Tell me with whom you associate with, and I tell you who you are." With Papa Kröning that would have been difficult.

He knew three days before his death that he would die. He told no one except his wife's sister, to whom he sent a telegram, which said:

"Please come immediately, I have at most three days to live." She arrived a day after his death to Muttel's great surprise and relief.

Muttel told Mother, that he had laboured up the five flights of stairs, looking very tired and pale. He put an arm around her, kissed her and said:

"You have always been so good to me." Then he laid down on his bed and went to sleep. Muttel Kröning had sat by his bed all night and had taken her leave from her beloved man. Mother was the first person to be with Muttel after Papa Kröning's death.

He was still waiting for his coffin when two officials arrived at his room from the Protestant Relief Work Office and collected the typewriter and some of his papers.

There was an ocean of people at the funeral. Muttel, her sister, mother and the three of us in a tight knot at the graveside. Günter and Benno right behind us and Anton Novak, the nameless one, and all the workers from his office in the *Silberne Fischgasse* making an outer circle around the grave. The vicar held a long and moving funeral service in the open in this beautiful grave yard. Ancient trees made a ceiling with buds ready to burst, very fresh young green everywhere, and comforting heat oozing from the ground. The freshly dug earth smelled good and wholesome at the graveside, bunches of flowers everywhere. The air was full of renewal, hope and wondrous beauty.

Something strange happened to me, while I was listening to the vicar. Some time ago, we met Papa Kröning in the street and his enormous and tall frame came to a halt right in front of Mother, and ended up on my foot. I tried to free myself but couldn't and Papa Kröning did not realise he stood on my foot. I looked up but could not see his face because his middle stood out too far. With my toes squashed and in pain I waited until he finished talking to Mother and moved on. Now I distinctly felt him as close as on that occasion, only he did not stand on my toes. It was a very strange but comfortable sensation. I looked around because I was so sure I would see him. The disappointment and sudden realization that I would never ever see him again, made my eyes sting. I still felt his nearness, and I squared my shoulders. Papsel wasn't dead.

They lowered him down carefully and Muttel was crying bitterly. Looking at Muttel, I had another sensation. I felt, that taking leave of a person was very sad when you knew you would never see them again in this life, this parting was the unbearable thing about death. For the person itself, to die was an extension of life. It was always worst for the people left behind. Papa Kröning was going home. I could see all that so clearly. I wondered how I suddenly knew that. I also realised, that I was not a child anymore. In a very few weeks I would be eleven years old.

After Papa Kröning's death things happened very quickly, his diligence started to pay off.

Günter found his parents, his brother Werner and sister Lieselotte. They lived in a village outside the little Spa town of Bad Kissingen, where they had two rooms in an old farmhouse.

Benno's family arrived and with that Benno disappeared from our lives. We only saw him sometimes on his bicycle, a highly prized acquisition, which he called his 'wire donkey'. Without stopping he would madly wave an arm and shout a Silesian greeting, weaving dangerously with his handlebars, trying not to get caught in the tramlines. He was a changed and happy man, acting crazy to those who didn't know him.

Onkel Jo von Göeczy found Tante Fee and his family; they now lived in a camp near Hanover.

The Jews were collecting throughout Germany to go to the Holy Land, which was given to them by the English to be their new home and which they claimed was theirs by right. If the Holy Land was free to be given away to the Jews, why couldn't they have gone there before, before all the horrors started? It was very puzzling and strange.

With so many people leaving Germany, apartments were now available and we were allocated a large one on the third floor of a beautiful big house, surrounded by fruit trees and a big court yard leading into another garden at the back. The house was completely untouched by the war and belonged to a chocolate manufacturer. We divided the apartment in half and one half was as big as Grandfather's entire accommodation was in the Von Stauß Straße, and the other half was ours. We had two rooms and a kitchen. The bathroom and loo which we shared with Grandfather. Günter had a bed in the living room which doubled up as a sofa during the day. We looked forward to the move.

The Von Der Tann Schule was vacated and reverted from being a field hospital to being a school again. We had a protestant school. The funny thing was, that we lived very close to the Von Der Tann Schule and had a long way to the Pestalozzi school which was our school up to now. After the move, we would live opposite the Pestalozzi school, with the same distance to the new school. Grandfather said walking was healthy.

That spring of 1947 Ise had to leave her fire station home too. They were allocated two rooms in barracks which were vacated by the American forces. A new town had been built for them outside Regensburg and they moved there with their families who joined them from the States.

Before we could move into our lovely new home, we had to go and clean the apartment which the previous occupants had probably left in a hurry and were therefore unable to clean it for the new owners. The place was in a frightful mess.

It was an elegant apartment with all modern conveniences in perfect working order. How it could have become so grubby was a mystery. The kitchen sink was blocked with gunge and awfully smelly. The little larder at the end of the kitchen had rotting foodstuffs in it. Unfortunately it was too rotten to be used.

The loo was very stained and also very smelly.

Mother, Günter, Bine and I and even little Tissi, who was just a shadow of a little girl, worked hard and enthusiastically, to make this our very own beautiful new home.

With a stick and an old spoon tied to the end of it I attacked the loo until it was white and shining, and each time the cistern had filled again I pulled the chain. In the end there was only the smell of fresh water in the loo. I polished the seat and lid until it shone in its original mahogany red. I scrubbed and polished the linoleum floor and then I polished the brass end on the china handle of the chain and the brass door handles and sliding lock.

Then I attacked the bathroom with 'Vim'. I took great pleasure in getting it all to look white, gold and elegant. Every time I made something else emerge from its grimy darkness, I called out: "come and look at this!" And everybody came running and admiring. Bine and I were competing in getting things clean and shining. Tissi eagerly ran around, trying to help everybody.

The kitchen sink next. Mother and Günter were painting the rooms and doors. Grandfather had been able to get the paint.

We had a beautiful balcony, which had sun most of the day. We scraped the parquet floor with wire wool and bits of glass to get it into a golden honey colour and then we waxed it and with the weighted floor polisher got it to a fabulous shine. A palace couldn't look more elegant.

I could hardly wait to move in. I was allocated a small corner in the room adjoining the balcony, so that I had two windows, one down onto the road and one onto the balcony. All the windows and balcony door had roller blinds. My little bay corner was just big enough for my bed and a makeshift desk to do my homework away from the others. A chair and chest of drawers made a kind of fourth wall. This balcony room was almost twice as large as the *Bauernzimmer* in the old place and we only used it for sleeping, apart from myself. I used my corner as a separate room, where I worked. An adjoining room was our living room, down the corridor was the kitchen, larder, bathroom and cloakroom.

The move was close to my birthday. As a present I had a recorder. Mother had remembered. I could learn to play an instrument.

Arnold came with two big brown paper bags full of shopping from the PX. It was bulging with food and something was smelling delicious. I sniffed the air and wanted to poke my nose into the bag, but I waited patiently.

Arnold also had a big square parcel which he put on the table. Shyly and awkwardly he pushed it towards Mother. His clumsy wrapping undoing itself already.

"This is my contribution to this beautiful new apartment. I hope you will be very happy here." Giving the parcel another push he said:

"Open it!" Mother unwrapped it and held a stunning copy of the Mona Lisa in her hand. It was made in such a way, that it looked like the hand painted real thing. It was beautiful and our very first picture to hang up. All the beautiful pictures we used to have were gone, gone in the war. Arnold stood in our middle, very pleased and happy with himself, happy to make us happy. I took his hand and looked up at him. He squeezed it and smiled down at me.

Here, now, I would start my new life. The air was fresh with optimism and hope and my heart was singing.

✻✻✻

1948 The family

Valentine   Arnold

44

It was before sunrise on a Sunday morning in the summer of 1953. The sleepy dairy man crossed the yard to start milking, inadvertently kicking a bucket as he entered the gloomy cow house. There were cunning new milking machines, which had just come onto the agricultural market, but farmers were still struggling to recover from the war, and to install these machines was very expensive. Milking here was done by hand by the dairy man and one helper. When it was my turn, every two weeks for one week, I had to milk seven cows before breakfast, an occupation which I found comforting and peaceful. Soon I learned to aim jets of milk at the cats who waited eagerly along the wall opposite, expertly opening their mouths to catch the warm cow juice, their little tongues licking any droplets from their long whiskers which had not found their mark.

I shivered in the early dawn, as I got ready to cycle to Köfering in Lower Bavaria, some 130 km distance. Since I started my agricultural apprenticeship, I had to attend college four times a year for a residential week, and our college was at Köfering. When I had absolved my three years, I would have to become a residential student there. I was now nearly completing my second year.

My first farm had been a small place not far from Regensburg; four cows, two dreadful old nags, a team of oxen, chickens and four pigs. A big market garden, where the farmer's wife grew asparagus and other choice vegetables for the best hotels in Regensburg, mostly still occupied by Americans. The farmer and his son grew potatoes, wheat, barley, oats and rye, sugar beets and maize.

She was a hard task master, who worked a maid, the family and myself from four in the morning until nine at night. I had every sixth Sunday off and was free to go home for the day on an old and rusty bike.

A refugee family with nine children, occupied half the farmhouse, which irritated *her* dreadfully and the maid and I seemed to be on the receiving end of all her frustrations. My contract was binding, I could not change to go to another farm, until my year was up. The maid left around Christmas time, pleading homesickness.

I left there with such joy, to go to this magnificent, solitary farm in the Upper Palatinate, sitting among its own fields and forests, with the River Vils running right through it. This farmer was a horseman with every fibre in his body. The farm was called Laubhof, a proud and beautiful place. Among other things it was a stud farm for strong, sturdy farming horses. Two Noriker Coldblood stallions, sixteen hands, one bay and one chestnut, one Heavy Rhineland Coldblood stallion, chestnut roan with flaxen mane, also sixteen hands and a snow white Bavarian Rottaler stallion, a Warmblood. These stallions occupied one stable, several mares for breeding stood in another one, and adjoining that, were 4 working teams, of which 3 consisted of geldings. There were of course also the foals and yearlings. Horses galore. The stallions were seldom used for work in the fields and had to be ridden out regularly for exercise.

There was also a bull, who was kept very busy by visiting cows, one hundred and twenty pigs, around a hundred free range chickens and an enormous market garden, with acres of tomatoes, strawberries, cabbages, carrots and in fact anything a good cook needs to feed her family throughout the year. Every morning at dawn, the greengrocers from Amberg and surrounding towns came to collect the fresh produce of the season.

There were several hundred turkeys, geese and ducks, most of whom had to forfeit their lives around Christmas time. Everybody with two hands would sit in the slaughter house, kill them skilfully, bleed them and pluck the feathers, carefully separating the down, to get the birds ready for the Christmas market.

Last autumn we made Sauerkraut, in big stone vats, about eight feet deep. It was terrific fun, stamping layers of finely shredded cabbage and salt until there was no air left and the cabbage was covered in its own juice, and layer by layer we grew out of the vat, joking and laughing and good natured teasing all around.

When I drove the huge tractor into a draining ditch, because I had misjudged the width of it and fell over the side of the earth bridge, the farmer laughed.

"We'll make a good man of her yet," and sent Heiner off to get two teams of horses to pull me out. Red faced I waited for Heiner's return. I never drove the tractor into the ditch again.

The farmer soon realised my fondness for horses, and detailed me more than the others, to work with them. During the haying, all the teams, including the stallions, were constantly on the move, going out empty, carefully filling the wagon, driving home with a full load, and unloading. The farmer never wanted to see anybody idle. To see someone having a rest, would change the colour of his face into pure purple. We had competitions, as to who turned the empty wagon around the fastest for reloading. As soon as the last of the hay was stashed in the barn, we turned the team, and standing on the wagon, drove the fork deep into the wood for support, and using our knees as shock absorbers and the reins gripped tightly, we galloped the horses back to the field, giving the laden wagon a wide berth on its way up to the barn. Schorschl (little George) who was the tallest of the male apprentices, and really knew how to handle horses, often said, grinning, that the Romans in their chariots could learn a thing or two from us. Well, we were pretty good, and so often I wished that Robert could see me now.

Life was good here on Laubhof. We were all appreciated, treated as equals, worked extremely hard and always as a team and had cause for happy laughter. There were 3 male and 3 female apprentices, and although I belonged to the male apprentices, being female, I had to do one week in 4 in the kitchen, which I did not enjoy all that much, especially since my fellows, being male, did not have to do it. But even in the kitchen I found great satisfaction; to see the hungry pack come in for a meal and enjoy the food, which took all morning to prepare and cook, and, I had the edge on my male fellows.

Herr Ulrich came out of the front door, sniffed the air and decided what sort of weather we would have that day. It promised to be a clear, blue and warm summer's day.

"You'll get wet today, there'll be heavy rain in the afternoon." He was never wrong. I wondered how he did it. He looked up into the air, watched the clouds, felt the breeze and made a decision.

"I have the triangular army tent section, with the pointed bit at the back and the wide bit over the handle bars, I should be alright." I was busy fastening the Rucksack on the luggage rack at the back.

"Put your gumboots on to keep your feet dry," he added. I didn't want to wear my gumboots, they didn't go with my bike. They were horrid smelly things, used to muck out the pigs, the cows and the horses. There was so much mucking out to do. Sometimes I thought that farming evolved around the mucking out, stacking the pile, loading it and spreading it on the fields. But even that was healthy, reassuring and fruitful.

I had a new pair of green shoes, elegant, with crepe soles, my first new pair after the war *and* bought with my own money, by myself. But Herr Ulrich was right. I would put my beautiful shoes into my Rucksack to keep them nice.

The farmer came over. He put his large, gnarled hand on my bicycle's shiny, chestnut brown leather saddle.

"Give your bike a rub down when you get home tonight. Stop it from rusting." He stood back and we both looked at my bicycle. Herr Ulrich's face had once been smashed in by a horse, as it kicked out and caught him fully. When I first came here, I found it very difficult to read his expression, to see his moods, but now, I could feel his moods, read how he felt in the way he spoke, watch for the tell-tale change of colour in his face. He was a kind and fair man, a lot of fun and a good laugh, but when roused, his temper was something to behold.

"A good buy." He meant my cycle, which had been delivered only three weeks ago. I had chosen it from a catalogue, payed a deposit of which Grandfather had paid half, and after six more monthly instalments, it would be mine for ever. It was a mountain-touring cycle, sky blue and silver-chrome, three gears, back pedal brake, shock absorber in the saddle shaft, air pump, leather toolbar with all necessary tools and repair kit under the saddle. Five year guarantee for the gears, but twenty five year guarantee for the frame! It was a perfect dream, admired by all with a certain envy. Even the lads and lasses from the villages around came to look at and discuss my bicycle on Sunday afternoons, seriously considering such a purchase themselves. Every speck of dirt and dust was immediately and carefully polished away by anyone who spotted it first.

Frau Ulrich appeared in the courtyard with a big parcel of packed lunch and a beer bottle of milk.

"Give Fräulein Becher this and my regards." She handed me a second parcel which smelled deliciously of Speck. Fräulein Becher, the head mistress at college, and Frau Ulrich graduated together before the war and stayed friends.

A last check, hand shaking, good wishes and I kicked my bike off the stand and swung myself into the saddle. It was sheer pleasure riding this bike.

"See you in a week!" In fast gear I peddled down the road to Amberg with the iron foundry belching black smoke day and night, 365 days a year, on the horizon to the right. Every night the sky above the foundry was crimson.

Amberg was a beautiful medieval town, still totally surrounded by a thick wall. It was our *Kreisstadt*, county town, and I had come here to the market, showing off our horses which were for sale.

It was still only five o clock in the morning and I planned to be in Schwandorf by ten. There were mountains, which would be too steep to peddle up, and I would have to push, making up for time on the way down on the other side. I should be home by two, I calculated, and have the afternoon and evening with Mother and the sisters, and continue the next morning early, to be in Köfering by eight.

It had not been easy to leave home two years ago, but there was little else for me to do at the time, and since I had come to the Laubhof, I had never regretted having made the decision to become a graduated farmer, specializing in horses. It was a great career and mine would be a wonderful life. People always have and always would need horses.

The road between Amberg and Schwandorf lead through endless forests. It was so quiet, no traffic at all. A deer was peacefully grazing at a clearing, a shaft of sunshine finding its way through the thick forest, highlighting the colour on its back and the dewdrops on some blades of grass. Her fawn standing on her inside, almost completely hidden from the road. The wild flowers shone brilliantly among the tall grasses.

Effortlessly and silently I cruised past, enjoying the scene, the forest, the bicycle, the trip, life.

Clouds gathered indigo, purple and black as I came out of the forest. I stopped briefly. The land spread vast into the distance below me, the Naab making a silver band right through to the horizon, where the purple clouds met the earth. I descended fast into the Naab valley. Just before Burg Lengenfeld it started to pour. I found a barn by the road and pushed the bike inside, sat in the hay and had an early lunch.

When I had finished eating, I rested contentedly, waiting for the rain to ease, hopefully stop. At midday I decided to cycle on in the rain. Water soon collected in a puddle on my tent cape, where it was spread between the handle bars, but it kept my knees dry. Soon however it dripped down in streams and straight into my boots, which I had to empty regularly to ease the weight. Then the water ran down my neck and eventually I was wet, even underneath my tent covering. I entered the Regen valley, and cycled along this peaceful river. Nature here was undisturbed, the road not surfaced and there were many potholes to be avoided, full to the brim with rainwater, and I hated my beautiful bicycle getting all muddy. However, I could wipe it afterwards.

Gallingkofen. Now it would be downhill all the way, Stadt am Hof, which was the town at the other end of the Steinerne Brücke. I had to come across this bridge, because they still had not been able to finish rebuilding the Nibelungen Brücke, which had been a motorway bridge across the Danube before the war. Some panic stricken idiot had even blasted the Steinerne Brücke in the last minutes of the war, and blown away an eight hundred year old arch, just by the Brückentor. A miracle that the Bridge Gate had not been too damaged by this stupid blunder.

It was still raining heavily, and I slithered on the cobbles, trying to avoid the tramlines.

I cycled up the Maximilian Strasse and stopped at the Parkhotel, wondering whether Arnold was at home, but then looking down at myself, decided against it, hopped back onto the wet saddle and made it for home. I pushed my bike in to the stairwell, down the five steps to the cellar ante room and then bounded upstairs, two at a time. It was three o' clock. Timing wasn't bad.

Mother and the sisters had been waiting, and as I entered I was surrounded, all my wet things torn off me, an old American dressing gown thrown over my shoulder and then they dragged me into our living room. My sisters *always* complained about the farm smells, which seemed to linger on me. They wrinkled their noses and squeezed their nostrils. They also called me *Bauerntrampel*, which meant clumsy peasant. I decided to ignore their ignorance.

The table was laid, a fresh strawberry cake, a cherry cake, whipped cream, good china, real coffee filling the room with a delicious scent. The sun had found a hole in the purple clouds and sparkled on the beautiful silver on the table. I counted the cups and saucers. There were seven of them. I looked at Mother and she said:

"Grandfather and Tata are coming too." I still looked at her, surprised. She laughed.

"Things are alright at the moment, I think Tata's good influence on Father is finally paying off."

Tata was Edith Kilian, who had married Grandfather in 1949, and after she had got used to suddenly being Frau Baronin von Stückerodt, had turned out to be a lady. It took her nearly three years, sorting out the various family connections, and to work out her exact status, which was very important to her, and exactly what we were doing there, living so close to Grandfather, when it would have been so much more convenient, had we lived at the other side of the moon. She soon realised Grandfather's stressed and mixed up feelings, sorted them out and put things right. She was a fair and unbiased lady.

Grandfather and I had always had a special relationship. I think it was our mutual love for horses, a kindred spirit which was special to us and which we both recognised. But there was also the fact, that I would not be intimidated by him, even answered back on several occasions. Mother was horrified and told me to show respect. Grandfather and I respected each other, and Tata welcomed my visits, because it put Grandfather into a good mood.

"Ah, Angela, time for a game of cards?" his face would light up as soon as I entered. He hardly ever heard my knock, he was getting deaf. Strangely though, he could hear things he wasn't supposed to hear.

I hoped very much, that Mother and her father would put their differences aside and be friends again, like they were after the trial.

It was a truly happy and united coffee round that afternoon, Grandfather, Tata, both in love and happy with each other's company, happy also to be in *our* sitting room, Mother beaming, her eyes sparkling like the silver on the table. Bine and Tissi looking in wonderment at Grandfather, not believing what they saw, still a little suspicious. Günter, who by now had been fully accepted into the family, as a deputy brother, his family in Bad Kissingen and ours had become good friends.

Bit by bit the cakes disappeared, the cream also vanished. Mother went to make some more coffee and Grandfather lit a cigar.

We sat and talked and talked, and nobody wanted to break up the round. When it became dark outside, Mother and I lit a candle and then sneaked into the kitchen and made smorgasbord, laying it out on three large platters. We put smoked ham, Cervelat, Salami, soft cheese and Emmental, Roquefort and Bierwurst on rye bread, wheat bread and Pumpernickel. We also sliced some rolls and made 'small bites', then garnished the platters with tomatoes, gherkins, parsley and bits of apples. They looked gorgeous. From the larder we got some homemade sloe wine and took everything into the sitting room. A chorus of "Ah" greeted us as we entered, and Bine and Tissi quickly took the coffee things out and laid a new table. The session continued happily and harmoniously until bedtime.

We discussed Mother's new job, which she had had difficulty in getting. She was a state registered nurse, but all papers verifying this fact had been lost, burnt, gone in the war, along with a lot of other important papers. She had to locate fellow nurses, professors and examiners, which was time consuming and difficult. But she had located enough witnesses to get new papers, and anyway, nurses were in great demand.

Bine was leaving school soon and decided to become a nanny. She would like to work with children. She also planned to go to England and work in a home for mentally handicapped children near Birmingham.

Mother and Arnold were in limbo, because our father was still missing without a trace. She would have to have him declared dead, and that was something she was not prepared to do. I hoped very much, that she would take some steps soon to free herself of this marriage. I realised long ago, that it was over, even at the time when we were in Silesia, just before we travelled to East Prussia, nearly ten years ago. Mother deserved a good man by her side. All her young years had been spent alone. Hard years. Mother's and my eyes met.

"I meant to ask you for a very long time. Have you ever found out anything of the people in Lichtenau?" I wondered constantly what became of all the people we came to love in Lichtenau.

Slowly, Mother got up and went over to a very small little chest of drawers. She came back and handed me a letter.

"I received this two years ago. I didn't want to tell you until you were older. I think now you are ready to read this. It is from the two ladies who lived in the loft of the schoolhouse in Lichtenau, the two who knitted the pretty cardigans you had for Easter, remember?"

I remembered the two ladies.

"Miss Schorn and Miss ..." I couldn't remember her name and looked at the end of the letter.

"Miss Hegarn." Mother nodded.

"Read the letter. It is very sad, I must warn you. At the time I tried to find people who were in Lichtenau and who could maybe tell me what became of everybody. This is her second letter to me." I took the letter and went into my corner of the room, which still had my desk and things and my bed. I sat down on my bed and started to read. It was dated Berlin, April 1949.

Dear Frau Gerret.

Thank you for taking all this trouble and for the parcel with the warm clothes, the coffee, the milk powder and the dried potatoes. We have no food here other than the strict rations which the planes fly in day and night. Day and night, day and night every three minutes. Thank your American friend, who was able to smuggle this parcel onto one of the planes. These planes and the men who fly them are a true modern day miracle.

Now to answer your questions. I am afraid, there is nothing but sadness and despair to report. Our escape from deportation or even death was ironic.

The Russians arrived a few months after your departure. We stayed, simply because we had nothing to lose or gain. There was nowhere for us to go in Berlin or anywhere else. All we had was in our attic room.

A week after the Russians arrived here, they herded all the villagers into the little square by the church, and there they waited until everybody, even the farmers and labourers from the neighbourhood, farmer Graf and the Kramps and everybody, were gathered. They were freezing in the icy cold. Our warm clothing had been taken away. I saw no sign of the Russian or Polish prisoners from the moment the Soviets arrived. There was a whisper that they might have been shot for having worked on the farms.

The villagers were separated into groups, farmer Graf, the Bürgermeister, the vicar, the teachers and all landowners in fact, were led away. I can still see Frau Kramp with the new born baby and all her boys walking away. She was crying so.

The Russians had separated the men from the women, but they left together, that same day. The last we saw of them was the column they formed, slowly walking down the Mehlsacker road. We never saw them again. It was said, that they had been sent to Siberia.

All the land was taken over by Russian labourers. We watched the beautiful, fruitful land perish around us in the two years we had to live there. All machinery, ploughs, wagons, threshing machines, everything, was sent to Russia in 45. The new farmers had no tools to work with. All was left to total ruin. Little Mother Poschman and her sister died of starvation.

In the spring of 1947, with the melting snow, a grave was found in the forest just outside of Lichtenau. It was rumoured that the bodies belonged to the Polish and Russian POWs, and that would explain why we were not permitted to gather wood, mushrooms and berries in the forest.

Fräulein Schorn and I went regularly to the Kommandantur and applied to be let out and go to the West. Fräulein Schorn's body was violated several times, and I made her stay in our attic room. I was miraculously spared this terrible ordeal. In the end it was quite easy, for all German speaking people, who had not been killed or deported, to get exit papers.

Frau Gerret, when we left Lichtenau, a handful of German speaking people, nobody who lived there while you were here, remained. We were not allowed to take anything with us, and on the train to freedom, our clothes were stolen from our bodies. We arrived at Frankfurt an der Oder, naked, starved and frozen.

Frau Gerret, the Russians are subhuman. To call them animals, is an insult to the animal kingdom. We are cold and starving now, but we are free. Thank you again for the parcel, and I look forward to a possible reunion in the future.

Very respectfully yours
Dorothea Hegarn

After all that I had heard in the years since the war, the news this letter contained, did not shock me. It really only confirmed what I had known in my heart already. It helped, to know for sure. I folded the letter and returned to the table.

Grandfather now turned to me and said:

"Put it behind you. You have started a new life." and then he asked:

"And what of your plans, after you come out of Agricultural College?"

He was right. I had finished grieving, although my feeling for Robert was different. It helped to know, that he lay in that beautiful forest, where the fairies lived and where we picked berries. It was a good place. I survived and I had to get on with life. I looked at Grandfather. He too had survived. I took a deep breath. Glad and proud to be asked, I answered:

"I have five practical years after that, and some of that I can take abroad. I have chosen Finland, the nearest country to East Prussia I can find, where I am permitted to go. After that I shall also go to England, because I think I would like to learn that language. Then I will be back and prepare myself here for my Masters. I have already started to save money for my fare to Finland." Grandfather smiled contentedly:

"Good, you have your future sorted out. Very good. I shall advance the fare money for you and Bine, should you both find that you have not saved enough and also need some travel money too. You shall pay me back when you can afford it."

I looked at my grandfather and our eyes met. He gave me an encouraging and reassuring twinkle. I loved this man. I got up and put my arms around him.

"Thank you Grandfather, thank you for everything.

✻✻✻

Looking back, I see my world has sunk into darkness and ashes, but not extinction. New growth and new life is everywhere. I felt that we were brave, surely, we have strength, but we also have fear, fear of the unknown. We started anew in this sinister, changed world, in this strange land, among strange and lost people.

It will be good in the end. Time has healed some wounds.

✻✻✻

The author

After leaving school at age16, August 1952, Angela Valentine worked as an agricultural apprentice. After three years, she passed her test and entered the Agricultural College in Regensburg. After graduating Angela spent three years in Finland, England and Ireland. When she returned, she went to Business college and ended up working for the German Railways in Basel. She later went on to London to work for the German airline, Lufthansa for ten years. She married a New Zealander and had two children, Sarah and Peter. Once Angela's children had grown up and left home, she started producing small wooden furniture. Later, she worked and managed an art and craft shop. Angela's true passion is writing and painting and she continues to do that most days. The Dark Edge of the Rainbow is her debut novel.

novum 🔶 PUBLISHER FOR NEW AUTHORS

The publisher

> *He who stops being better stops being good.*

This is the motto of novum publishing, and our focus is on finding new manuscripts, publishing them and offering long-term support to the authors.
Our publishing house was founded in 1997, and since then it has become THE expert for new authors and has won numerous awards.

Our editorial team will peruse each manuscript within a few weeks free of charge and without obligation.

You will find more information about
novum publishing and our books on the internet:

www.novum-publishing.co.uk

Rate this book on our website!

www.novum-publishing.co.uk